EARTHSHIP

EVOLUTION BEYOND ECONOMICS

Michael E. Reynolds

Les Lawson
Southern Highlands Mortgage
(706) 781-2992

SPECIAL THANKS

Claire Blanchard
 for grinding out this production from start to finish

Mary Stone
 for office support during production

Tom Drugan and **Marty Remaly**
 for graphics

Peter Kolshorn
 for rear cover photograph and running construction crews during production

Jonah Reynolds
 for computer graphics and photography

Joe Hoar and **Justin Simpson**
 for contributions to component design.

Nick Stallard
 for electrical design and production of POM

Gerry and **Dennis Weaver**
 for ongoing involvement in the Earthship concept

Tanya Parks
 for running Solar Survival Press and

Chris Simpson, my wife for continuing to deal with a fanatic.

EARTHSHIP VOLUME III

CONTENTS

INTRODUCTION

ENTRY OF THE WEAVER EARTHSHIP AT R.E.A.C.H., NEAR TAOS, NEW MEXICO

JUST AS THE SUN ALLOWS NO DARKNESS
THE LAKE ALLOWS NO DRYNESS
THE WIND ALLOWS NO CALM
THE RIVER, NO SILENCE...

THE EARTHSHIP ALLOWS NO POVERTY

EARTHSHIP AT BEAVER SPRINGS, MONTANA

INTRODUCTION

Global observations continue to show that the earth and its inhabitants are in a precarious situation. Politics, economics, and religion all present shallow solutions to a confused, disenchanted global populace. Politicians promise jobs. Economists analyze markets and play games while religious leaders perform crystalized ceremonies that have little to do with today's world. Meanwhile people are jobless, homeless, starving and dying, or if they are lucky, just unhappy and apathetic.

Why make jobs? Why should our lives (our existence) depend so much on a thing called the economy? Even religions which were founded on a spark of inspiration have now become dogmatic institutions that function with money. The all-encompassing economic dinosaur is too large to be changed or significantly influenced by *anybody* or *anything* and doesn't even notice the people it is supposed to serve. It eats everything in its path (including the souls of men) and then leaves excrement so physically and emotionally vile to both people and planet that life itself is beginning to look questionable. What if we slowly abandoned this dinosaur, using it for what it's worth as we sail into another dimension of existence? This thought will not be too exciting for those who want wealth and power. But then what is wealth and power and do these words have anything at all to do with **living**?

Let's imagine we are going to give all people all the necessities of life. This thing called economics need not be so much a part of this.

The extras of life should be the fuel for the economy - not the necessities.

What are the necessities? **SHELTER, ENERGY, FOOD, WATER, AIR.** These necessities should not be subject to the perversions of the economic dinosaur. The capitalist game can still be played with VCR's, lawn mowers, hair dryers, clothes dryers, etc. but the necessities of life should be made easily available to all, independent of economics. Education should be aimed at this, politics could be aimed at this, even religion can guide us toward a survival that transcends the economic dinosaur.

We spend our time and money developing faster cars, taller buildings, better TV's, and so on while people are freezing, starving and shitting in the streets of our polluted and dying cities. Is there a bee in any hive that is not provided for? Is there a tree in any forest that does not have soil for its roots? Is there an elk in any herd that cannot graze (well actually all of these are on their way out with the rest of us!). But humans have no system for all like these other creatures. It is still possible for us to achieve this however. ***A system for all would manifest the necessities of life for all while perfectly interfacing with the planet that we are all traveling on.***

One conceptual approach to this *system for all* is a single vessel, available to all, that independently provides the necessities of life. Somehow every adult human should get one of these. The Government could provide them; foundations could provide them; even the wealthy could provide them, but this is a dream. These factions all are slaves themselves of the economic dinosaur. **We must invoke the necessities of life for ourselves.** We must take what is "out there" and build ourselves vessels that will provide the necessities of life - SHELTER, ENERGY, FOOD, WATER, and AIR - survival beyond economics. This is what the ever evolving Earthship concept is after - a survival guide for a civilization that has turned on itself. Is it possible for all people to have the necessities of life without pollution, politics, or economics (all of which are synonymous)? Yes it is. We must continue to evolve the vessel and to help others get it, for there is no peace in a world of haves and have nots.

In the Colorado mountains, the steep downhill grades have built in safety spurs off of the main road. These spurs (or runaway truck ramps) are short uphill unpaved diversion lanes that occur every few miles. Often, large semi trucks experience brake failure and find themselves rolling down the hill at an increasing rate of speed, at some point getting out of control and crashing. The uphill safety spurs are there to absorb the out of control momentum of the truck and bring it to a halt without a catastrophe. The driver only has to be aware enough to change the direction.

Hence, life on this planet is much like a giant semi truck rolling down a hill. We are trying to put on the brakes. Examples of this "braking effort" are: auto emissions control, industrial emissions control, waste dump clean up efforts, recycling etc.

All of the above are genuine efforts of "putting on the brakes" but unfortunately the momentum of the giant truck is too much for any braking effort. *We are out of control.* No braking effort by any politician can stop us. We must steer the "truck" ourselves into another direction that (like the runaway truck ramp) *absorbs the momentum of our current downward plummet* and avoid catastrophe.

How close are we to catastrophe? Mexico City has air four times dirtier than that which makes healthy people sick. Eastern Europe has thousands of starving people. The USA has thousands of homeless people. Political corruption is as rampant as any plague that history records.

How do we change that direction? We have discovered that a little fire can warm us and cook our food. So we move toward fire. We make more and more fire. Then we learn that too much fire can burn our house down and kill us. A little fire is helpful, too much fire destroys.

We know that a little water is good to drink, bathe in, and cook with, but too much water washes away our houses and drowns us. We have learned these lessons about basic phenomena like fire and water. Our economic and political systems are much like fire and water. A small amount of each can be an asset to our lives. A large amount can devour us. People all over the world are drowning in economic turmoil and being burned alive by political corruption. Why must these phenomena stand between us and our existence? Can't we steer ourselves in another direction without the permission of our failing economic and political systems? We are relying on them to put on the brakes but they are failing. We are unaware of the fact that we can steer the giant truck into another direction ourselves. **<u>We</u> can take the steering wheels of our world and change the course.** As with the truck, a sharp turn would be tragic but a slight turn in another direction, little by little, absorbing the momentum of our current direction, can save us from catastrophe.

There are things we must take charge of. There are a few defined necessities of life that we must pull out of the fire and flood of the political and economic turmoil. SHELTER, ENERGY, FOOD, WATER, and AIR.

No political or economic system should stand between a human and her/his right to the above necessities. We must invoke these necessities for ourselves and we must show and help our "relatives" to have the same. We are talking about a <u>global human partnership for survival</u>. Look at a bee hive. Are any bees not provided for? Look at a tree. Are any leaves not allowed to tap in to the branch? Why are some humans on this planet provided for and others left to starve? If you are naked in 10 below zero weather and you have a very expensive warm glove on your right hand, that hand will be very comfortable until the rest of your body dies. We must realize that the globe is one body much like the human body. If the people on one small elite part of the planet are happy and well cared for, they will be very comfortable until the rest of the planet dies. **The whole body must be equally cared for to avoid specific damage *that will ultimately affect the whole body*.** The bottom line is that *all the people must help all the people*. We cannot wait for or rely on politics or economics to do it for us.

With these thoughts in mind we present Earthship Volume III.

DEGAN AND SEAGAL EARTHSHIP, SANTA FE, NEW MEXICO

ONLY AFTER THE LAST TREE HAS BEEN CUT DOWN,
ONLY AFTER THE LAST RIVER HAS BEEN POISONED,
ONLY AFTER THE LAST FISH HAS BEEN CAUGHT,
ONLY THEN WILL YOU FIND
THAT MONEY CANNOT BE EATEN.

CREE INDIAN PROPHECY

PART ONE
EARTHSHIP EVOLUTIONS

EARTHSHIP AT REACH - TAOS, NEW MEXICO

EARTHSHIP AT 1,400 FEET IN BOLIVIA SHOWING THE DIFFERENT GREENHOUSE ANGLE
FOR THE HIGHER SUN NEAR THE EQUATOR

1. STRUCTURAL EVOLUTIONS

AS EARTHSHIPS ARE BUILT ALL OVER THE USA AND OTHER PARTS OF THE WORLD, WE CONTINUE TO EVOLVE THE TECHNIQUES, DETAILS AND PERFORMANCE. THESE EVOLUTIONS ARE DISCOVERED BY OWNER/BUILDERS, CREW MEMBERS AND ARCHITECTURAL STAFF MEMBERS. WE THANK EVERYONE FOR HELPING US CONTINUE TO MAKE EARTHSHIPS BETTER AND EASIER TO BUILD. AT THIS POINT WE SEE NO END TO THE EVOLUTION AND IMPROVEMENT OF THE EARTHSHIP BOTH IN TERMS OF STRUCTURE AND SYSTEMS. WE ARE JUST SCRATCHING THE SURFACE OF A CONCEPT THAT WILL SAIL US THROUGH THE FUTURE AT PEACE WITH OUR ENVIRONMENT. STRUCTURAL EVOLUTIONS ARE PRESENTED IN THIS CHAPTER ALONG WITH OTHER TECHNIQUES AND INFORMATION THAT WE HAVE BEEN REQUESTED TO PROVIDE TOWARD MAKING ALL ASPECTS OF THE EARTHSHIP MORE EASILY WITHIN THE GRASP OF THE OWNER/BUILDER.

graphics by   .....Claire Blanchard
photos by   .....Chris Simpson, Ken Anderson,
                        Tom Woosley

CONCRETE SPACER BLOCKS

Earthship Volume I (page 95) shows half blocks made of treated wood covered with plastic. There are two conditions where these blocking situations occur. Both of these conditions can be executed with concrete rather than wood as an alternate and sometimes easier method of forming blocking. *We must point out that a planned arrangement of empty tires before pounding can avoid most blocking.*

A half block that occurs in the middle of a row can be made by nailing a double thickness of metal lath to the tire on either side of the space to be filled. 2" galvanized roofing nails are used as they are long enough to get a good grip into the tires well yet still short enough to drive into the tires very easily. If there are any spaces where the concrete can fall through, fill them with cardboard before pouring the concrete.

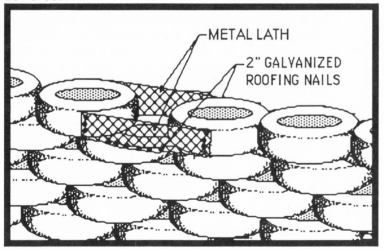

Once the lath is secured to the tires you can begin pouring in the concrete. The concrete is a 3-4-5 mixture of 3 parts cement to 4 parts sand and 5 parts gravel plus a small handful of engineering fibers which we recommend for all concrete. The engineering fibers can be obtained from a local redi-mix dealer. The concrete should be poured level with the top of the tires to receive the next course.

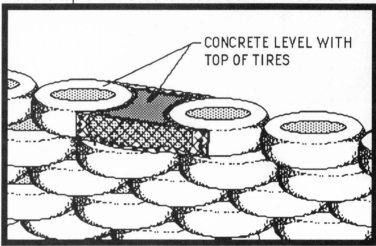

CONCRETE HALF BLOCKS

Half blocks on the ends of the tire walls can be formed with a similar procedure. The metal lath is nailed on one side of the tire with 2" galvanized roofing nails, wrapped around the tire below, and then nailed to the other side of that same tire. The lath is also nailed to the top of the tire below to hold the concrete in as shown in the following diagram.

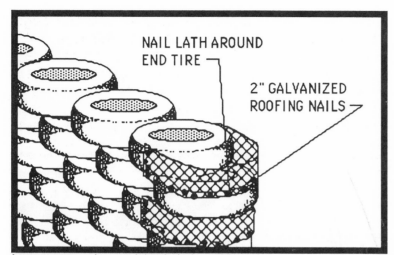

NAIL LATH AROUND END TIRE

2" GALVANIZED ROOFING NAILS

In an extra large block it is some times necessary to use baling wire added as shown below to strengthen and keep the shape of the lath as it can sag when the concrete is poured.

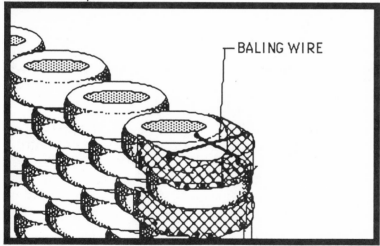

BALING WIRE

Now the form is ready to be filled with concrete.

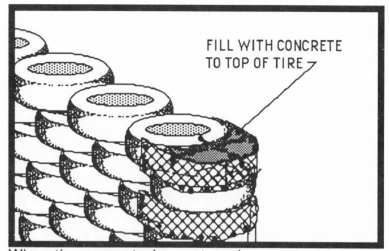

FILL WITH CONCRETE TO TOP OF TIRE

When the concrete has set up (usually overnight) you can begin pounding the course of tires above. If you stop tire pounding an hour or two before the end of the day, you will have time to form the lath, and pour all the concrete blocks so that they can harden overnight and be ready for more tire pounding the next morning. The advantage of concrete is that it is faster, cheaper, and uses less tools and materials than the wood technique. The advantage to the wood technique is that you don't have to wait a day for the concrete to set up in order to pound tires on top of it. This is really the only advantage of wood, therefore we recommend the new concrete blocking technique wherever time allows. If time is a factor and you still want to use concrete blocking, there is a trick to continue pounding tires with a wet concrete block. It requires that you pound the tire at another location such as further along the tire wall or on the ground next to the tire wall and then lift or slide the tire into place gently over the wet concrete (see page 5).

GREG AND MARJORIE HARFORD'S EARTHSHIP SHOWING CONCRETE HALF BLOCKS.

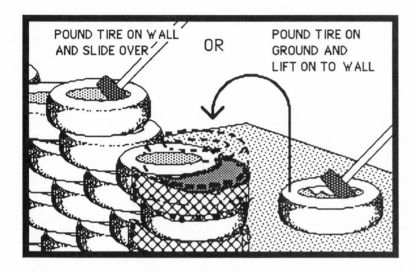

POUND TIRE ON WALL AND SLIDE OVER

OR

POUND TIRE ON GROUND AND LIFT ON TO WALL

RAMMED EARTH SPACER BLOCKS

We have also developed a rammed earth spacer block. The advantages of this method are cost and environmental factors relative to less use of concrete. The only cost is a double piece of lath, 6 mil plastic and a handful of nails. The earth is free. Compare this to the concrete block where you have to purchase sand and cement in addition to the lath and nails. The basic difference is in the strength of the two materials. In situations where strength is a major concern, such as an extreme load (or half blocks at the end of a tire wall) we recommend the use of the concrete blocking. In many situations though, the rammed earth block is cheaper, quicker and easier, and is constructed as follows.

A double layer of metal lath is nailed on to the tires as shown for the concrete blocks <u>with additional nails at the bottom of the lath to the tire below</u>. Use plenty

of nails to withstand earth ramming. Then the inside is lined with two layers of 6 mil plastic.

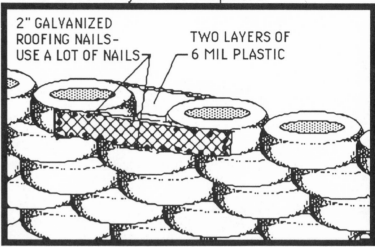

2" GALVANIZED ROOFING NAILS- USE A LOT OF NAILS

TWO LAYERS OF 6 MIL PLASTIC

Now the dirt is shoveled in a little at a time and tamped down with the sledge hammer. It is best if the dirt is slightly damp. This process of filling and tamping is repeated until the block is full and level with the tires on either side of it.

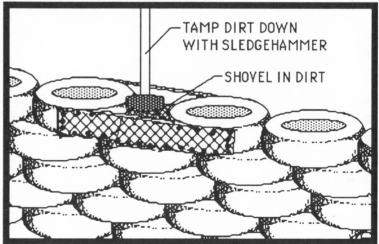

TAMP DIRT DOWN WITH SLEDGEHAMMER

SHOVEL IN DIRT

Rammed earth spacer blocks require a much more serious and conscientious job in forming and nailing the lath than on concrete spacer blocks as the lath must withstand the ramming of earth. *We do not recommend rammed earth <u>half</u> blocks on end walls.* Concrete is the best material here.

CAN AND CONCRETE BOND BEAM

The can and concrete bond beam is most effectively used on a building that has a <u>steep roof slope</u>. In this situation the tires do not end on a level course but are stepped up, sometimes many steps.

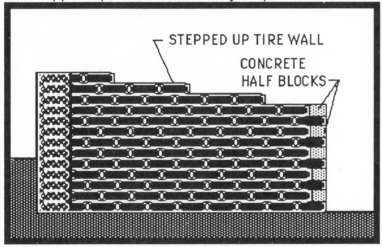

The concrete bond beam connects all the levels together much easier than the stacked wood blocking steps required with a wood plate bond beam. The can and concrete bond beam provides a <u>continuous</u> platform for the roof structure. Another advantage of the concrete bond beam is the reduction of wood used in the Earthship. In many cases concrete is cheaper than wood and requires fewer tools. *Concrete is ultimately a more permanent material than wood.*

The first step of the bond beam is to hollow out the center of <u>every tire</u> on the top course to receive the bond beam.

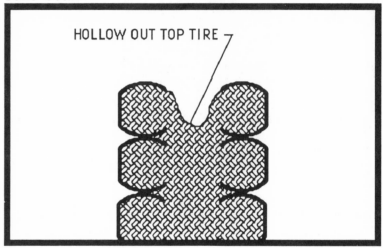

This connects the concrete bond beam to every tire on the top course. Drive a 3'-0" rebar deep into the tire coursing leaving 6" sticking up above the top of the tire. Try to aim the rebar between the tires on the second course down so you don't have to pound the rebar through the rubber casing.

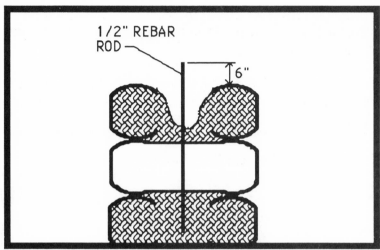

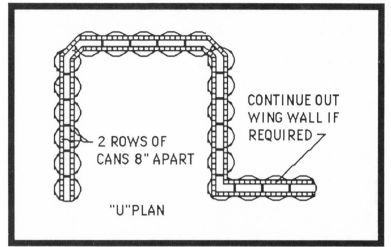

When all of the rebar has been placed you can begin laying cans at the top of the tire wall. Two rows of cans are laid leaving a space between that is a minimum of 8 inches wide. See page 158, Volume I for laying cans.

When the can walls are complete, (2) 1/2" rebar are installed horizontally in the space between the cans. This rebar should run continuously. The twenty foot lengths should be overlapped 18" where necessary and joined with baling wire to achieve a continuous length of rebar throughout the bond beam.

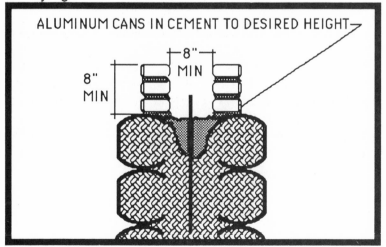

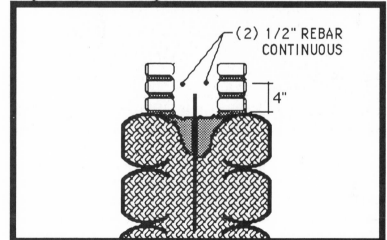

This horizontal rebar should be installed at 4" above the top of the tire. This can be achieved by wiring it in place with baling wire or by pouring the bond beam 4" thick, laying the rebar on the wet concrete and then continuing the pour. <u>Never</u> leave a horizontal cold joint.

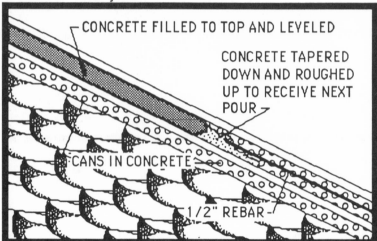

When the concrete is poured into this cavity, it is best to pour the beam all at once as any cold joints in the concrete will weaken this structure. If cold joints do occur, taper the pour off and rough it up to receive the new pour.

After the concrete is poured and while it is still wet, provisions must be made for roof structure. If vigas are used, a vertical rebar with a 3" hook on the end is placed in the wet concrete at the required viga locations. The rebar must be left sticking up about 10" to allow roof slope shimming for vigas (see Earthship Vol. I, pages 104 - 109).

Notice that the top of the concrete bond beam is level and stepped. Never attach vigas to a sloped bond beam

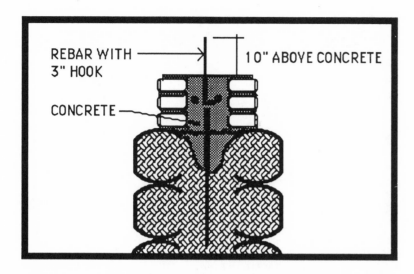

REBAR WITH 3" HOOK

10" ABOVE CONCRETE

CONCRETE

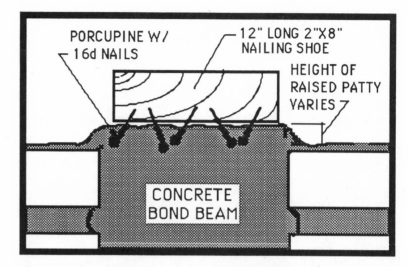

PORCUPINE W/ 16d NAILS

12" LONG 2"X8" NAILING SHOE

HEIGHT OF RAISED PATTY VARIES

CONCRETE BOND BEAM

Vigas are not available in many places so we have evolved a truss system that can be used when heavy timber is not available. If trusses are used, a wood nailing shoe is cleated into a raised patty on the wet concrete bond beam. The shoe is made from 1-1/2" thick pressure treated 2" x 8" lumber and is 12" long. It is porcupined (see Earthship Vol I. page 157) with 16d nails and set into the wet concrete.

These wood "shoes" allow anchoring and shimming of the trusses to an appropriate slope. Be sure that these shoes are installed level and not sloped. Never install trusses on a sloped shoe. See photograph oposite page one.

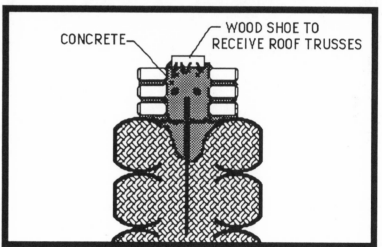

CONCRETE

WOOD SHOE TO RECEIVE ROOF TRUSSES

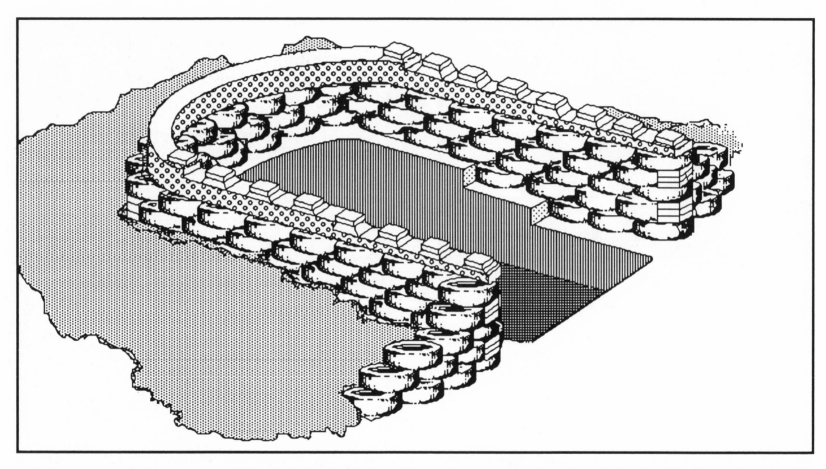

TYPICAL EARTHSHIP "U" WITH CAN/CONCRETE BOND BEAM AND WOOD NAILING SHOES FOR TRUSS MOUNTING.

10

EARTHSHIP AT 14,000 FEET IN BOLIVIA SHOWING THE DIFFERENT GREENHOUSE ANGLE FOR THE HIGHER SUN NEAR THE EQUATOR

11

Depending on the conditions of the tire wall, the horizontal rebar will either slope down continuously or step down as shown in the next two diagrams.

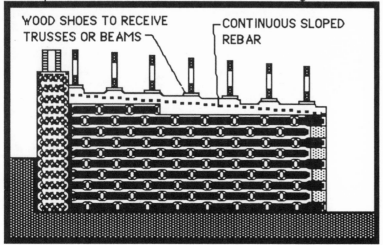

WOOD SHOES TO RECEIVE
TRUSSES OR BEAMS

CONTINUOUS SLOPED
REBAR

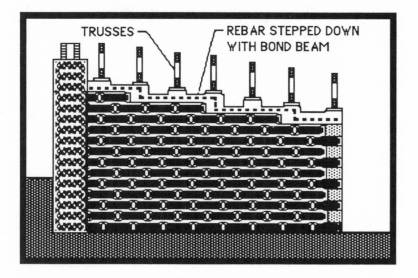

TRUSSES

REBAR STEPPED DOWN
WITH BOND BEAM

REBAR PINNED PLATES

In some situations, Earthships are built with only one to three courses of tires on a gentle slope. For these Earthships we have an alternate method of anchoring a wood bond beam plate to the tires - the rebar plate anchor (See Earthship Volume I p. 101-103 for wood bond beam plates). This method can save time and money since it does not require any concrete.

3 foot lengths of 1/2" rebar are hammered down through the pounded tire with a sledgehammer at least 18" into undisturbed soil (or 3 tires deep), leaving 6" to 8" sticking out above the tire.

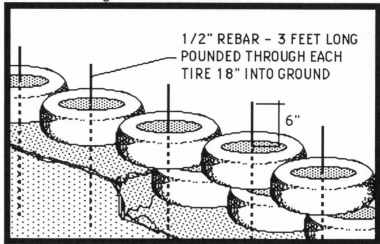

1/2" REBAR - 3 FEET LONG
POUNDED THROUGH EACH
TIRE 18" INTO GROUND

6"

Then the first layer of 2"x12" pressure treated lumber is set over the tires and rebar. *Be sure to lay down 6 mil plastic over the tires first..* Marks are made, where holes will be drilled, at the location of the rebar anchors by placing the 2x12 plate over the rebar stakes and tapping it with a hammer. Make pencil marks where the dents are.

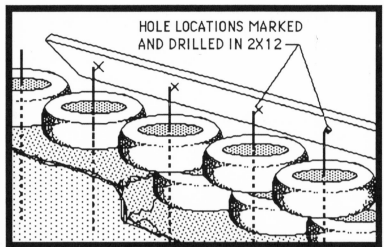

The plate is then placed on the tires and the rebar that is sticking up from the plate is now bent over with a steel pipe and snugged up with a sledgehammer. Make notches in the second 2 x 12 with a chainsaw where the bent rebar is so the second plate lays flat on the first plate.

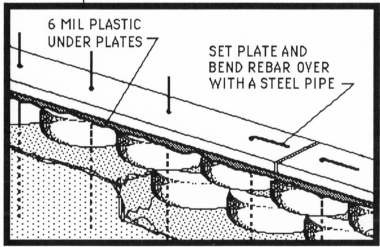

Finally the second layer of 2x12 lumber is nailed on

with 16d nails. Keep upper layer joints away from lower layer joints.

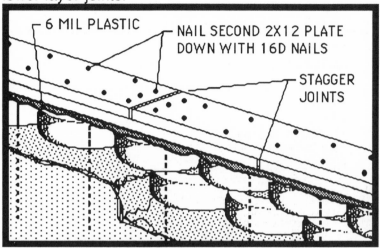

An alternative method is to place and nail both plates and install rebar pins through them afterwards.

HOMEMADE TRUSSES
PANEL TRUSS
The truss as a roofing system has several advantages. Trusses are lighter and easier to handle than a viga or beam. Some areas do not have access to timber for vigas or beams so trusses are a must in these areas. Trusses also allow an increased depth of insulation in the roof. Custom trusses can be constructed with minimal tools on the job site or purchased from a local building supply store. The truss is a flat box type and is constructed of panels made from 2"x4" stock lumber. The depth and number of panels in the truss will depend on the span of the room and the roof loads to be carried. 3'-0" is an average size of the panels. If large snow or wind loads are possible in your area, trusses should

be checked out with a local engineer, truss manufacturer or SSA.

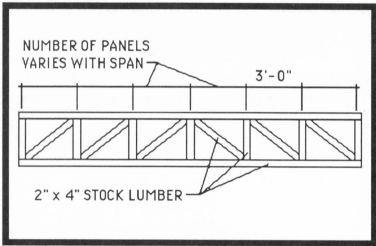

The 2x4 members of the truss are connected together with metal plates nailed into the lumber. These metal plates are called truss plates and can be obtained from a building supply store.

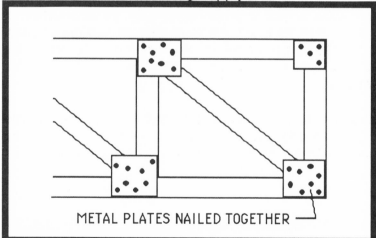

Trusses are mounted flush with the outside of wood shoes.

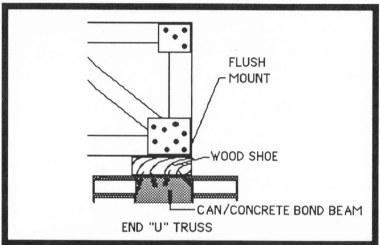

At the center walls the trusses overlap on the wood shoe.

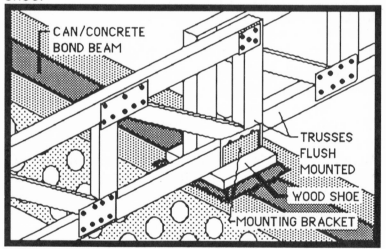

The truss can be mounted on the prepared shoe block (previously set in the bond beam) with metal brackets available at a building supply store.

14

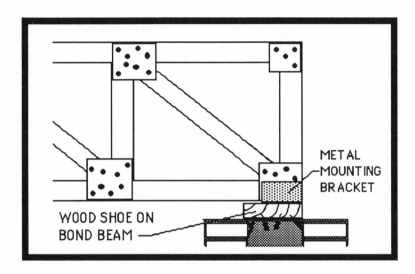

METAL MOUNTING BRACKET

WOOD SHOE ON BOND BEAM

If you are in an area that may receive heavy snow or wind, or if your span is more than 18'-0", you may require additional reinforcing of the trusses. It is important that you consult your local structural engineer or SSA for assistance.

Although this panel truss design is simple, it does require some carpentry skill and quite a few tools. An inexperienced builder can make a dangerous mess of this truss. Therefore we have a second truss design that literally anyone can make. We call it the "idiot truss". It is actually much safer and stronger. It does cost a little more in materials. This truss is constructed of 2x4 stock lumber and 5/8" CDX plywood. It should be constructed on a flat surface and requires minimal tools such as a circular saw, square, and hammer along with nails and liquid nails. First the plywood is cut in half so that you have (2) 2'x8' sheets of plywood. Cut the length so that

joints in the plywood do not occur near the center of the truss.

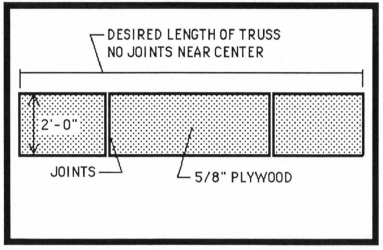

DESIRED LENGTH OF TRUSS
NO JOINTS NEAR CENTER

2'-0"

JOINTS

5/8" PLYWOOD

Then 2x4 stock lumber is glued and nailed around the edge of the plywood as shown on the following page. The bottom and top 2x4's should be continuous and if possible should be one piece of wood. If joints are necessary they should occur away from the center and away from other joints. **No joints of any kind occur within 3'-0" of middle.**

Use 8d nails for the top 2x4 plate. Tack the bottom plates on with 8d nails but use 16d nails staggered every 6" to secure them permanently. Use Liquid Nails on all 2x4 plates.

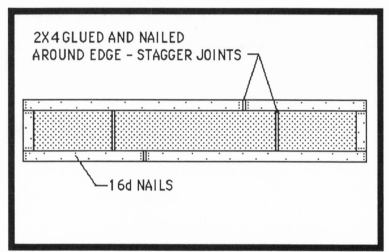

2X4 GLUED AND NAILED
AROUND EDGE – STAGGER JOINTS

16d NAILS

Now 2x4 strips are glued and nailed over the plywood joints as shown below.

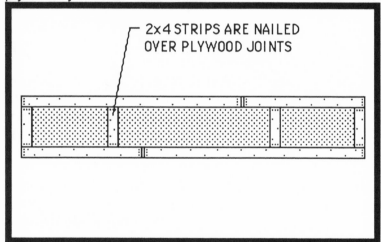

2x4 STRIPS ARE NAILED
OVER PLYWOOD JOINTS

Now the truss is turned over and an additional 2x4 is glued and nailed along the bottom only, plus a small (2'-0" min.) piece of 2x4 nailed where the joint in the 2x4 on the other side occurs.

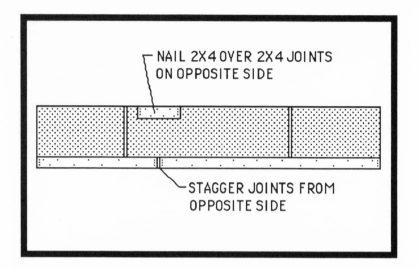

NAIL 2X4 OVER 2X4 JOINTS
ON OPPOSITE SIDE

STAGGER JOINTS FROM
OPPOSITE SIDE

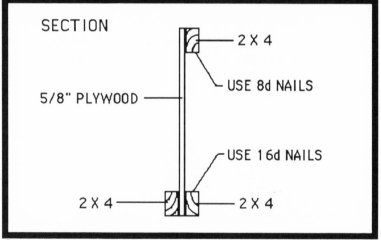

SECTION

2 X 4

USE 8d NAILS

5/8" PLYWOOD

USE 16d NAILS

2 X 4

2 X 4

Once again, the important thing to remember is that *none of the joints in plywood or 2x4 occur next to each other*. Now the truss can be installed as shown on opposite page. These trusses will span up to 22' at 2'-0" O.C for loads up to 50 PSF. For longer spans or larger loads check with SSA or an engineer.

16

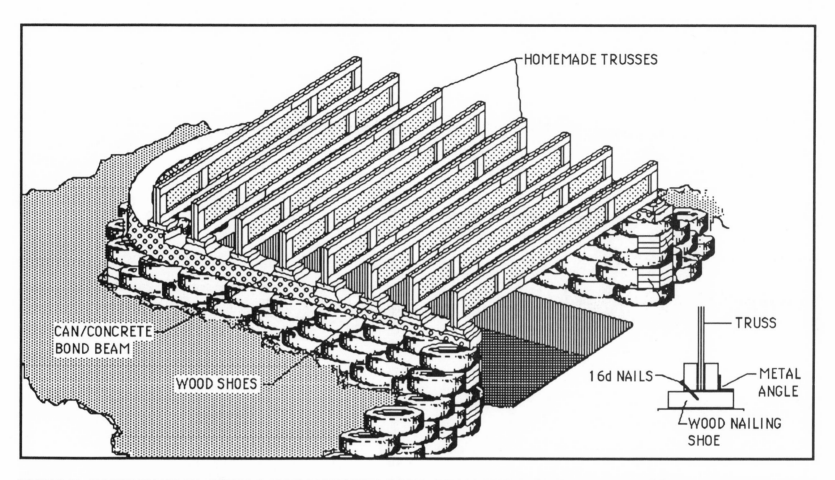

HOMEMADE TRUSSES

CAN/CONCRETE
BOND BEAM

WOOD SHOES

TRUSS

16d NAILS

METAL
ANGLE

WOOD NAILING
SHOE

TYPICAL EARTHSHIP "U" WITH CAN/CONCRETE BOND BEAM AND HOMEMADE TRUSSES. TRUSSES CAN BE ANCHORED TO NAILING SHOES WITH 16D NAILS AND/OR METAL ANGLES NAILED TO TRUSSES AND TO NAILING SHOE.

COLD AREA
GROUND INSULATION

In areas where the tire structure of the building is above the frost line or where the frost line is very deep (4'-0" or more), additional insulation may be required around the perimeter. In this situation, the tire wall is completed and the voids between the tires *on the outside of the building* are filled with mud or cement the same as the interior. (see Earthship Vol. I pages 174-5)

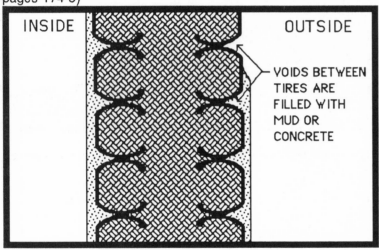

Then, before the earth is bermed up against the tires, a layer of 2" rigid perimeter insulation is nailed (with 16d nails and roofing disks as washers) to the tires as shown in the following diagram.

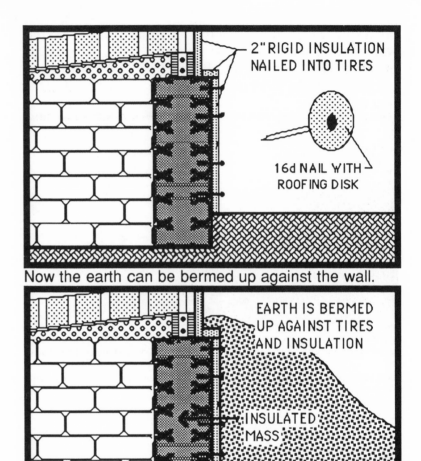

Now the earth can be bermed up against the wall.

BATTERED TIRE RETAINING
WALL AND WING WALL

On some steep sites or where Earthship walls are well below normal grade, a <u>retaining wall</u> may be necessary to hold back the surrounding earth. The construction of the leaning or battered tire retaining wall is as follows. The first course of tires is pounded at the base of the area to be retained. A flat area of undisturbed earth must be cleared for these tires to rest on.

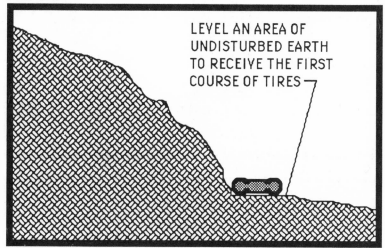

LEVEL AN AREA OF UNDISTURBED EARTH TO RECEIVE THE FIRST COURSE OF TIRES

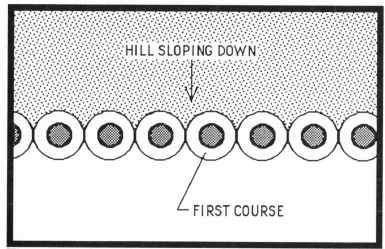

HILL SLOPING DOWN

FIRST COURSE

The second course of tires is staggered like bricks the same as building a vertical tire wall, but it also

steps back. An arc can be added for strength but is not always necessary. The distance the tires are stepped back on each course depends on the severity of the slope that is to be retained.

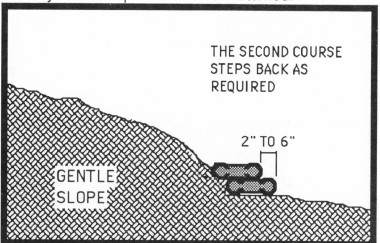

THE SECOND COURSE STEPS BACK AS REQUIRED

2" TO 6"

GENTLE SLOPE

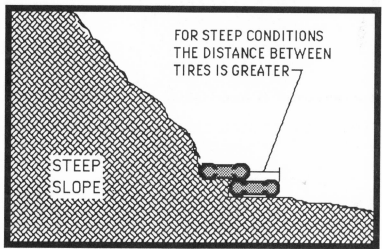

FOR STEEP CONDITIONS THE DISTANCE BETWEEN TIRES IS GREATER

STEEP SLOPE

A steep slope requires more step distance.

19

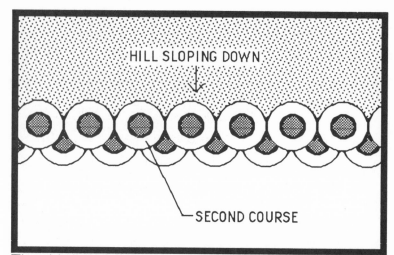

HILL SLOPING DOWN

SECOND COURSE

The third and following courses are set in the same manner of leveling and stepping back until the desired height is reached. Make sure you compact the earth behind and under the wall as you go up.

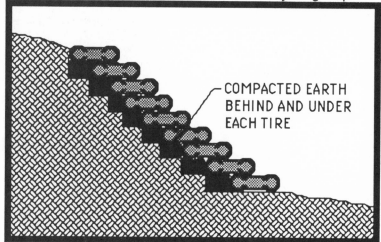

COMPACTED EARTH BEHIND AND UNDER EACH TIRE

All tire walls retaining earth should lean into the hill they are retaining. This is true for all wing walls as well.

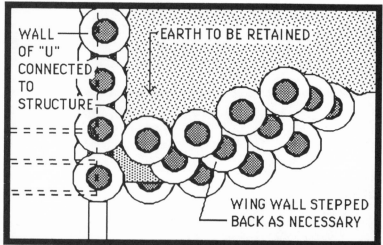

WALL OF "U" CONNECTED TO STRUCTURE

EARTH TO BE RETAINED

WING WALL STEPPED BACK AS NECESSARY

The wall of the "U" is supported by the roof diaphragm and does not have to be arched or battered like the free unsupported walls that are not connected to structure. If the wall is retaining fill, the fill must be compacted to 90% under the wall.

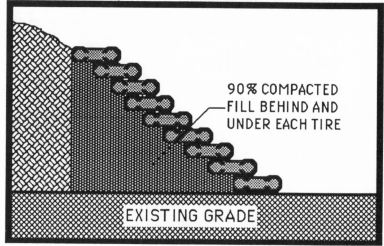

90% COMPACTED FILL BEHIND AND UNDER EACH TIRE

EXISTING GRADE

TIRE RETAINING WALL BEHIND EARTHSHIP IN JAPAN.

21

STEEP SLOPE SECTIONS

For those sites that have a steep slope, we have designed two level Earthships that can accommodate the steep terrain. These are not two story structures but rather two levels stepping back into the hill as shown on the following pages. SSA should be involved in terms of guidance and/or architectural details for these situations.

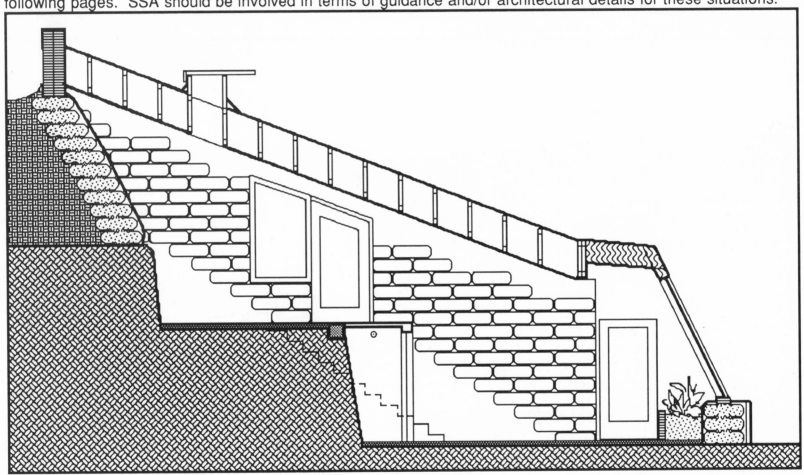

THIS CONFIGURATION IS MORE ECONOMICAL AS IT DOESN'T REQUIRE GLAZING ON THE SECOND STORY.

These structures require more money in terms of architectural drawings and more money in terms of construction. Also the warmest rooms tend to be on the upper level since heat rises. This sometimes requires ducts for air movement.

The overlap can be very small or large as the following diagram suggests. A large overlap can accommodate a tall space for fruit trees.

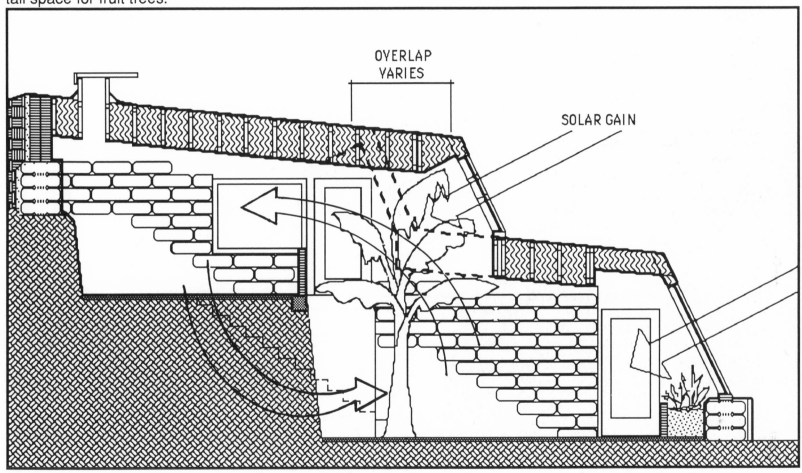

THE CONFIGURATION OF THIS ROOF PROVIDES FOR A SECOND ROW OF SOUTH FACING GLASS TO HEAT THE UPPER LEVEL.

Two typical sections can be stepped up a hill without any unusual details as shown below. They can be joined by an interior staircase carved up under the front face of the upper "U".

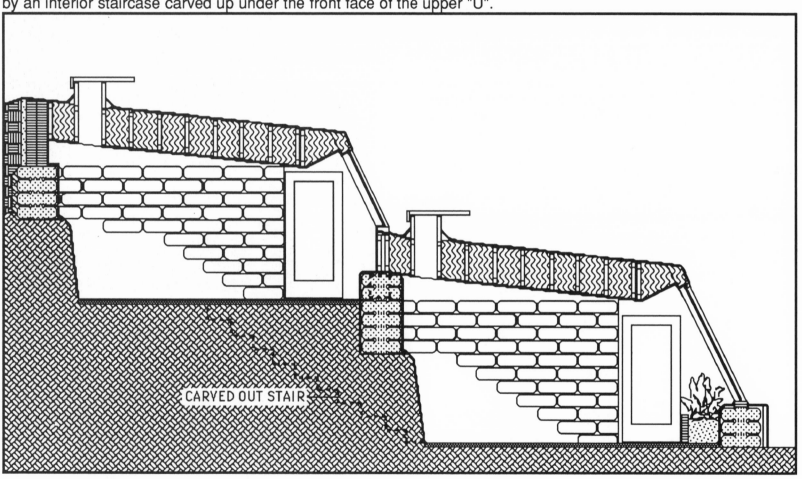

CARVED OUT STAIR

24

NEW GUTTER DETAILS

In areas with very cold winter temperatures the gutters, presented in Earthship Volume II, located at the top of the front face shade themselves and for that reason are prone to freezing and ice dams.

A new gutter detail, located at the bottom of the front face alleviates this problem as sun can reflect off the glass face and melt the ice dams. Also this is where the house loses heat so it is a warmer place than the location of the upper gutter. This gutter works best for south sloping roofs that do not have a kick up in the front.

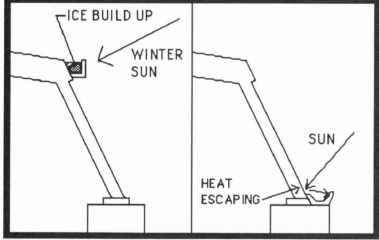

The new indoor cisterns can eliminate gutters all together. In many cases this is easier and cheaper. See chapter 2, pages 44 to 47.

If you don't want water running down your front face, another gutter detail idea is shown below.

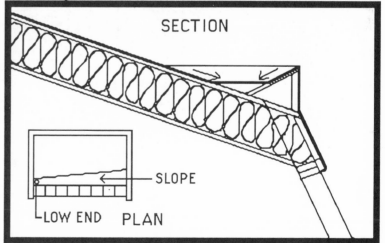

This is achieved with plywood and 2x6 or 2x8's. Making it higher at one end will direct the water.

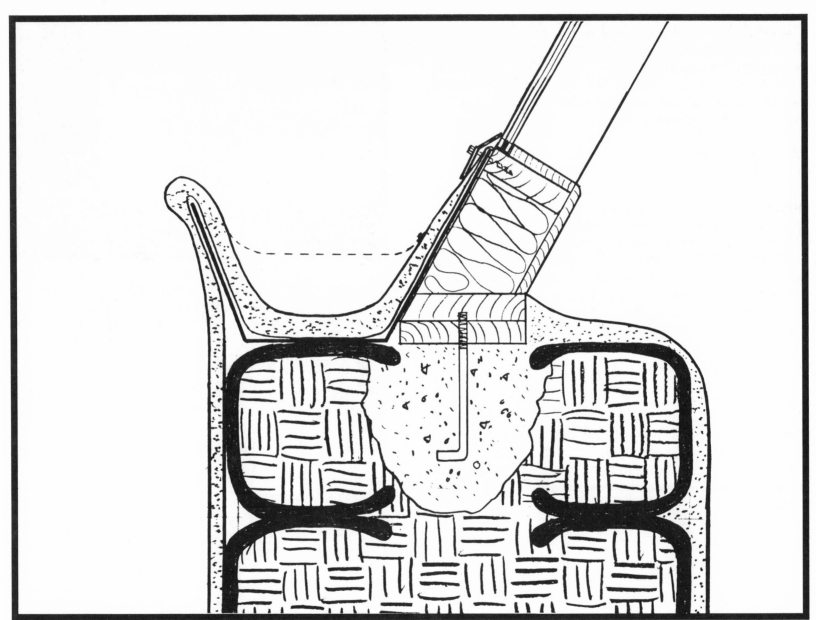

GUTTER DETAIL AT THE BOTTOM OF THE FRONT FACE.

26

FLOORS - MUD AND FLAGSTONE

Both flagstone and mud floors are laid directly on an earth subfloor. In arid climates this is fine. If there is a possibility of dampness, lay down a 6 mil plastic vapor barrier on the earth subfloor before starting your mud or flagstone floor.

MUD FLOORS

A mud floor is very similar in construction and finishing to an adobe mud wall finish and with the addition of oil coatings or sealers can be very durable. It is not, however, recommended for use in high traffic areas near exterior doors or wet areas like bathrooms. The process of applying the mud floor will usually occur in three steps which should correspond to the finishing of the rest of the building. In general the floor is the last part of the building to be finished so it is important to make sure that when you are ready to do your last coat of mud on the floor that the rest of your finishing has been done.

The first step in applying a mud floor is to level the dirt subfloor to a reasonably smooth surface. Make sure all areas of fill (such as plumbing trenches, low spots, etc.) are tamped and compacted before starting your floor. You will want to establish the desired height of finished floor. The subfloor is leveled about 2 1/2" below the proposed finish floor height.

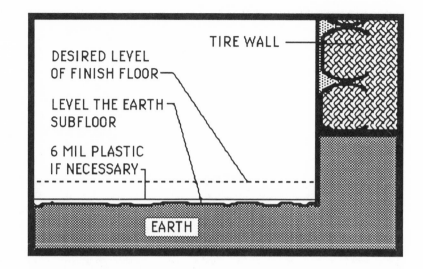

The floor can now be covered with the first of two scratch coats of mud. The mud is typically a mixture of one part sifted dirt to one part sand, 4 or 5 large double handfuls of chopped straw per wheelbarrow load and water to a fairly thick consistency. For the scratch coat, the sand can be course or fine. If you use the dirt from your site you will have to sift it through a 1/4" hardware cloth screen for the scratch coats. This hardware cloth can be attached to a simple frame of 2x4 lumber for easier sifting. You will have to vary the quantity of sand added depending on how sandy or clay your soil is. The dirt is the "glue" for the mixture. The sand keeps the mud from cracking and the straw makes a structural web throughout. You will find the correct proportioning by trial and error as you work through the mud in the building. If you get cracks in your scratch coats, add sand to the mixture.

27

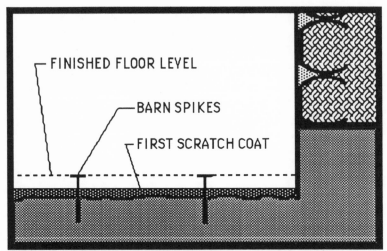

FINISHED FLOOR LEVEL

BARN SPIKES

FIRST SCRATCH COAT

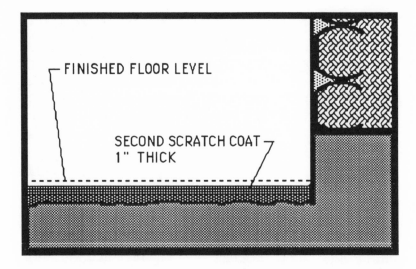

FINISHED FLOOR LEVEL

SECOND SCRATCH COAT
1" THICK

The first scratch coat is applied to level and smooth the surface of the subfloor. The mud can be poured or shoveled on and is then troweled flat with a square trowel and leveled. After the mud is level, it is scratched to roughen the surface for receiving the next coat (see Earthship Vol. I, p. 177 for scratcher). The thickness of the first coat will vary because of irregularities in the subfloor. Sometimes it is necessary to drive barn spikes into the subfloor and level them all with each other (with a builders level) to establish a level surface at the height of the finished floor. These spikes are removed during the final coat. After the first coat is completely dry, the second coat is applied in the same manner but should be about 1" in thickness.

The final or "finish" coat has a slightly different mixture. The quantity of sand should nearly double the quantity of dirt so it will be 2 parts sand and 1 part dirt and a slightly larger quantity of straw can be added. The sand for this coat should be fine plaster sand. It is during this coat that you remove your grade stake spikes. Again it is troweled with the square trowel as smooth as possible and left to set up until it is firm to the touch but still damp. It is best to keep this coat between 1/2" and 3/4" thick.

The last step is to retrowel the mud by first misting it with a plant spray bottle filled with water and then troweling until it is slick (see Earthship Volume I, P. 178 for misting mud). For this step a "pool" trowel that is more flexible and round on the ends is recommended. This step can be repeated the following day if cracks begin to occur.

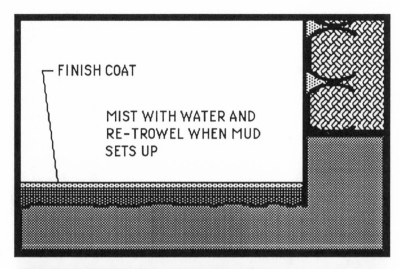

FINISH COAT

MIST WITH WATER AND
RE-TROWEL WHEN MUD
SETS UP

When the mud is completely dry it can be sealed to create a very durable surface. The most commonly used sealer for mud is boiled linseed oil mixed half and half with mineral spirits. This thin mixture soaks into the mud 1/2 to 3/4 of an inch and dries quickly. It is applied with a brush like paint and usually takes three coats to cover and soak in evenly. Each coat soaks deep into the mud floor giving you a thick 1/2" layer of hard oiled mud. A fourth coat of two thirds oil and one third mineral spirits can be added for more durability. *Make sure every coat is totally dry before applying another.* If a pool of oil does not soak in, wipe off the excess. Compared to other floor sealing products, the linseed oil is a fairly organic way to seal. Another product that can be used after 3 coats of the oil mixture is satin finish Varathane which, unlike the linseed oil, gives the mud a more shiny finish. These floors are very beautiful and reasonably durable for areas that aren't exposed to wet muddy shoes and grit. Heavy furniture should have coasters to keep pointed legs from denting the mud floor.

FLAGSTONE FLOORS

Our method of laying a flagstone floor begins the same way as a mud floor. You must first level the subfloor reasonably flat as shown in the previous discussion. Allow 3" to 3 1/2" for the total thickness of the floor. Then you will want to lay out your stones, cutting and fitting a small area at a time.

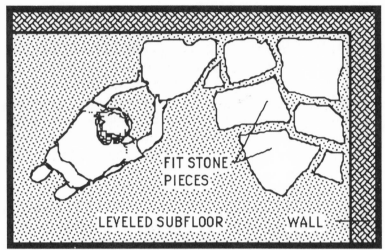

FIT STONE PIECES

LEVELED SUBFLOOR   WALL

The flagstone can be trimmed with a hammer and cold chisel or scored on the back side with a circular saw and masonry blade and then chipped off. If you take the time to work out a good "puzzle" you should have very little cutting.

The joints between the stone can vary between 1/2" and 1-1/2". Once you have laid out a small area, you can begin setting the stones in concrete. The mixture for concrete is 1 part cement to 3 parts concrete sand plus the addition of a hand full of structural engineering fibers. The brand of fibers you purchase will recommend the correct quantity to add. Fibers can be purchased at a concrete and gravel yard. Concrete sand has particles (aggregate) up to 1/2" diameter, whereas plaster sand has very fine particles. Concrete sand is cheap but not good for plaster or grout. Plaster sand is more expensive and is not necessary for laying the stone.

Next pour out the concrete onto the subfloor at least 1 1/2" to 2" thick and set the flagstone, one piece at a

time, in the concrete. Wet the stone and push it down lightly into the concrete leveling it in all directions at the same time.

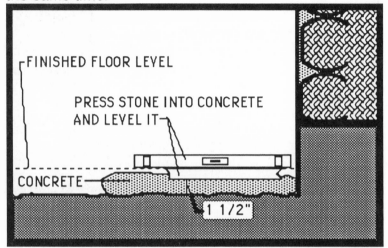

FINISHED FLOOR LEVEL

PRESS STONE INTO CONCRETE AND LEVEL IT

CONCRETE   1 1/2"

Now set the second and all other stones similarly, leveling them with the first stone. When you are finished with the area for that day be sure to remove any concrete from inside the joints as you will want to fill them with grout later. Hollow out all joints between stones to at least 1" deep to allow for finish grout. Also, you must thoroughly sponge off each stone as concrete is very hard to remove once it dries.

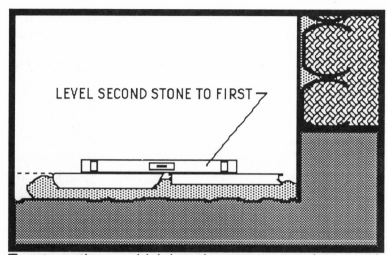

LEVEL SECOND STONE TO FIRST

To strengthen cold joints between one days work and the next it is a good idea to set some long 20d nails into the edge of the wet concrete about 3" apart. This will give the new concrete something to grip onto. Never leave a vertical area of concrete to be joined to later.

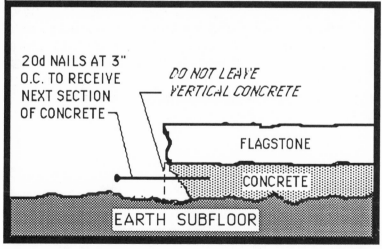

20d NAILS AT 3" O.C. TO RECEIVE NEXT SECTION OF CONCRETE

DO NOT LEAVE VERTICAL CONCRETE

FLAGSTONE

CONCRETE

EARTH SUBFLOOR

GROUTING AND SEALING

Grouting can begin as soon as the concrete is set up, usually overnight. There are several types of material that can be used for grout, the cheapest being cement. A mix of 1 part cement to 3 parts fine plaster sand with water mixed to a paste. This will be light grey when it dries. Other products specifically made for grout can be purchased at your local building supply and are generally applied in the same manner.

The joint is dampened and grout pressed in with the side of a triangular pointing trowel to fill up all of the voids. It is a good idea to chop the cement into the joint to make sure all voids are filled.

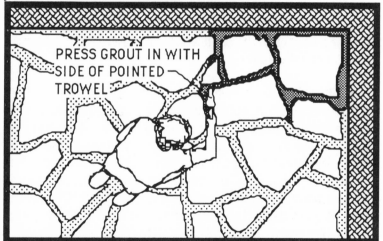

PRESS GROUT IN WITH SIDE OF POINTED TROWEL

Then, using the trowel, the grout is smoothed out level with the top of the flagstone. When the grout starts to become firm it can either be smoothed out with a sponge float or troweled to a more shiny finish with a small pointing trowel. The latter is a more difficult finish.

31

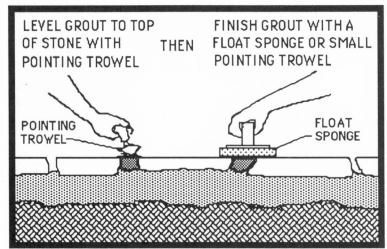

LEVEL GROUT TO TOP OF STONE WITH POINTING TROWEL — THEN — FINISH GROUT WITH A FLOAT SPONGE OR SMALL POINTING TROWEL

POINTING TROWEL

FLOAT SPONGE

It is very important to remove any grout that has gone onto the stone as it will stain and be very difficult to remove later. This can be done by repeatedly wiping the stones with a wet sponge towards the grout joints.

Once the grout is dry, the flagstone can be cleaned thoroughly with a scrub brush and water to prepare it for sealing. When the flagstone is dry, a mixture of half boiled linseed oil and half mineral spirits is painted on. Usually three coats are necessary. *The oil should dry completely between coats. Do not allow pooling.* Due to the nature of this work we recommend knee pads and a respirator, if desired, during the oiling process.

If you prefer to use large floor tile instead of flagstone the procedure for setting, grouting and sealing tile is identical to flagstone.

FINISHING EARTHCLIFFS

There are two methods suggested for finishing earth cliffs; a mud plaster finish and a cement plaster finish. The mud plaster finish would be used in areas where you are sure that your Earthship is far enough away from the water table and therefore, will not encounter any moisture or dampness. Like the mud floors, the mud plaster is a mixture of mud, sand and straw with water added. The mix is 1 part dirt to 1 part sand and 4-5 handfuls of straw for usually two coats of scratch mud, then 1 part dirt to 2 parts sand with 4-5 handfuls of straw for the finish coat.

The earth cliff is dampened with a sponge or splash brush and water. Then the mud plaster is applied directly on the earth cliff with a trowel, either square or round pool type. The object of plastering is to fill in the "low" spots or dips in the earth cliff in layers until it eventually becomes a flat, even surface.

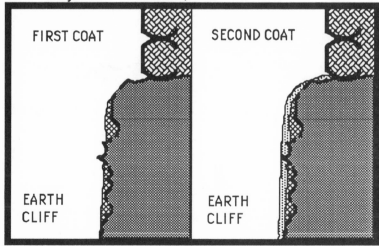

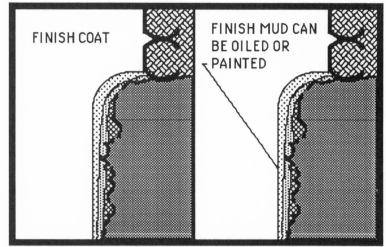

Remember to scratch the mud between coats to roughen the surface. The finish coat is retroweled and misted in the same manner as the finish coat on the mud floor (see page 26 this chapter and Earthship Vol. I p. 178). When the mud is dry it can be sealed with the same linseed oil/mineral spirits mixture as the floors. Another good finish for mud walls that does not effect the light color is called "Z- Seal" by Z- Brick.

If there is any chance of moisture, being close to the water table, or a flaky earth cliff we recommend a cement plaster coat over the rough earth cliff. This will protect the structure of the earth cliff and help seal out moisture. This plaster mix is 1 part cement to 3 parts plaster sand and structural fibers. It is applied with a trowel as shown above, and may take several scratch coats to cover properly. After the cliff is covered with 2 scratch coats of cement plaster you may continue with mud plaster for your finish coat. It will be sealed as above. We have also used stucco (a cement base color finish coat) for a finish in cement plastered earth cliffs. This provides a moisture resistant finish.

HANGING EARTHSHIP DOORS

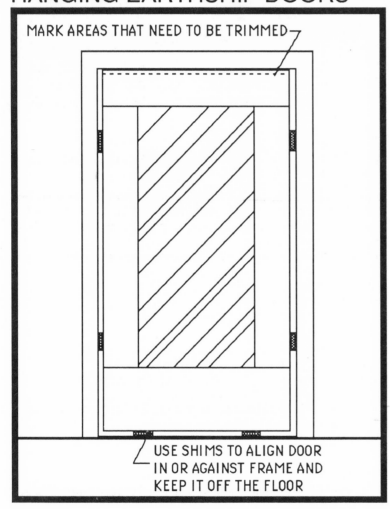

MARK AREAS THAT NEED TO BE TRIMMED

USE SHIMS TO ALIGN DOOR IN OR AGAINST FRAME AND KEEP IT OFF THE FLOOR

After a door is completed (as per Earthship Volume II pp 163-176) it is ready to be hung. This process begins by fitting the door into or against the frame and marking areas that need to be trimmed for a proper fit. Next, trim the door down as per the marks with a plane or sander using coarse paper. It is best to trim the door a little on the small side as swelling sometimes occurs with weather changes.

Now you are ready to mark and install the hinges. Be sure that you have purchased the appropriate size hinge for your door as a heavy door can pull a small hinge out. We usually use (3) 3 1/2 inch butt hinges per homemade door. Begin by measuring and mounting the hinges *on the door jamb* in their desired location. There are 2 methods for this. One method exposes the whole hinge and is very easy. This is the flush mount method.

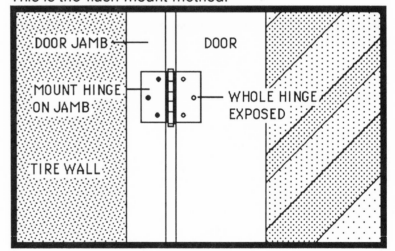

DOOR JAMB   DOOR

MOUNT HINGE ON JAMB   WHOLE HINGE EXPOSED

TIRE WALL

Another method requires recessing the hinge into the inside of the jamb. This is called the "let in" method.

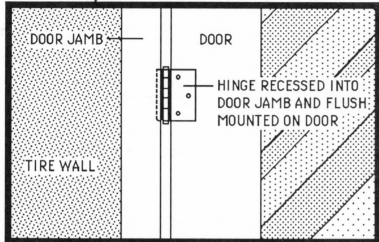

Now the hinge must be recessed into the jamb with a chisel.

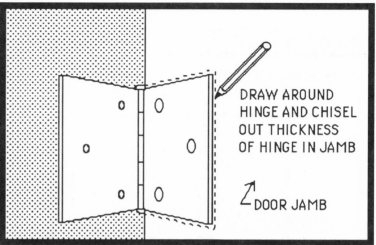

This method requires unpinning the butt hinge and reversing it.

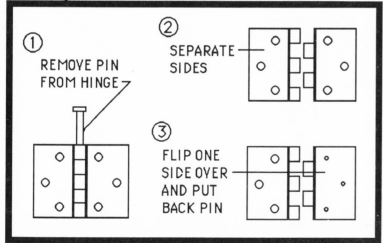

The hinge is recessed just enough to be flush with the jamb. Notice that the pin is not let in - just the leaf of the hinge.

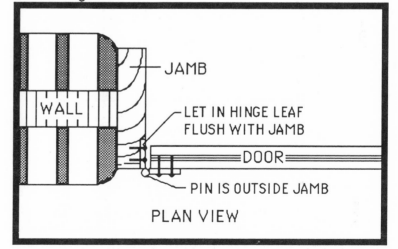

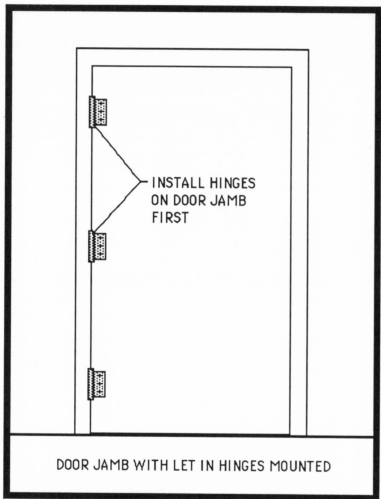

INSTALL HINGES
ON DOOR JAMB
FIRST

DOOR JAMB WITH LET IN HINGES MOUNTED

The door is now placed in the frame exactly as you wish it to hang. Use wood shims to raise it off the floor to take into account for carpet, threshold and/or weatherstripping where applicable. Make sure it is almost touching the top of the jamb. Then, while holding it in place, screw the hinges into the door. Hinges usually come with short screws. We advise

replacing these screws with longer screws of the same diameter. This will work much better for the heavier door. Screws should go through the plywood diaphragm.

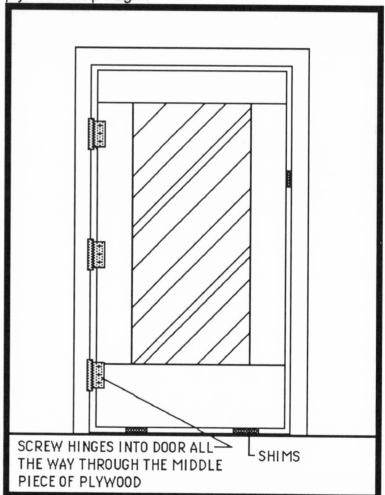

SCREW HINGES INTO DOOR ALL
THE WAY THROUGH THE MIDDLE
PIECE OF PLYWOOD

SHIMS

After the door is hung, a final sanding or trimming can be done if necessary. Installation of the door stops is done as follows. Begin by selecting the desired width (2" to 8") of 1" stock lumber and then measure and cut pieces for the sides and top. Now glue and nail the stops in place while another person holds the door steady and flush with the jamb on the opposite side to ensure a flush fit. Start with the top stop then add the sides

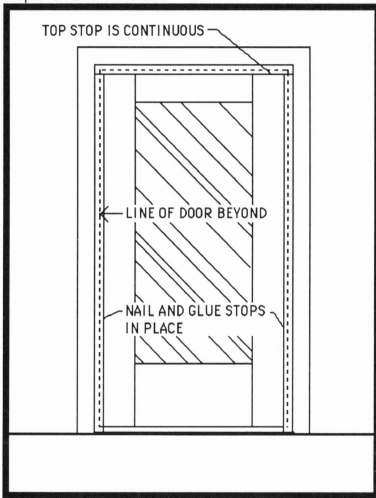

TOP STOP IS CONTINUOUS

LINE OF DOOR BEYOND

NAIL AND GLUE STOPS IN PLACE

Your door is now ready for handles or other hardware available at your local building supply store. Be sure to measure the thickness of the door before purchasing these supplies as Earthship doors can be slightly thicker than conventional doors.

If you are installing cabinet doors the stops are not necessary. A simple magnetic catch installed anywhere opposite the hinged side of the door is all that is required.

ROUND AND ARCH WINDOWS

The construction of a round or arch window in a single or double can wall can be done by building the can wall up to the desired level and location of the window. Then cut the shape of the window out of a sheet of rigid foam insulation. Cut two or more layers if necessary to get the thickness of the can wall. The layers can be joined together with some long nails like 10" barn spikes from both sides.

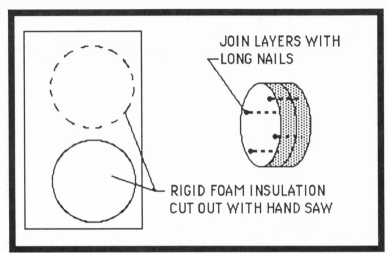

JOIN LAYERS WITH
LONG NAILS

RIGID FOAM INSULATION
CUT OUT WITH HAND SAW

Now your form is placed on the wall and the can work continues around it until the wall is finished.

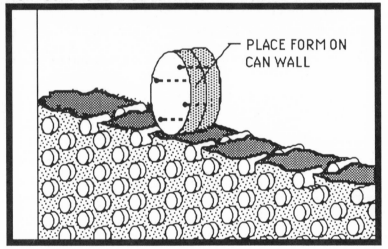

PLACE FORM ON
CAN WALL

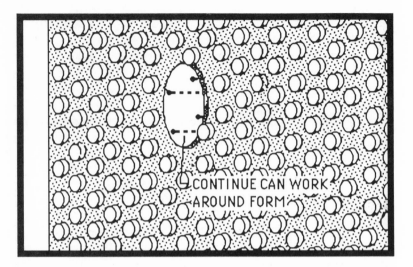

CONTINUE CAN WORK
AROUND FORM

When the wall is complete and you are ready to install the glass, the form is removed. If the form will not come out by sliding it, then break the foam up with the claw end of a hammer until it comes out. Now you can make a template or take measurements for your glass.

The glass is set into the hole by making a small ridge of concrete around the opening to receive the glass. This ridge serves as a stop and should be on the outside - the glass sets on the inside of this ridge.

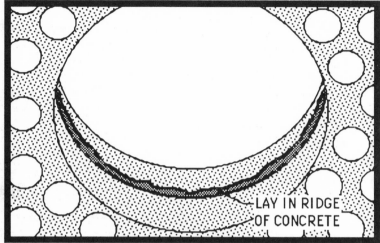

LAY IN RIDGE OF CONCRETE

When the concrete is hard, set the glass in on rubber shims and put another ridge of mud plaster all around the *inside* to hold the glass in place. We use mud plaster here so the glass can be easily replaced if broken. Now plaster up against the glass with mud inside and cement plaster outside. Slope the plaster at the bottom so water will run away from the window.

HOMEMADE OPERABLE HOPPER WINDOW

The advantages of this new homemade operable window that fits into the lower front face are many. It is cheaper, it has better insulative value than the commercial hopper window and since it is made on site, it can be any size. The third factor is important because tire coursing varies making standard size windows more difficult to plan for and install.

The first step to constructing this window unit is to frame out the desired rough opening in the tire wall.

This frame is attached to both the front face plates and the tires below it.

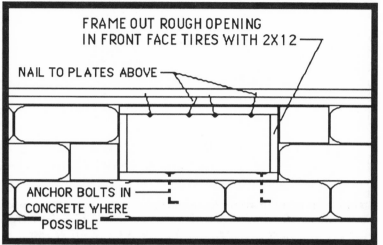

FRAME OUT ROUGH OPENING IN FRONT FACE TIRES WITH 2X12

NAIL TO PLATES ABOVE

ANCHOR BOLTS IN CONCRETE WHERE POSSIBLE

Then the operable part of the window is made by cutting out a piece of rigid insulation, slightly smaller than the opening to allow space for the tin wrapper.

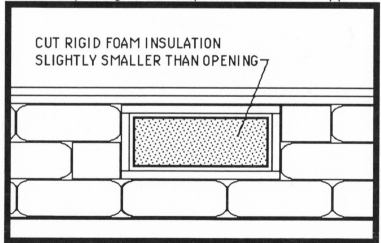

CUT RIGID FOAM INSULATION SLIGHTLY SMALLER THAN OPENING

Now begin to wrap the foam with galvanized tin cutting off the excess with tin snips.

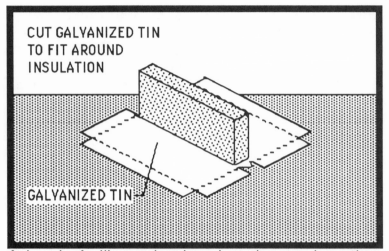

CUT GALVANIZED TIN
TO FIT AROUND
INSULATION

GALVANIZED TIN

A bead of silicone is placed at the overlaps then those overlaps are riveted together with a simple riveting tool available at any hardware store.

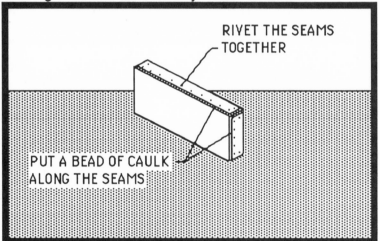

RIVET THE SEAMS
TOGETHER

PUT A BEAD OF CAULK
ALONG THE SEAMS

Now it is ready to install in the rough opening. The tin wrapped insulation unit is placed in the opening with the seams toward the inside of the building. Then the hinges are installed.

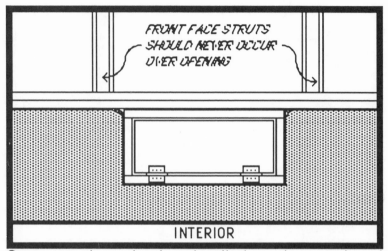

FRONT FACE STRUTS
SHOULD NEVER OCCUR
OVER OPENING

INTERIOR

Stops are then glued and nailed on the exterior of the opening. 1" stock lumber can be used for these stops. Each piece is cut to fit and then glued and nailed in place. Weatherstripping can be used if necessary to get a tight seal.

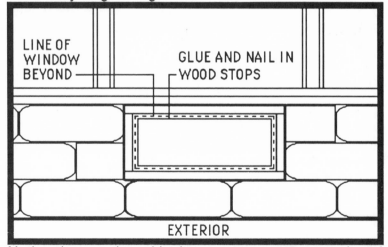

LINE OF
WINDOW
BEYOND

GLUE AND NAIL IN
WOOD STOPS

EXTERIOR

Notice the weather skirt (riveted and caulked in place) and sloped lower stop. These are important to keep the unit from leaking.

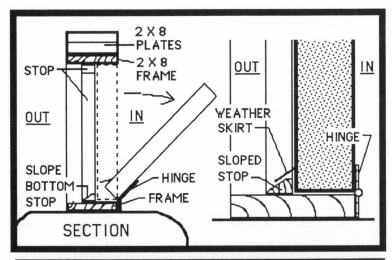

SECTION

2 X 8 PLATES
2 X 8 FRAME
STOP
OUT
IN
OUT
SLOPE BOTTOM STOP
HINGE
FRAME

OUT
IN
WEATHER SKIRT
HINGE
SLOPED STOP

ADDING ON A "U"

There are two methods of adding another "U" on to a completed building. Either of these methods used to add a "U" can be done at any stage of completion of the original Earthship. The first of the two methods does not disrupt or require any alterations of the original structure. You simply add another "U" 8 to

10 feet away from the original "U" and connect the in between space with a short greenhouse hallway. The advantage of this method is that adding another "U" does not have to be taken into account during construction of the original Earthship. The disadvantage is that it leaves a space or hallway between the two rooms but this always has a use and is in most cases desirable.

Begin by determining the correct distance away from the existing "U" that you will build the addition. This distance is based on the strength of the soil. If the soil is hard and does not crumble easily, you can build as close as 8 feet. If the soil is crumbly or unstable you will need to build at least 12 feet away. The next step is to mark the perimeter of the room with string and lay out the first course of tires on the ground as per Earthship Vol. I, pp. 90-93. The new "U" ties right into the wing wall of the existing "U".

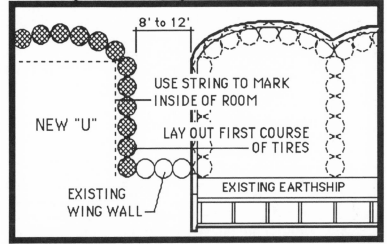

8' to 12'
NEW "U"
USE STRING TO MARK INSIDE OF ROOM
LAY OUT FIRST COURSE OF TIRES
EXISTING WING WALL
EXISTING EARTHSHIP

Then continue building the "U", excavating, pounding the tire walls, installing the bond beam and roofing, as you would with any Earthship.

41

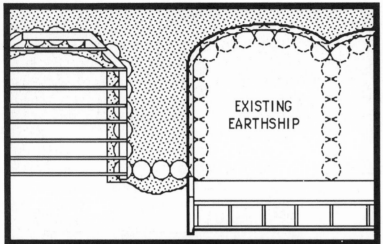

Now you will install the greenhouse of the new "U" in plane with the existing greenhouse.

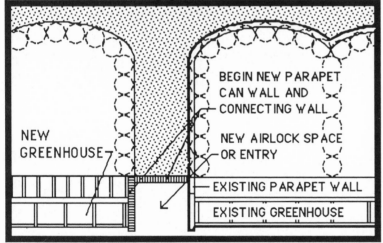

BEGIN NEW PARAPET
CAN WALL AND
CONNECTING WALL

NEW AIRLOCK SPACE
OR ENTRY

NEW GREENHOUSE

EXISTING PARAPET WALL

EXISTING GREENHOUSE

This connection between the old and new structures can be finished and serve as an entry airlock or hallway connecting the two "U"s as in the following diagram. It can also be left open as in the photograph opposite.

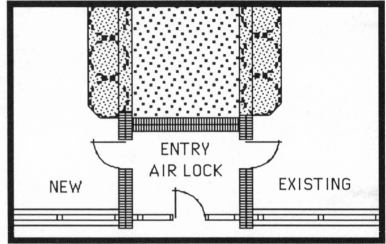

ENTRY
AIR LOCK

NEW   EXISTING

The second method of adding on to a completed Earthship is planned for *in the original structure*. During construction of the original Earthship a stub tire wall is left sticking out of the back of the last "U" where you plan your future addition. This stub serves as the connector for the new tires.

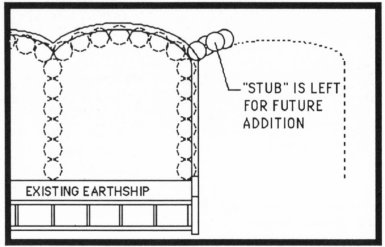

"STUB" IS LEFT
FOR FUTURE
ADDITION

EXISTING EARTHSHIP

42

EARTHSHIP IN TAOS, NEW MEXICO WITH A "U" ADDED ON

The stub can be buried during the original construction and re-excavated when and if you do your addition. The addition is laid out and built as per Earthship Volume I. The procedure for tire pounding and excavation are identical to that of the original Earthship.

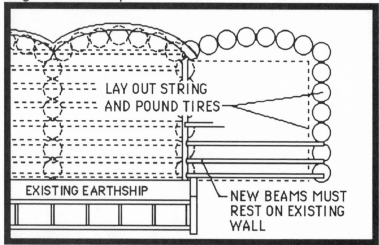

LAY OUT STRING
AND POUND TIRES

EXISTING EARTHSHIP

NEW BEAMS MUST
REST ON EXISTING
WALL

The vigas, trusses or roof beams for the new addition must rest on the existing wall of the original building. This requires some planning ahead when you originally detail this wall. It must be set up just like a typical wall between two "U"s in the original building. See Earthship Volume I, P. It can be temporarily capped with plywood and roofing paper or plastic and rigid insulation. It can even be buried. You simply have to remove this detailing to get to the bearing plate for the new beams.

As the Earthship continues to evolve, there will be more new details and more questions will arise. Future books will continue to respond to our development and your requests.

2. MECHANICAL EVOLUTIONS

AS THE EARTHSHIP ITSELF EVOLVES, SO ARE THE VARIOUS MECHANICAL SYSTEMS EVOLVING. JUST AS THE HUMAN BODY IS A RESULT OF THE VARIOUS SYSTEMS THAT SUPPORT IT- (CIRCULATORY SYSTEM, NERVOUS SYSTEM, RESPIRATORY SYSTEM, ETC..) SO MUST THE EARTHSHIP BE A PRODUCT OF THE SYSTEMS THAT SUPPORT IT. IN VIEW OF THIS WE HAVE REALLY FOCUSED ON MAKING THE EARTHSHIP SYSTEMS BOTH UNDERSTANDABLE AND AVAILABLE TO THE COMMON EVERYDAY HUMAN AT NO EXPENSE TO THE PLANET. ***WE ARE SIMPLY ADAPTING OUR NEEDS TO THE ALREADY EXISTING ACTIVITIES OF THE PLANET.*** WHY PIPE WATER LONG DISTANCES FROM A CENTRALIZED COMMUNITY WATER SYSTEM, OR UP FROM AN EXPENSIVE WELL THAT NEEDS SIGNIFICANT ELECTRICAL POWER, DEPLEATS AQUIFERS AND LOWERS THE WATER TABLE, WHEN WATER FALLS FREE FROM THE SKY? WHY HAVE A CORPORATE OR POLITICAL "MIDDLE MAN" BETWEEN US AND OUR ENERGY NEEDS? OUR VESSEL MUST BE DESIGNED TO SAIL WITH THE FORCES THAT EXIST ***BEYOND HUMAN CONTROL AND EXPLOITATION.*** THESE FORCES WILL BE THE "MENTORS" OF THE FUTURE.

Graphics by .....Tom Drugan, Claire Blanchard
Photos by .....Pam Freund, Tom Woosly

An understanding of mechanical systems for most humans is limited to what is within reach of their fingertips. It is understood that when you flip a switch on the wall, a light comes on. When you turn on the faucet, hot water comes out. When you pull the handle on the toilet, it flushes. Little thought is given to where the electricity comes from or what kind of nuclear waste was produced to generate it. How many of us even know where the power plant is that supplies our power. Few people ever wonder which water table is depleted to bring them water and what chemicals have been added to it. Where does the sewage go after it is flushed and which rivers and lakes are polluted by it?

The condition of our planet tells us we must now begin to take responsibility for what happens beyond the reach of our fingertips. We must begin to reconsider the source of these utilities, our access to them, and how we dispose of the waste produced. The mechanical systems of the Earthship confront these issues *directly*. We call this direct living (see A Coming Of Wizards, chapter 5). Source, access and destination are all contained within the Earthship, *within the reach of our fingertips*. There is no mystery involved in Earthship electricity. There is no unknown source of water. There is no magical black hole that sucks up all our sewage. Instead, we work in harmony with the earth to deal with these issues - taking what it has to give us *directly* and giving back what it wants to receive. With this harmony ringing in our minds we evolve the Earthship mechanical systems.

INDOOR WATER CATCH

Water falls from the sky. If your area has more than 8" of total precipitation per year, your roof can catch enough water for domestic use. This is assuming you are using a dry toilet (solar or compost), low flow faucet heads, and reusing your grey water for plants. In Earthship Volume II we discussed the use of holding tanks *outside* the Earthship for storage of water. We found this to work very well but we found something better. The cost of making an *indoor* water catch is less than the cost of buying and delivering the 3000 gallon galvanized storage tanks we have used in the past. The roof can drain directly into this indoor reservoir now and avoid the considerable expenses of pipes and funnels to get the water from the roof to the outside reservoir.

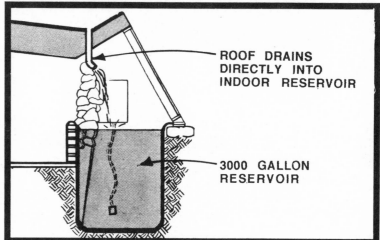

ROOF DRAINS DIRECTLY INTO INDOOR RESERVOIR

3000 GALLON RESERVOIR

There is also less chance for ice dams and snow blockage when using a direct roof drain. Standard commercial roof drains available through SSA are recommended.

AN INDOOR WATER CATCH AT **REACH** NEAR TAOS, NEW MEXICO

The indoor water catch is both better and cheaper as it also dispenses with the need for underground freeze proof piping from the outdoor reservoir to the inside of the dwelling. Another advantage is the presence and sound of water in the dwelling as a small water fall must be incorporated to keep the water circulating thus keeping it fresh. The roof drain can direct the water to this waterfall so the waterfall becomes the "source" of water for your reservoir. The only disadvantage is that some space is required in the building for the reservoir, usually about 8'-0 in diameter and 8'-0" deep.

DETAILS AND SPECIFICS
An easy indoor cistern is made by digging into the ground, down 5'-0" from floor level and building up 3'-0" from floor level with a single can wall.

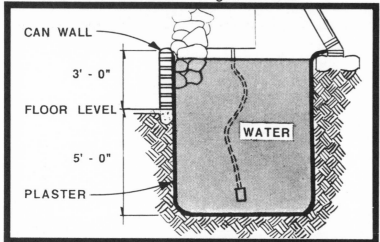

In most cases the earth is stable enough to plaster with a cement plaster (1 part cement to 3 parts sand plus engineering fibers) right on the earth cliff of the hole that has been dug out. It is best to apply about 4 scratch coats so that you have a 1 1/2" to 2" thick *slab* of

concrete forming the cistern. Remember that this is a structural situation and that the plaster is just a technique for building up the structural slab. The engineering fibers are a <u>must</u>. *This is not just a plaster job.* After each coat, be sure to scratch it well. Then apply a 5th coat smooth troweled using a swimming pool trowel (see Earthship Vol. I p. 177 for scratcher and trowel). It is important to apply the final smooth coat in one application to avoid cold joints in the final surface.

If the earth is not stable enough to hold a good cliff, then a can wall must be taken all the way down to the bottom. This can wall must set on a small footing with continuous rebar. The same 5 coat plaster job is then applied to the can wall.

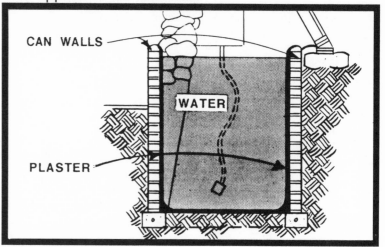

The shape of the cistern does not have to be a perfect circle but it should be slightly curved on all sides for structural integrity and easy plastering with no seams or corners.

can it be more than 3000 gallons

48

Metal lath should be applied to areas where the can wall of the cistern meets the tire wall or another can wall of the building.

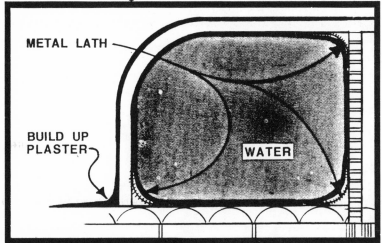

Whenever there is a change of materials or a cold joint, metal lath is always applied lapping well onto both surfaces for plaster preparation. Plaster should be built up on the outside of these areas (where applicable) to work against the force of the water pushing out.

The water is funneled into the cistern from the roof via "crickets" on the roof. A cricket is a term used for added planes on a roof surface to slope water in a specific direction. This is very similar to the water management on the ground surface around the outside of the Earthship.

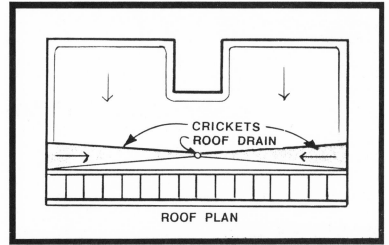

ROOF PLAN

The crickets are made by framing with 2x4's and adding plywood to the roof surface creating a slope toward the drain. The plywood is then roofed with the same material as the rest of the roof.

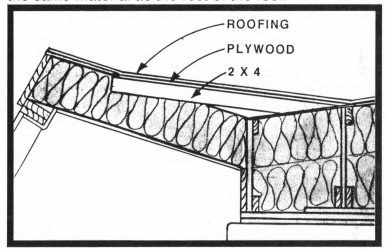

49

We have not found any material that is as easy to apply and as economical as the Brai or Firestone roofing (two different brands of modified bitumen roofing material) which we recommend in Earthship Volume II. This roofing comes with a mineral surface that protects it from the sun. It also comes without the mineral surface. We call this naked Brai. Both types have to be painted as the chemicals in the roofing can leach into the water. We recommend the naked roofing as it is easier to melt together and easier to paint. We have found an acrylic roof paint that protects the roofing material from the elements and creates a "drinkable" surface, preventing the roofing chemicals from leaching through. This coating is billed as a roofing material also and can be obtained through Solar Survival Architecture. It is applied like paint in three coats - a primer and two finish coats. Regular outdoor latex paint can be applied over this

for color. The reservoir must have one 4" overflow for every 6" inlet. The roof must have one 6" inlet for every 1200 square feet of roof surface. The overflow can be detailed as illustrated in the diagram below.

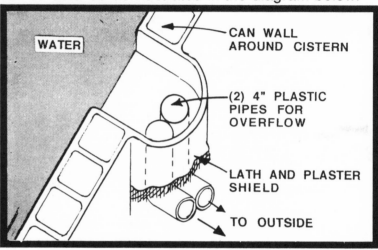

When the reservoir is against the front face an alternate overflow detail can take water out under the front face framing.

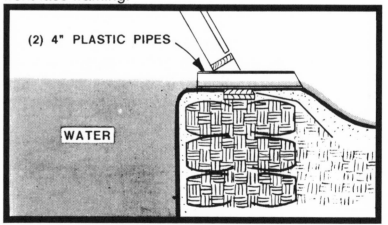

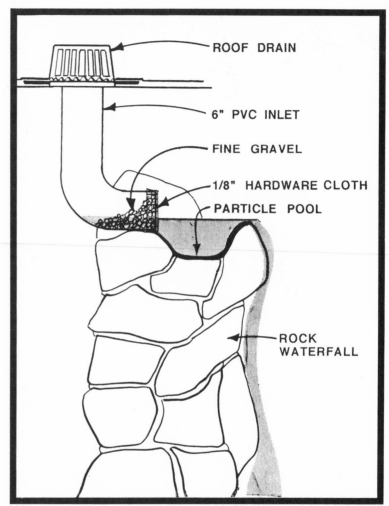

ROOF DRAIN

6" PVC INLET

FINE GRAVEL

1/8" HARDWARE CLOTH

PARTICLE POOL

ROCK WATERFALL

The six inch inlet from the roof drain is covered with a screen (1/8" hardware cloth) to hold in some fine gravel as a preliminary filter to keep particles from flowing into the reservoir. The inlet can then be placed directly over the waterfall so incoming water is simply *a waterfall* into the reservoir. Sometimes a particle pool is incorporated to allow particles to settle and be caught before the water tumbles down the waterfall.

We have also evolved a sand filter in the bottom of the reservoir. This makes cleaning the filters (outlined this chapter page 52-54) not necessary as often. The sand filter is detailed on the following page. The sand filter takes up 2'-0" in the bottom of the reservoir so this requires a deeper excavation in order to achieve about 3000 gallons of water .

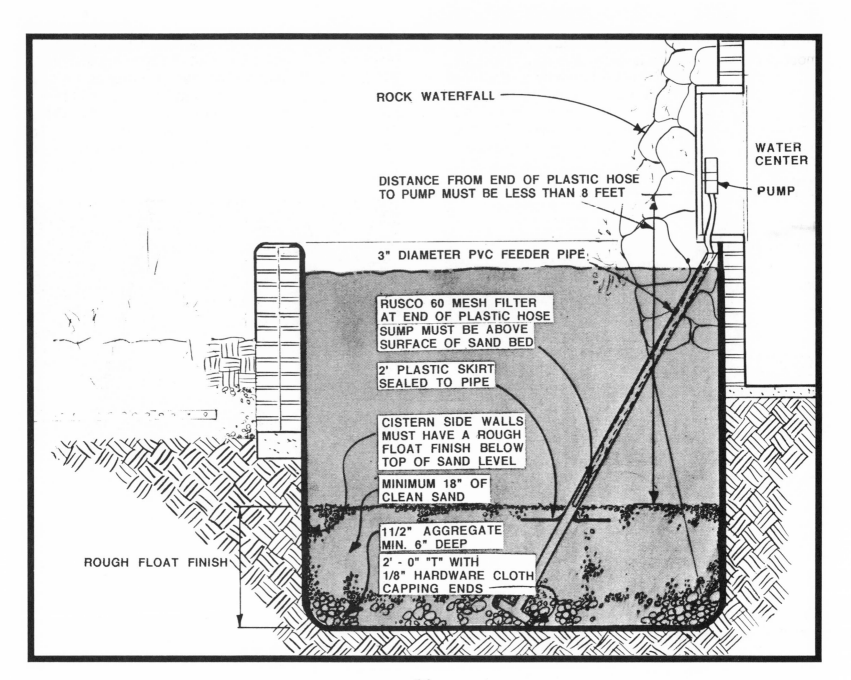

ROCK WATERFALL

WATER CENTER

PUMP

DISTANCE FROM END OF PLASTIC HOSE TO PUMP MUST BE LESS THAN 8 FEET

3" DIAMETER PVC FEEDER PIPE

RUSCO 60 MESH FILTER AT END OF PLASTIC HOSE SUMP MUST BE ABOVE SURFACE OF SAND BED

2' PLASTIC SKIRT SEALED TO PIPE

CISTERN SIDE WALLS MUST HAVE A ROUGH FLOAT FINISH BELOW TOP OF SAND LEVEL

MINIMUM 18" OF CLEAN SAND

11/2" AGGREGATE MIN. 6" DEEP

2' - 0" "T" WITH 1/8" HARDWARE CLOTH CAPPING ENDS

ROUGH FLOAT FINISH

52

The water in an interior reservoir must be circulated most of the time to keep it fresh. We accomplish this with a small D.C. pump hooked directly to a 60 watt solar photo-voltaic panel. Thus the water is circulating automatically whenever the sun is out. This is independent of the *house power*. The D.C. pump requires a 60 mesh Rusco filter to protect it. The following diagram schematically illustrates this system.

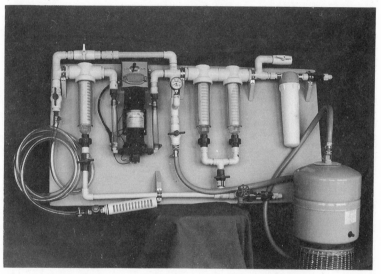

PV PANEL

WATERFALL

D.C. PUMP

PATH OF
CIRCULATING WATER

We have incorporated this pump and filter into the Water Organizer Module (WOM) described in the following pages.

WATER ORGANIZER MODULE (W.O.M.)

The indoor water catch also makes the location of the main 12 volt, D.C. pump for house water pressure more flexible. This pump has to be within 15'-0" horizontally of the reservoir and within 8'-0" vertically of the bottom of the reservoir. This pump must be

installed with a bank of filters as illustrated in the diagrams on pages 43 and 44 of Earthship Volume II. We have found that finding parts for and assembling this pump and filter arrangement is not within the normal procedures provided by local plumbers. Anything *out of the ordinary* is very expensive so we are now providing the pump-filter arrangement ready to install. We present the Water Organizer Module (WOM).

The above WOM is for an outside reservoir. When the indoor cistern is used, the waterfall pump is included as in the photo on the following page.

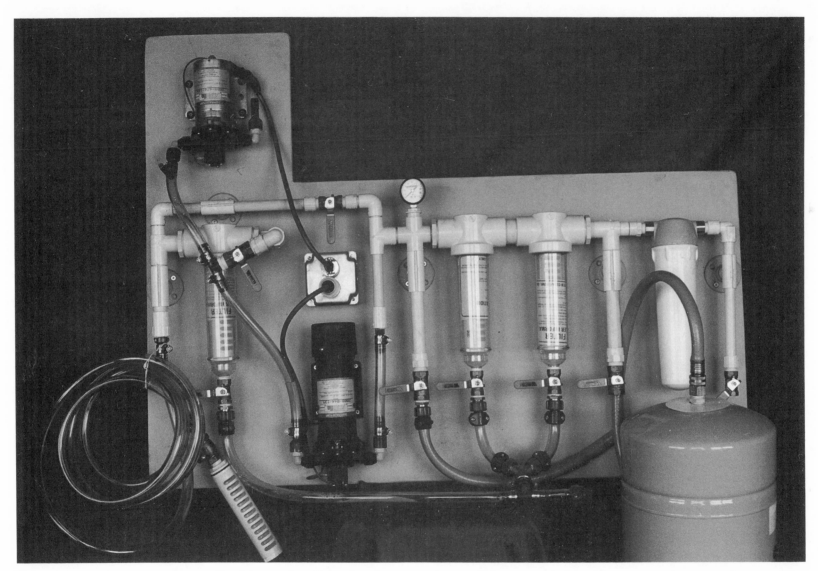

This unit screws on your wall. Your plumber simply hooks into familiar fitting on the right side of this panel (see photo). The panel comes with or without the water fall pump, thus there is a W.O.M.

for outdoor and for indoor water catches. The following diagram is the ideal installation of this panel with an indoor reservoir and water fall.

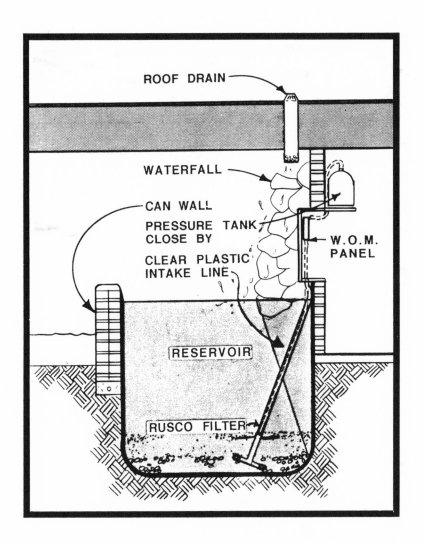

ROOF DRAIN

WATERFALL

CAN WALL

PRESSURE TANK
CLOSE BY

W.O.M.
PANEL

CLEAR PLASTIC
INTAKE LINE

RESERVOIR

RUSCO FILTER

This unit will provide on demand water pressure without a pressure tank. However, a pressure tank of any size will prolong the life of the pump. The pressure tank builds up pressurized water and stores it so the pump doesn't have to come on every time the faucet is turned on. A small pressure tank (3 gallons) comes with the WOM for this purpose. A large conventional pressure tank (60-80 gallons) provides pressure for more faucets on at once. This large tank costs about $400 and about $200 for installation. In cases of a tight budget this more expensive pressure tank can be added later. The WOM is already set up for it. The tank can be remote from the WOM but should be nearby to avoid pressure "quirks" in the system.

The clear plastic hose going from the water organizer module to the bottom of the reservoir has a 60 mesh filter on the end of it. This hose and filter comes with the water organizer module. If a sand filter is used this hose and filter are placed down the plastic feeder pipe of the sand filter (see page 49).

The following diagrams illustrate filter cleaning and operation of the water organizer module. The Rusco sediment filters do not require replacement, just cleaning. The same is true for the Katadyn drinking filter.

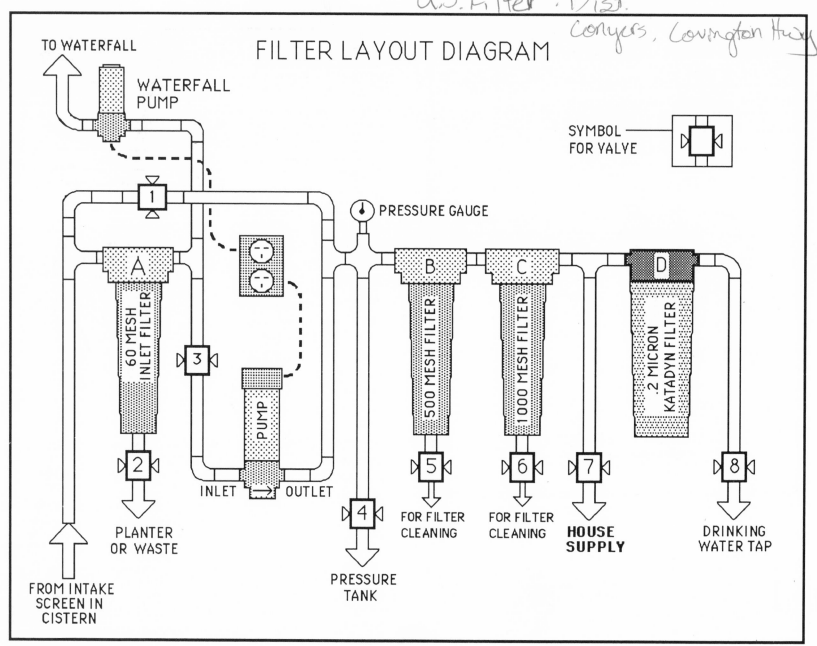

FILTER LAYOUT DIAGRAM

U.S. Filter & Dist.
Conyers, Covington Hwy

TO WATERFALL

WATERFALL PUMP

SYMBOL FOR VALVE

1

PRESSURE GAUGE

A

60 MESH INLET FILTER

INLET → OUTLET

PUMP

B

500 MESH FILTER

C

1000 MESH FILTER

D

.2 MICRON KATADYN FILTER

2

3

4

5

6

7

8

PLANTER OR WASTE

FROM INTAKE SCREEN IN CISTERN

PRESSURE TANK

FOR FILTER CLEANING

FOR FILTER CLEANING

HOUSE SUPPLY

DRINKING WATER TAP

56

FUNCTION *	1 VALVE	2 VALVE	3 VALVE	4 VALVE	5 VALVE	6 VALVE	7 VALVE	8 VALVE	NOTES
NORMAL OPERATION	CLOSED	CLOSED	OPEN	OPEN	CLOSED	CLOSED	OPEN	OPEN	Closing valve 3 while pump is plugged in can result in damage to pump. Pump should be unplugged for all functions other than normal operation.
BLOW DOWN FILTER A *	OPEN	OPEN	CLOSED	OPEN	CLOSED	CLOSED	OPEN	OPEN	Valve sequence 3,1,2, reverse for normal operation.
MANUAL CLEANING FILTER A	CLOSED	OPEN	OPEN	OPEN	CLOSED	CLOSED	OPEN	OPEN	After opening valve 2 open filter body just enough to admit air and drain filter. Then remove drainline and filter body and clean with soft brush.
PRESSURE PRIMING *	OPEN	CLOSED	OPEN	OPEN	CLOSED	CLOSED	OPEN	OPEN	"Crack" inlet line at pump port. Open valve 1 just enough to purge air, when air is expelled, close valve 1 and re-tighten inlet line.
BLOWDOWN FILTER B *	CLOSED	CLOSED	OPEN	OPEN	OPEN	CLOSED	OPEN	OPEN	Open valve quickly, close slowly.
MANUAL CLEANING FILTER B	CLOSED	CLOSED	OPEN	CLOSED	OPEN	CLOSED	CLOSED	CLOSED	Valve sequence 4,7,8,5. Clean same as filter A then reverse sequence.
BLOWDOWN FILTER C *	CLOSED	CLOSED	OPEN	OPEN	CLOSED	OPEN	OPEN	OPEN	Open valve quickly, close slowly.
MANUAL CLEANING FILTER C	CLOSED	CLOSED	OPEN	CLOSED	CLOSED	OPEN	CLOSED	CLOSED	Valve sequence 4,7,8,6. Clean same as filter A then reverse sequence.
CLEANING FILTER D KATADYN	CLOSED	CLOSED	OPEN	CLOSED	CLOSED	OPEN	CLOSED	CLOSED	Open filter body just enough to admit air and let excess water drain through filter C. Remove filter body and clean. Clean ceramic candle as per katadyn instructions

* BLOWING DOWN FILTERS AND PRESSURE PRIMING REQUIRES ADEQUATE WATER IN PRESSURE TANK.

1. The pump ports are plastic. Use care when tightening connectors to the ports. Finger tight should be sufficient.

2. The Shurflo pump has an internal pressure switch set to turn on the pump at 25 PSI and shut it off at 45 PSI.

3. The pump will not be able to prime itself if:
A- The water level in the cistern is more than 8 feet below the pump. B- There is no outlet open on the outlet side of the system. C- There is even a minute leak in the inlet side of the system.

4. Clogging of the screen at the end of the cistern intake line or of filter **A** can quickly damage pump. Always watch that filter **A** is clean and always inspect and clean the intake screen when filter **A** is cleaned. Be especially vigilant if cistern water is dirty. If pump becomes noisy unplug it and inspect screen and filter immediately.

5. Do not use hose for Katadyn water line since pressure stored in the inflated hose could rupture the ceramic filter element if the pressure were suddenly reduced on the inlet side of the filter.

6. There is a 15 amp fuse in the receptacle box to protect the pump. If pump does not energize when plugged in shut off circuit breaker and inspect this fuse.

7. The air cushion of the pressure tank should be pre charged to approximately 2 p.s.i. less than the cut-in pressure of the pump which is 25 p.s.i. Therefore precharge the tank to 23 p.s.i.

8. If you have begun collecting water from your roof before it has been sealed (especially with a brai roof), you will have acummulated some foul looking and smelling construction water. This bad water can leave a permanent odor and taste in your filters.

Therefore, when the water system is first put into use it is recommended that the cistern be emptied and cleaned, and then refilled with clean water. If this is not possible then temporarily remove the inside candle of the Katadyn filter for the first 3 - 4 weeks. This will prevent it from picking up any taste or odor that may have accumulated in the tank during construction.

INDOOR *CONTAINED* GREY-WATER ABSORBING TANK

Early grey water systems simply split the grey water from the black water and took it outside to various planters. We have also taken the grey water from individual plumbing fixtures and piped it to specific indoor planters as outlined in Earthship Volume II p.p. 53-55. With the increased need for food production in an Earthship we have started providing more than just *token planters*. Another consideration is that health officials as a rule are generally not going to approve of *any* grey water going outside the dwelling on the surface of the ground no matter how well kept the planter is. The point they make is that if someone has a disease like hepatitis, takes a shower and the shower water runs outside, *a neighbor child could play in it and be exposed to hepatitis.* We must deal with grey water totally inside a closed system - nothing leaves the dwelling. This, plus the fact that more space is needed for food production, has led us to create an indoor contained greywater absorbing tank that can support a virtual jungle. We are now dedicating major amounts of space to grey water absorption and food production. The floor plans following illustrate the size and integrated use of the contained "jungle" tank.

58

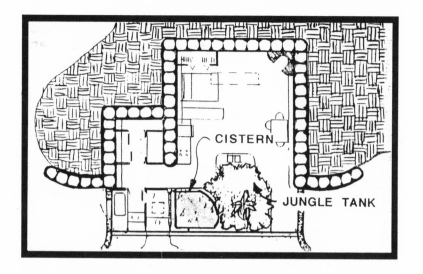

CISTERN

JUNGLE TANK

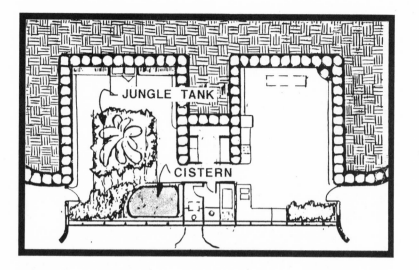

JUNGLE TANK

CISTERN

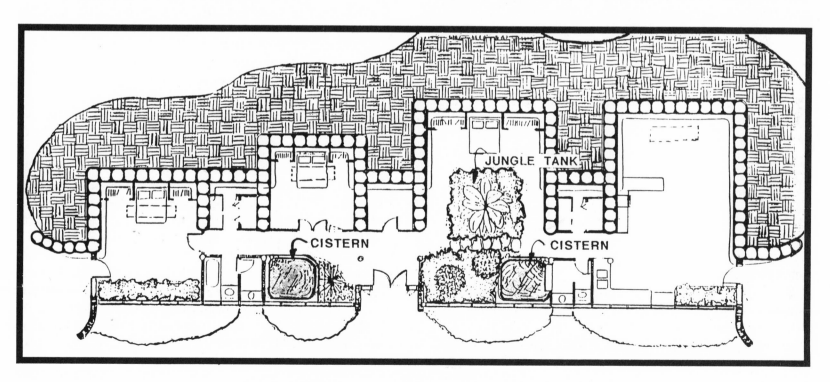

JUNGLE TANK

CISTERN

CISTERN

59

INTERIOR JUNGLE AT THE OFFICE OF SOLAR SURVIVAL ARCHITECTURE, TAOS, NEW MEXICO

We are digging down in the jungle space and <u>lining it with a rubber membrane</u>. We basically *roof it* with the Brai, Firestone, or EPDM roofing. It is now actually an *indoor tank*. We then distribute the grey water from a 4" perforated pipe manifold through gravel on the bottom of this tank. Over the gravel we have a foot of top soil. Between the top soil and the gravel we have a layer of aluminum screen to prevent dirt from leaching into the gravel. Fine (1/4") gravel placed between the soil and the base gravel will accomplish the same thing as the aluminum screen.

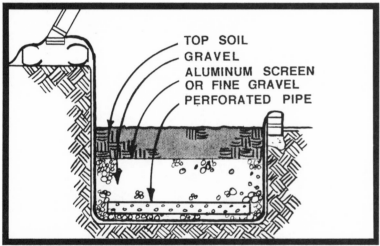

TOP SOIL
GRAVEL
ALUMINUM SCREEN
OR FINE GRAVEL
PERFORATED PIPE

The result is a large, lush growing area that is also a grey water treatment **container**. The point is that the water is <u>contained</u> and <u>used</u> by the plants.

The water actually passes through the gravel for the entire length of the tank getting cleaned and filtered as it goes. It then collects in a well at the opposite end of the tank where a second collection 4" manifold pipe is placed (see diagram on the following page).

The photograph below in a grey water absorbing tank under construction

A stand pipe comes up from the collection manifold to accomodate a plastic hose going to a D.C. pump (the same pump used in the WOM). This pump facilitates reuse of the now treated water on the surface of the jungle tank or outside. The tank is sized with enough volume and planting that surface watering is a convenience not a necessity.

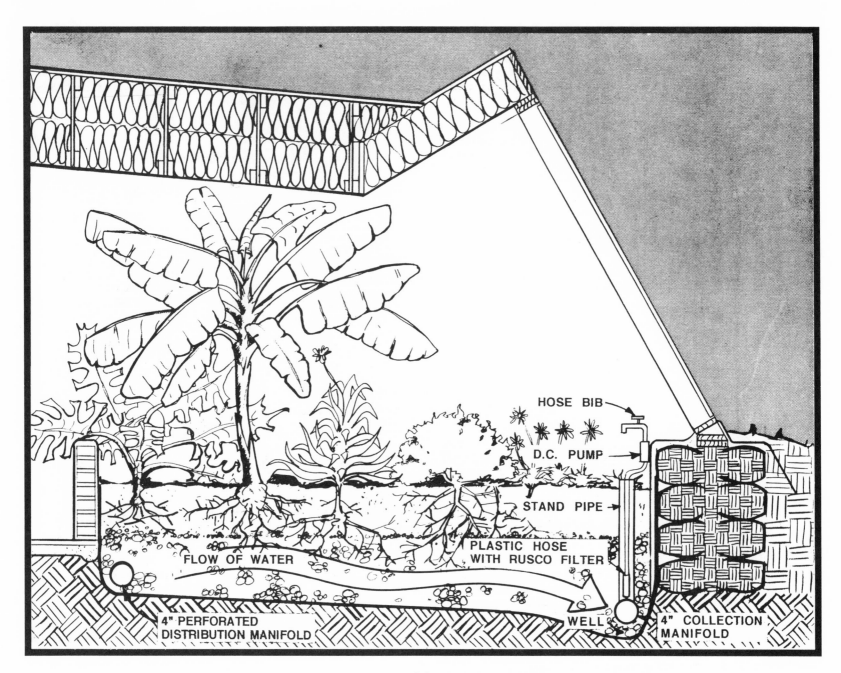

HOSE BIB

D.C. PUMP

STAND PIPE

FLOW OF WATER

PLASTIC HOSE
WITH RUSCO FILTER

4" PERFORATED
DISTRIBUTION MANIFOLD

WELL

4" COLLECTION
MANIFOLD

62

When this system is used in conjunction with a dry toilet (see Chapter 4) **no waste water leaves the building.** Nothing is absorbed into the earth.

Everything is contained and used to produce food and flora. The illustrates the basic concept in plan.

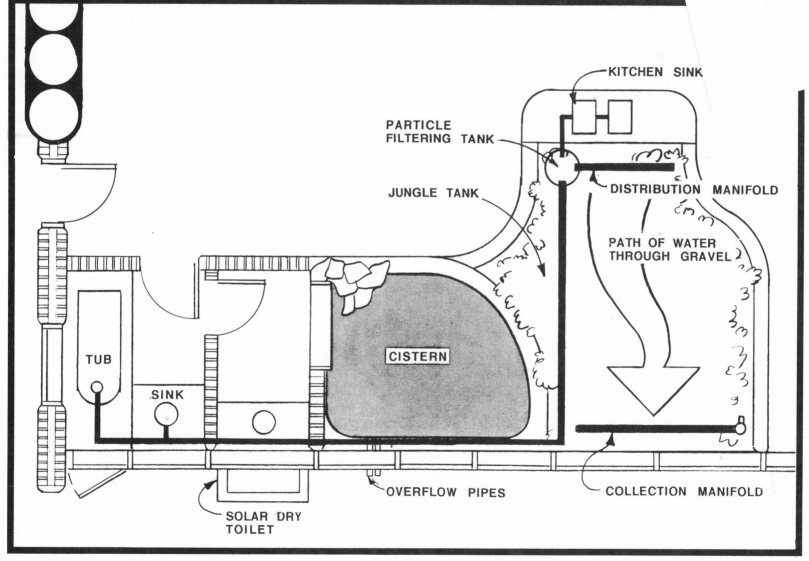

PARTICLE FILTERING TANK

JUNGLE TANK

KITCHEN SINK

DISTRIBUTION MANIFOLD

PATH OF WATER THROUGH GRAVEL

CISTERN

TUB

SINK

SOLAR DRY TOILET

OVERFLOW PIPES

COLLECTION MANIFOLD

basic objective of health officials is to <u>contain all</u> <u>grey water</u>. This contained grey-water-absorbing-jungle accomplishes that with an *already proven* method of processing - the wetlands approach. This contained grey water absorbing tank is similar to wetlands systems which have been used successfully to treat and absorb <u>black and grey</u> water outside. In our application *there is no black water* and **the entire system is contained inside**. The fact that we are not including toilet/black water makes it basically a much less serious <u>contained</u> wetlands system. Nothing is admitted to the surrounding environment. The jungle (via the tank below) takes it all. The plant roots reach down and absorb the moisture that is distributed throughout the gravel. The well and stand pipe provides access to treated water for outside or inside use. If you live in an arid climate and will need a lot of outside water, the depth of your tank can be shallow 2'-4". If you live in a wet climate and won't need much outside water, the tank can be deeper to store more water. The <u>shallow tanks will</u> <u>actually function better to filter and clean the water</u> <u>than the deeper tanks.</u> A plastic can with gravel on the bottom and a removable screen provides a preliminary filter (see diagram opposite) for particles and food chunks in the water. The lid of this container must be sealed with silicone to avoid odor. The lid is removed (usually every 2 months) for cleaning and must be re-siliconed when it is replaced.

This green (jungle) space can be sized according to volume of water usage, number of people, and fixtures. Originally we planned to isolate it with doors closing it off from the rest of the dwelling. We called it a "walk in septic tank". However, people began asking if they could put a couch and T.V. in the jungle room. One thing led to another and now we present the jungle room as study, living area or even a bedroom. We are basically integrating it into the entire dwelling.. People do not want to be separate from "the jungle". *They want to live with the plants*. The average exchange is healthy for both people and plants and the <u>containment</u> of grey water is achieved.

Description of elements in the following diagram:

1. Grey water from sinks, tubs, shower, and washer.

2. Grease trap filters out particles.

3. 4" deep fine aggregate.

4. Distribution manifold.

5. 16" deep medium aggregate.

6. 2" - 4" large aggregate.

7. 12" topsoil.

8. Roots and gravel filter to purify water.

9. Well.

10. Intake manifold with filter.

11. D.C. pump.

12. Faucet dispenses filtered water.

64

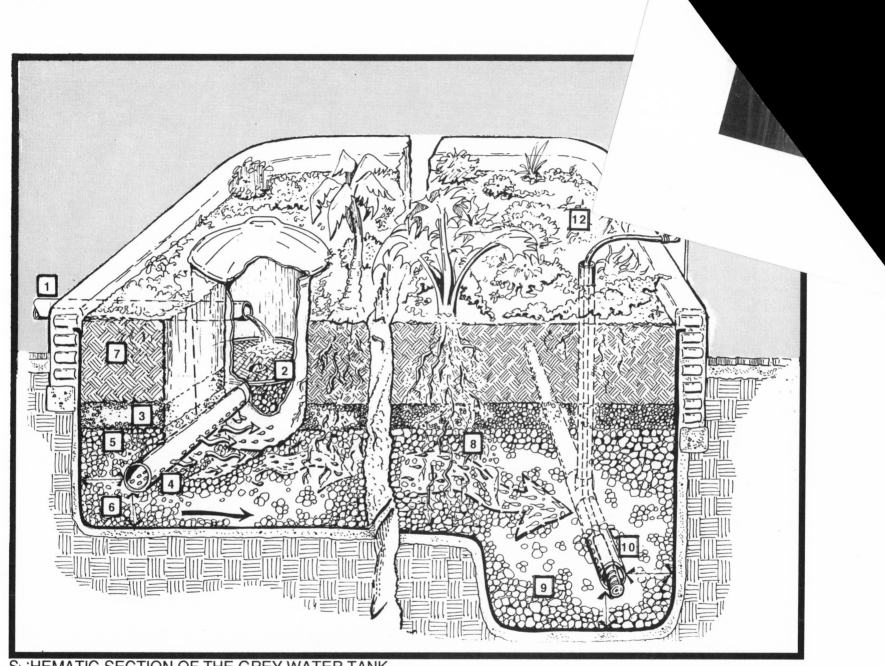

SCHEMATIC SECTION OF THE GREY WATER TANK.

GREY WATER ABSORBING TANK AND CISTERN UNDER CONSTRUCTION

66

POWER ORGANIZER MODULE (P.O.M.)

The electrical discussions in Earthship Volume II (pp 3-23) lead us to the diagrams of a power organizer on page 23 of that Volume. This module is equipped with conventional electrical circuit breaker boxes that any local electrician is accustomed to. The objective here being to allow the house to be wired <u>absolutely conventionally</u> so that local electricians would not have to deal with solar power. This concept (explained in depth in Volume II pp 11-12) has been successful. The Power Organizer Module itself has come a long way and is now available through Solar Survival Architecture. We have options on inverters (Trace or Photocomm) and our new module can now be expanded up to 16 panels before adding another whole module.

This unit is simply secured onto a wall with the batteries below and panels above. We now recommend that batteries be sunken into the floor for more protection and to provide flat floor space in front of the circuit panels and disconnects at the P.O.M. to conform to code. The battery box should be detailed as a "vault" with a 3 hour fire rating and should have a high and low vent to sweep battery gases out.

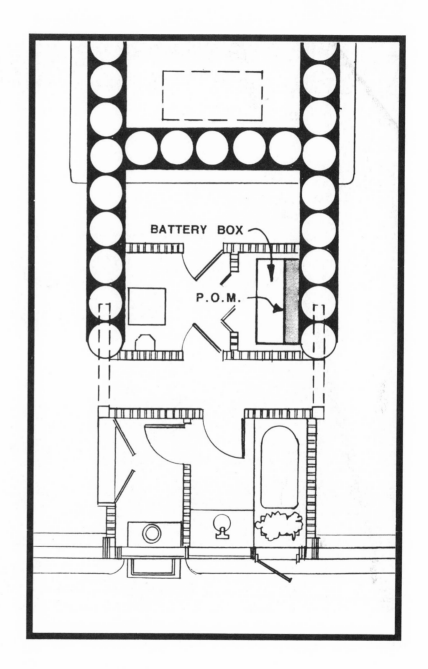

BATTERY BOX

P.O.M.

THE P.O.M.

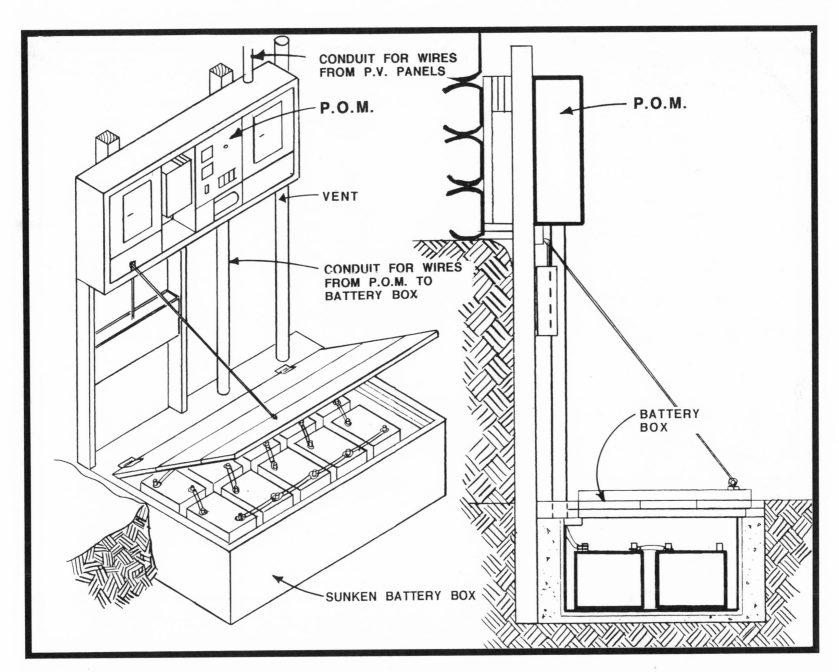

CONDUIT FOR WIRES
FROM P.V. PANELS

P.O.M.

VENT

CONDUIT FOR WIRES
FROM P.O.M. TO
BATTERY BOX

SUNKEN BATTERY BOX

P.O.M.

BATTERY
BOX

69

The basic P.O.M. was set up with eight 51 watt solar panels and ten 6 volt batteries. Two auxiliary panels could be added to that system for a total of ten panels. Two more panels could be added as a trickle charge independent of the P.O.M. disconnects and fuses. This basic unit has proven itself to provide ample power for a small household of 2 or 3 people. For slightly larger Earthships (2 bedroom, 4 people) we have now developed an oversized POM that will accommodate a larger load. This new unit will house a Trace 2500 inverter and have the capability to expand the system to 16 panels and 14 batteries. This new POM will allow the owner/builder to install the basic photovoltaic system (8 panels, 10 batteries) during construction. At a later date, if more power is required or if an additional "U" is added (or another family member is added) the system can be expanded *without any additional cost for modifications* other than the cost of panels and batteries. This expandable system will simplify wiring and reduce costs in larger Earthships. This is still a modular concept. The modules themselves are now capable of handling more power. A very large Earthship would still use a series of these simple power modules to avoid the costly, custom designed, hard to understand and maintain systems of the past.

The P.O.M.'s are developed and manufactured by Solar Survival Architecture and are up to the latest code and made with all UL approved components. The following page illustrates the complete hook up of this system. It is our objective to make the system easy enough for you or your builder to install the solar power and any typical electrician to wire the house absolutely conventionally. We still recommend keeping lights on D.C. power and outlets

on A.C. power as described in Earthship Volume II. This wiring can be achieved within the realms of conventional code (see Earthship Volume II pp 22-23).

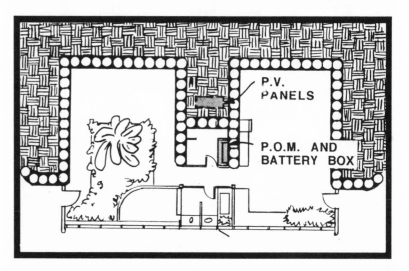

P.V. PANELS

P.O.M. AND BATTERY BOX

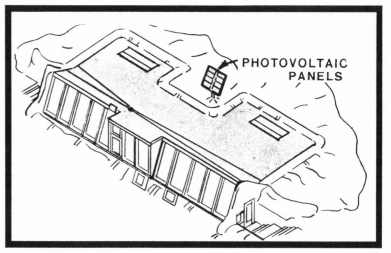

PHOTOVOLTAIC PANELS

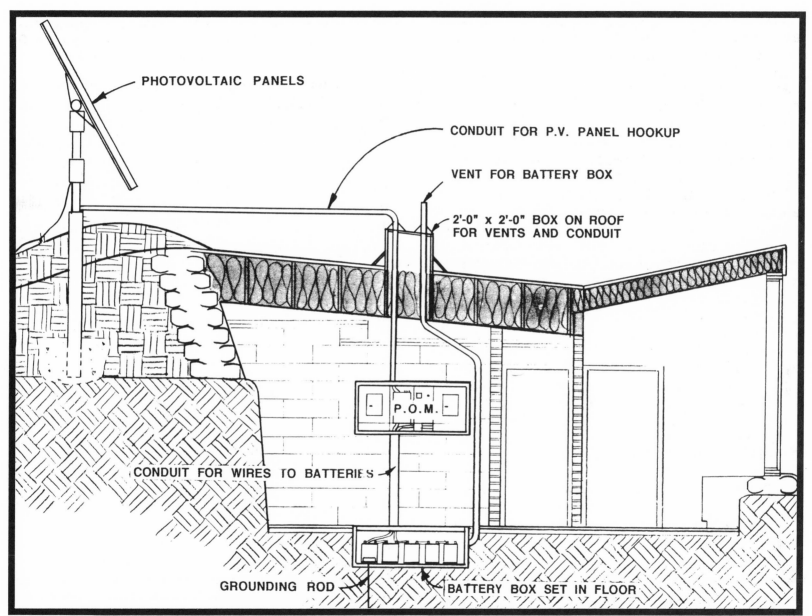

PHOTOVOLTAIC PANELS

CONDUIT FOR P.V. PANEL HOOKUP

VENT FOR BATTERY BOX

2'-0" x 2'-0" BOX ON ROOF
FOR VENTS AND CONDUIT

P.O.M.

CONDUIT FOR WIRES TO BATTERIES

GROUNDING ROD

BATTERY BOX SET IN FLOOR

SECTION OF MECHANICAL "U" WHERE POM IS HOUSED (SEE CHAPTER 14).

DIRECT VENT BACK UP HEATER

The ventless gas heaters discussed in Earthship Volume II, pp. 5 and 24 have proven very satisfactory in terms of a little back up heat during cloudy times in winter. Ventless heaters, however, are prohibited in some states and an alternative has become necessary. We have found a gas heater that vents through a wall up to 15" thick. Double aluminum can walls with 4" of rigid urethane in the middle are only 14" thick; they usually occur in the east and west ends of the dwelling.

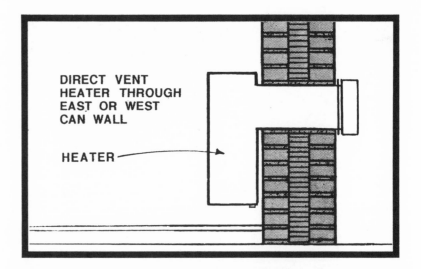

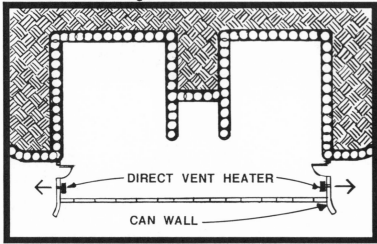

These are good places to install direct vent back up heaters. We have also used them under the front face windows.

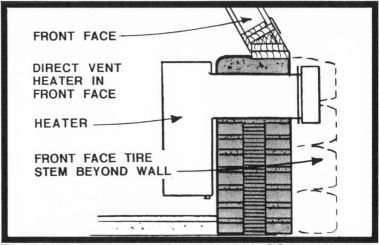

These heaters are available through SSA

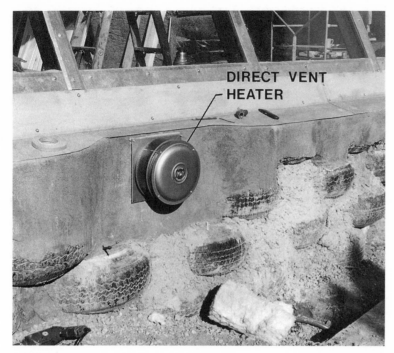

A direct vent heater through the front face tire wall shown above.

INSTANT "FIRED MUD" FIRE PLACE

Now that Earthships are being built all over the country, the adobe fireplaces described in Earthship Volume II are proving to be difficult to build in places where adobes are not available. Shipping them is possible but expensive and time consuming because of the weight. We have therefore developed an instant *fired mud* fireplace. SSA provides a bird cage type skeleton in a kit. It is simply a bunch of 3/8" rebar bent to fit together in a code fireplace configuration.

This bird cage oven is held together with baling wire and covered with metal lath. The lath is also attached with baling wire. This cage is set where you want the fire place with a 28" x 28" skylight type box in the roof for the flue to go through. This roof box is like the one described in Earthship Volume II, p. 108.

73

FIREPLACE WITH PRELIMINARY COATS OF MUD.   FIREPLACE WITH FINISH COAT OF MUD.

74

12" diameter galvanized stove or furnace pipe is then placed over the top neck of the cage. The neck is designed for this purpose. The stove pipe is run all the way through the roof and wrapped with metal lath. The lath around the furnace pipe is held on with baling wire. The damper is installed as per Earthship Volume II, pp. 115-117. Now you simply plaster this unit with the same mud from your site that you are using on the walls. You plaster both oven and stack and scratch the finish with a scratcher. Then you build a fire! The fire dries and "fires" the mud. This process is repeated over and over again until you have 5" thick of mud on the stack and 8" of mud on the oven. Then you apply a finish coat of mud as per Earthship Volume II p. 178. Do not fire this coat, let it dry like your walls. A 4" combustion air duct must be added as in Earthship Volume II, page 120.

Your plaster job goes up to the ceiling. You should temporarily fill the gap around the roof box with fiberglass insulation for protection during the firing process. After a 5" thickness of fired mud is achieved to the ceiling, remove the fiberglass insulation and fill the void with pumice-concrete mix, mud or concrete. You must have 8" of masonry around the metal flue for code acceptance. This requires a wider (28") truss placement where fireplaces occur. The pumice or mud fill goes to the top of the 2x12 roof opening box and then slopes up to the 12" metal flue. Brai roofing can now be applied up and over the box and up the slope of the pumice or mud fill. Stop the Brai about 1" from the flue and caulk the gap with silicone.

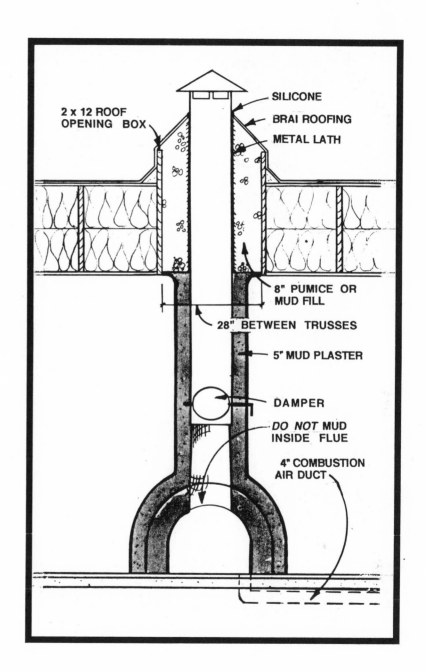

SILICONE

2 x 12 ROOF OPENING BOX

BRAI ROOFING

METAL LATH

8" PUMICE OR MUD FILL

28" BETWEEN TRUSSES

5" MUD PLASTER

DAMPER

DO NOT MUD INSIDE FLUE

4" COMBUSTION AIR DUCT

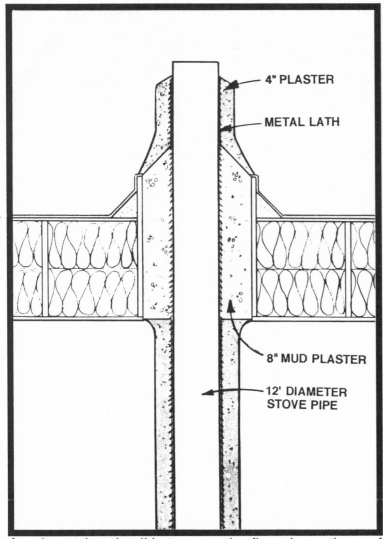

4" PLASTER

METAL LATH

8" MUD PLASTER

12' DIAMETER STOVE PIPE

An alternative detail is to wrap the flue above the roof with lath and plaster with several coats achieving a 5" thickness. This results in an adobe type chimney.

EQUIPMENT IN THIS CHAPTER - AVAILABLE FROM SOLAR SURVIVAL SALES

Power Organizer Module (POM) $1980. plus freight

Roof drain $135.   plus freight

Water fall pump $165.   plus freight

Water Organizer Module (WOM) $1000. plus freight
    w/ water fall pump $1200. plus freight

Direct vent heater   small $395.   plus freight
                        large $504.   plus freight

Brai or Firestone roofing
    check with local roofing dealer.

Acrylic roof coating $33./ gal
                                        plus freight

60 watt panel for water fall $335.   plus freight

Fire Place Kit $175.   plus freight

Pump, hose bib from jungle tank $165.   plus freight

EPDM tank liner - check your local roofing dealer

Prices subject to change after the printing of this book.

THE BENNSTROM EARTHSHIP AT R.E.A.C.H. TAOS, NEW MEXICO

77

LAW AS IT RELATES TO TIME
WHEN MURDER BECOMES LEGAL

MURDER IS ILLEGAL - **WITHIN A CERTAIN TIME FRAME.** IF SOMEONE PUTS A GUN TO YOUR HEAD AND PULLS THE TRIGGER, YOU ARE DEAD INSTANTLY. THAT IS ILLEGAL. IF SOMEONE POISONS YOU WITH A FAST ACTING POISON AND YOU DIE INSTANTLY, THAT IS MURDER. IF SOMEONE POISONS YOU WITH A SLOW ACTING POISON AND YOU DIE WITHIN A WEEK, THAT IS STILL MURDER. IF SOMEONE POISONS YOU WITH A POISON THAT ACTS VERY SLOWLY AND YOU DIE IN ONE MONTH, THAT IS STILL MURDER. THERE HAVE BEEN CASES OF SOMEONE POISONING THEIR SPOUSE WITH LEAD OVER A PERIOD OF A YEAR OR MORE. THESE PEOPLE WERE ALSO CONVICTED OF MURDER. WHAT ABOUT POISON OVER FIVE YEARS? IS THAT MURDER? WHAT ABOUT POISON OVER TEN YEARS? IS THAT MURDER? WHAT ABOUT TWENTY YEARS? WE ARE ALL PARTICIPATING IN A TOXIC LIFE STYLE THAT IS BASICALLY KILLING OTHER (FUTURE) HUMANS OVER A PERIOD OF **TIME.** STRANGELY ENOUGH, AT SOME POINT IN OUR WORLD, **TIME ALLOWS MURDER.** IF YOU CONSCIOUSLY PARTICIPATED IN ONE OF THE ABOVE (SHORT TIME FRAME) MURDERS, YOU WOULD BE CONVICTED AS A PARTICIPANT IN MURDER. YET WE ARE ALL PARTICIPATING IN LONG TIME FRAME MURDERS EVERY DAY. WE ALL USE, BURN, PURCHASE AND DISCARD TOXIC MATERIALS, SYSTEMS AND PRODUCTS. TIME SIMPLY PROVIDES A DISTANCE SO.......

WE DON'T HAVE TO SEE THE VICTIMS FALL.

PART TWO

NEW COMPONENT CONCEPTS

RESEARCH BUILDING AT SSA HEADQUARTERS

THERMAL MASS REFRIGERATOR AT R.E.A.C.H, TAOS, NEW MEXICO.

3. THERMAL MASS REFRIGERATOR

THE EARTHSHIP IS DESIGNED FOR MINIMAL ELECTRIC USE SO THAT THE SOLAR ELECTRIC SYSTEM CAN BE AS INEXPENSIVE AND LOW TECH AS POSSIBLE. A "DESIGNED DOWN" ELECTRIC SYSTEM IS DISCUSSED IN EARTHSHIP VOLUME II PP. 9-22. PURSUANT TO THAT DISCUSSION WE HAVE OBSERVED THAT THE SINGLE MAJOR DRAW OF ELECTRICITY IN EARTHSHIPS HAS BEEN THE D.C. REFRIGERATORS. THEY WORK GREAT BUT MONOPOLIZE 2 TO 4 PHOTO-VOLTAIC PANELS YEAR ROUND DEPENDING ON THE SIZE OF THE REFRIGERATOR. WE OBSERVED THAT THE MOST CRITICAL TIME FOR THIS CONSTANT DRAW OF ELECTRICITY IS THE WINTER WHEN DAYS ARE SHORT AND SUN LIGHT IS AT A MINIMUM. THIS IS ALSO THE TIME WHEN LIGHTS ARE USED MORE OFTEN DUE TO EARLIER DARKNESS. HERE IN THE WINTER WE SEE THE LEAST AMOUNT OF SOLAR POWER COMING IN AND THE MOST DAILY DEMAND. DURING THIS "WEAK" OR VULNERABLE TIME (FOR A P.V. SYSTEM) WE HAVE TWO CHOICES:

1. **BEEF UP THE SYSTEM JUST TO MAKE IT THROUGH THIS TIME**

2. **REDUCE THE USAGE DURING THIS TIME SOMEHOW.**

CAN THE NATURE OF THE EARTHSHIP AND THE PHILOSOPHY OF ALIGNING WITH NATURAL PHENOMENON AGAIN COME TO OUR RESCUE? YES, WE PRESENT THE "THERMAL MASS REFRIGERATOR".

Graphics by   Tom Drugan, Claire Blanchard
Photos by   Chris Simpson

Imagine you are from another galaxy and you are observing habits and activities of the human beings on Earth. Observation would reveal that these creatures build "boxes" to live in that shield them from the natural elements of the planet.

One such natural element is the sun around which the planet orbits. This sun is a natural source of heat and energy. The boxes shield and separate the humans from this heat. Then the humans manufacture their own heat inside the box using fuels extracted from the planet itself. *They turn their back on natural, "free" heat and make their own heat at great expense to both them and the planet.*

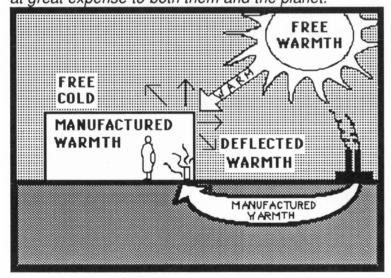

This in itself seems ridiculous, however closer observation reveals an even greater blindness in these humans. They heat the big box with manufactured warmth when natural warmth is available. Then inside the big heated box they build

another little box and they use the same manufactured energy to make that box cold *when cold is often naturally available just outside the heated box.*

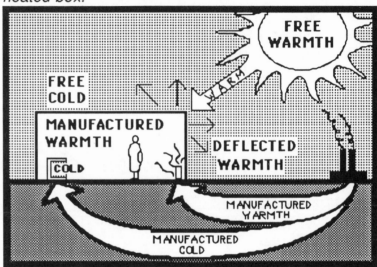

The way this looks from a distant view is quite absurd. The existing environment is COLD but with a source of HEAT "in the sky". The initial box wants HEAT but ignores this source of HEAT from the sky and uses a manufactured and transported form of the same type of energy. Then inside the initial box they do the same thing again. The little box wants to be COLD but ignores the COLD just a few feet away and uses the same manufactured energy to make COLD.

Maybe the problem is that humans can't get far enough away from themselves to see the obvious.

This chapter will pursue the obvious.

82

THE NIGHT COOLER CONCEPT

A simple example of the night cooler existed (and exists) in old buildings where single pane glass and thick walls created a deep window seat where food could be cooled simply by placing it on the window sill and closing off the warmth of the room with a blanket or panel of some type.

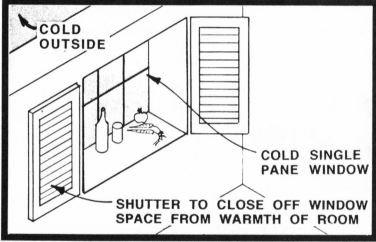

This was most effective on the north side of the building (in the northern hemisphere) where there is no solar gain on the window. If we take this concept which has been used out of necessity by many (who could not afford refrigeration) and attach it to the already explored concept of thermal mass and the temperature retention qualities thereof, we can have a modern refrigerator that in many areas requires half the energy from outside sources that conventional concept refrigerators do.

We are admitting the cold from the roof (as cold air is heavier and falls down) and storing it in mass much the same as the Earthship itself admits the heat of the sun and stores it in mass.

We have a little box inside a big box; both of which get what they need in terms of temperature from the "phenomenon at hand" rather than a power plant.

In many areas this concept would work as shown by opening to the night temperatures and closing to the day temperatures. The night temperature is allowed into the mass lined and insulated refrigerator space. This space is closed off during the day time and the mass enables it to retain the cold night temperature through the day. The process starts all over again by admitting the cold air again in the evening.

The range of use of this concept can be expanded by attaching a small DC cooling unit, run by P.V. panels. This cooling unit is similar to the one the Sun frost D.C. refrigerator (discussed in Volume II, p. 8 and 25) uses. The cooling unit runs quite often in the summer when there is plenty of sun to power it, but not at all in the winter when there is limited sun. Thus we have *eliminated the use of electricity for refrigeration in the winter.*

The refrigerated space which is in the center of the mass, surrounded by intense insulation, will render the summer use as efficient as possible by *storing* the cold air produced by solar electricity. When you open your refrigerator door and the cold air escapes, the mass quickly cools the space back down after the door is closed. The mass helps the D.C. cooling unit to work less often.

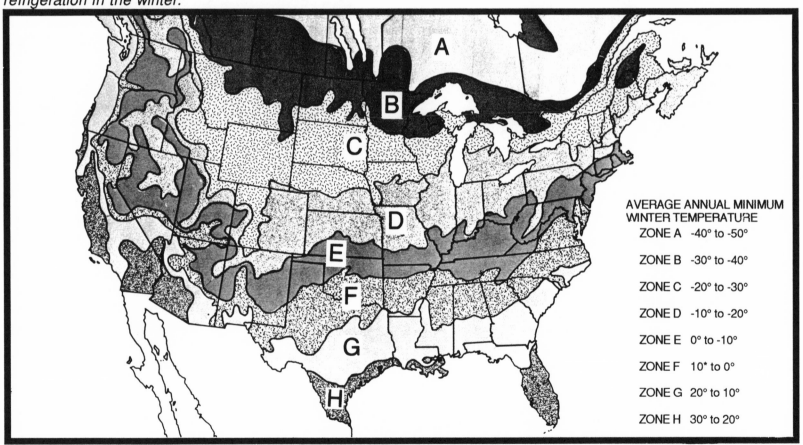

AVERAGE ANNUAL MINIMUM
WINTER TEMPERATURE

ZONE A -40° to -50°

ZONE B -30° to -40°

ZONE C -20° to -30°

ZONE D -10° to -20°

ZONE E 0° to -10°

ZONE F 10* to 0°

ZONE G 20° to 10°

ZONE H 30° to 20°

Even in areas where there is no winter freezing, the thermal mass of the night cooler helps *hold the cold* thus reducing the energy required for maintaining refrigeration. Standard refrigerators have only insulation. The night cooler has mass <u>and</u> insulation. In some areas this unit could be used without any auxiliary cooling unit. Any place that has freezing temperatures at night 90% of the time can have free refrigeration. In over half of the globe this concept could suffice without auxiliary power 50% of the time. This reduces the usage of power (solar or other), takes the winter strain off of P.V. power systems and in general puts us a step closer to non freon refrigeration. By *reducing the energy demand* on refrigeration systems on over 50% of the globe we have made the job of refrigeration easier. Now as we struggle toward non freon refrigeration, we at least have a smaller task.

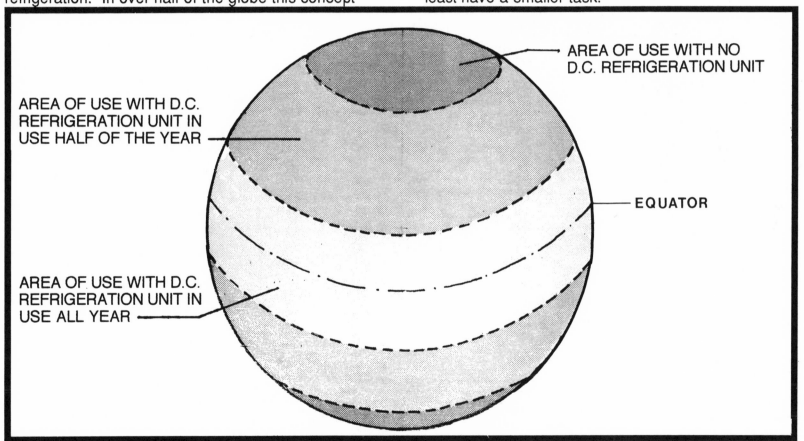

AREA OF USE WITH NO
D.C. REFRIGERATION UNIT

AREA OF USE WITH D.C.
REFRIGERATION UNIT IN
USE HALF OF THE YEAR

EQUATOR

AREA OF USE WITH D.C.
REFRIGERATION UNIT IN
USE ALL YEAR

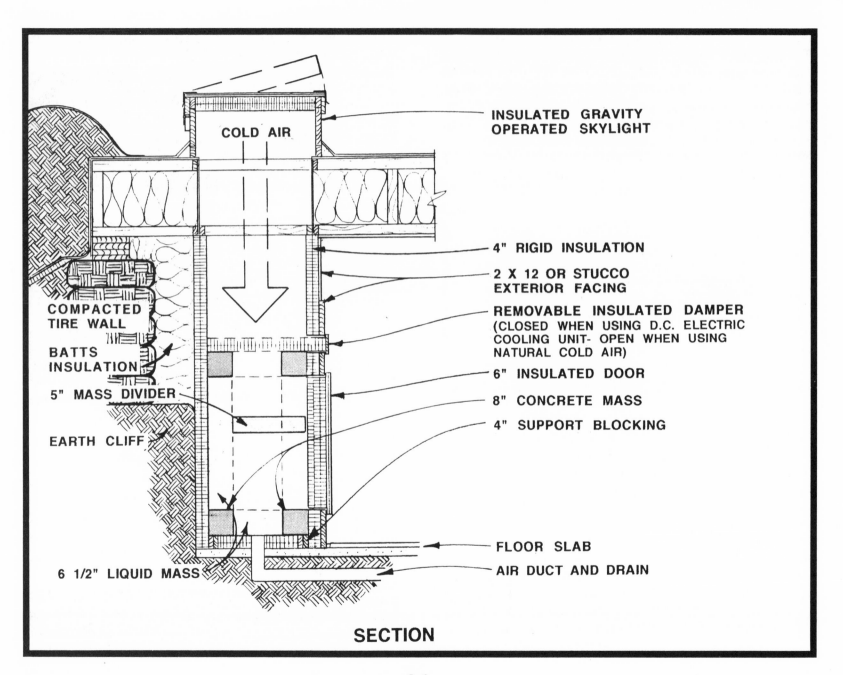

INSULATED GRAVITY
OPERATED SKYLIGHT

COLD AIR

4" RIGID INSULATION

2 X 12 OR STUCCO
EXTERIOR FACING

REMOVABLE INSULATED DAMPER
(CLOSED WHEN USING D.C. ELECTRIC
COOLING UNIT- OPEN WHEN USING
NATURAL COLD AIR)

6" INSULATED DOOR

8" CONCRETE MASS

4" SUPPORT BLOCKING

COMPACTED
TIRE WALL

BATTS
INSULATION

5" MASS DIVIDER

EARTH CLIFF

FLOOR SLAB

AIR DUCT AND DRAIN

6 1/2" LIQUID MASS

SECTION

86

The entire unit is surrounded by mass and insulation. The door is weatherstripped and is filled with 4" rigid urethane insulation. The duct to the roof is also insulated with 4" rigid urethane. The duct must be as wide as the space to be cooled plus the width of the mass. The higher the ceiling the farther the air has to travel, thus lower ceilings are better.

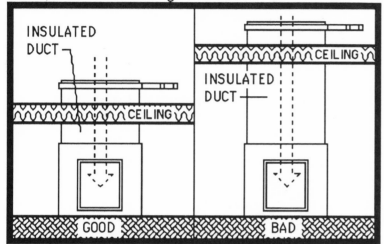

The duct has a standard (but solid insulated) Earthship gravity skylight (as detailed in Volume II) above. An insulated slide out damper is used to close the duct off from the cooled space during times when cool air is not coming in and you are trying to contain what you already have. This damper is also used when the D.C. refrigeration unit is the source of cool air as you are also trying to contain this cool air. In section the unit is a freezer space on top with a cooling space on the bottom. The cooling space can be about 2'-0" tall while the freezer space is about 12" tall. This 12" is important as this dimension is necessary to accommodate the cooling coils of the D.C. cooling unit. A 5" mass divider between the

refrigerator and freezer is made of sheet metal and filled with aluminum cans of cheap beer.

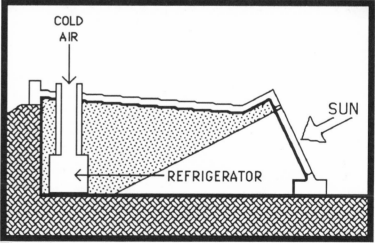

The unit must be placed out of the winter sun angle.

This means deeper into the "U" module. It is very massive, so to place it against or slightly recessed in a mass or cliff wall is a good idea.

We have observed that the incoming cold night air fills up the space and won't come in as much when there is no place for it to go. This allows cooling but never gets as cold as the outside.

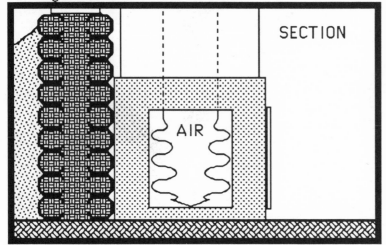

When there is a duct coming out the bottom to the outside, the cold air is pulled all the way through the unit and creates a constant flow of fresh cold air. This achieves temperatures as cold as the outside.

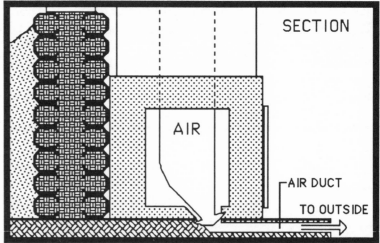

Now for an added benefit this "through air" duct can double as a fresh air duct for a nearby fireplace. It is sucked out through the fireplace chimney providing combustion air for the fireplace which stops it from sucking air through cracks around doors and windows. Whenever you burn a fire, you are cooling your refrigerator and storing cold for the next day.

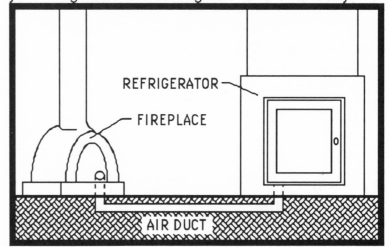

AIR DUCT

AIR
DUCT

89

SPECIFICS

Various experiments with concrete and water thermal mass have provided statistics for the following graph.

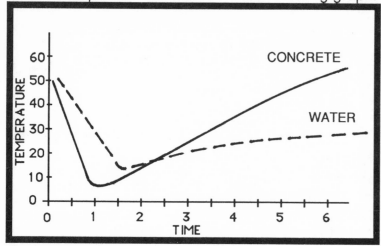

The results show that concrete gets colder faster but water holds the cold for a longer time. This means that a combination of concrete mass to get cold quickly and water mass to see you through a longer period of time is the best approach to building the mass for your "night cooler". We leave "pockets" in the 8" thick concrete mass walls to accommodate water (or cheap beer in aluminum cans) for the liquid mass. You want at least 70% of the mass to be liquid.

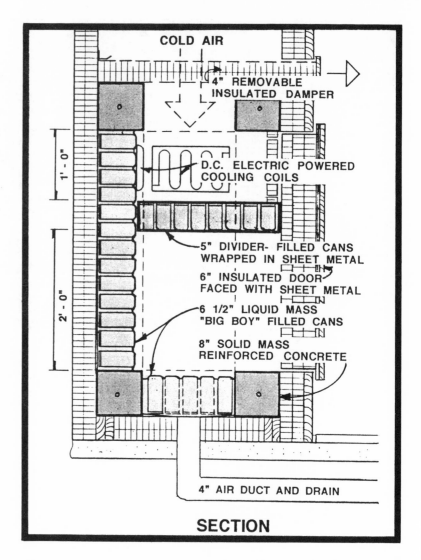

SECTION

The unit in plan is roughly a 2'-0" x 2'-0" space surrounded by 8" of thermal mass. The mass (at least 70% water) is surrounded by 4" of rigid urethane insulation.

90

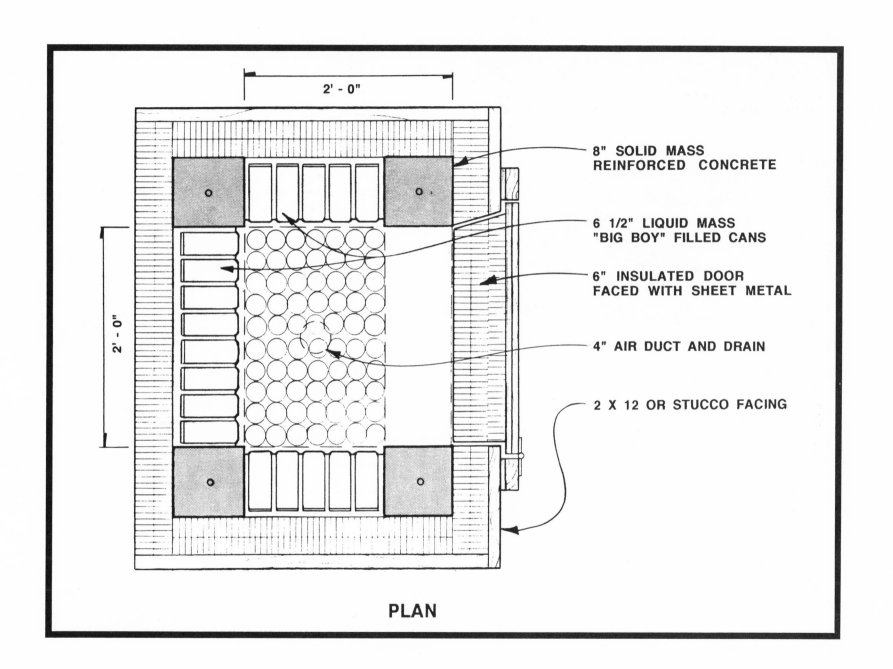

2' - 0"

2' - 0"

8" SOLID MASS
REINFORCED CONCRETE

6 1/2" LIQUID MASS
"BIG BOY" FILLED CANS

6" INSULATED DOOR
FACED WITH SHEET METAL

4" AIR DUCT AND DRAIN

2 X 12 OR STUCCO FACING

PLAN

91

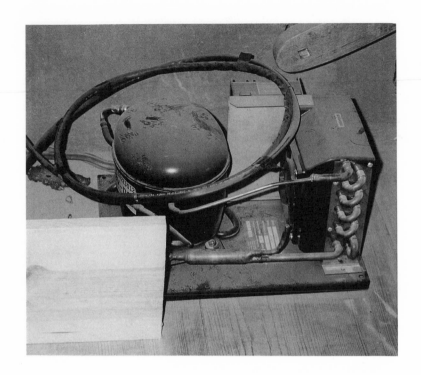

The DC refrigeration unit, shown opposite, or the night air has the capacity to freeze the upper (freezer) part of the unit. The freezer mass is connected to the refrigerator mass and consequently conducts the cold temperature into the lower compartment, thus cooling (not freezing) that area. The mass buffer between the two compartments also aids in <u>containing</u> the *freezing* temperatures while <u>conducting</u> *cold* temperatures. Thus we have a mass refrigerator with a freezer powered both by night temperatures and by the sun. We have taken another appliance and cut its power demand down thus allowing the home power system to be smaller, simpler, and less expensive.

Detailed construction drawings of the thermal mass night cooler are available from SSA. The D.C. refrigeration unit can also be purchased through SSA. These together are cheaper than the Sunfrost D.C. refrigerator and result in a significantly lower household electrical requirement.

Construction drawings for the thermal mass night cooler $100.00

D.C. refrigeration unit. $600.00

Prices subject to change after the printing of this book.

4. THE SOLAR TOILET

THE CONTINUED PRACTICE OF MIXING WATER WITH HUMAN EXCREMENT IS A WASTE OF WATER, A HAZARD TO THE ENVIRONMENT IN WHICH IT IS DUMPED, AND GENERALLY AN ENLARGEMENT OF THE PROBLEM. THE BEAUTIFUL TOWN OF TAOS, NEW MEXICO HAS A SEWAGE TREATMENT PLANT THAT CAN'T HANDLE ITS "LOAD" SO THEY ARE HAULING SLUDGE TO THE DESERT IN TANK TRUCKS AND PLOWING IT UNDER. FECAL MATTER WAS FOUND IN THE DRINKING WATER OF A PUBLIC SCHOOL IN THE CITY OF ALBUQUERQUE, NEW MEXICO. NEEDED GROWTH IN MANY URBAN AREAS IS LIMITED BECAUSE OF LACK OF ADEQUATE SEWAGE FACILITIES. WITH RESPECT TO ENERGY, HEALTH AND THE ENVIRONMENT, WE NEED TO QUIT MIXING OUR SHIT WITH WATER AND ALCHEMIZE IT INTO ANOTHER FORM. *WE NEED TO DO THIS ON A LARGE SCALE NOW.* IN AN EFFORT TO EVOLVE A VIABLE END TO BLACK WATER IN BOTH URBAN AND RURAL AREAS, WE HAVE USED AND LIVED WITH VARIOUS COMPOST TOILETS FOR ALMOST TWENTY YEARS. IN THE FIRST PART OF THIS CHAPTER, WE WOULD LIKE TO PROVIDE AN UPDATE ON THE RECOMMENDATIONS WE PRESENTED IN <u>EARTHSHIP VOLUME II</u> ABOUT THESE COMPOST TOILETS. THEN WE WOULD LIKE TO INTRODUCE A RADICAL NEW CONTRIBUTION TOWARD SOLVING THE PROBLEMS OF BLACK WATER. AS WE LISTEN TO THE EARTH, OUR OWN NEEDS AND THE VARIOUS ENVIRONMENTAL AUTHORITIES, AND TRY TO SATISFY ALL, WE INTRODUCE - THE SOLAR TOILET.

Graphics by   Tom Drugan
Photographs by   Peter Kolshorn / Tom Woosly

UPDATE ON COMPOST TOILETS

The REACH project has given us the opportunity to live with both non-electric compost toilets made by SunMar - the Centrex-NE (formerly WCM-NE) composter used in conjunction with Sealand 910 Traveler low flush toilet and the toilet/composter in one unit, the Excel- NE (formerly Sunmar-NE). Of the two, the most sensible and least expensive in terms of cost and installation is the SunMar Excel-NE.

The SunMar Excel-NE uses no water or electricity for composting. There is a small DC fan ($50) that is a must or it will stink. The fan uses a small amount of electricity (less than an efficient light bulb) and must be on *all* the time. It would be good to have a spare fan on hand as they are quite delicate and an imperative part of the unit. We once had a chipmunk crawl down the vent stack and get caught in the fan. Both chipmunk and fan were damaged beyond repair. Another time a fan just burned out. The unit begins to smell immediately after the fan quits working.

The unit must be used properly. We have found that almost any kind of composting "enhancers" will work such as sawdust, peatmoss, vegetable scraps, or leaves. Some form of composting aid must be added daily (like feeding a rabbit) and the unit must be tumbled after every use. The worst misuse of this unit we have seen is that some people do not understand the "back tumbling" process which is really how and why it works.

Every three weeks (assuming regular use) the tumbler must be turned backwards for about two revolutions. This unloads some of the contents from the tumbler into a tray in the bottom of the unit. This tray is a very important part of the process of getting the material dried out and harmless enough to put on the ground. The tumbler simply holds the contents separate from this tray and mixes it up as new contents are added. The material begins to break down here but never gets a chance to really dry out. The contents that have been back-tumbled into the tray are left undisturbed for about three weeks.

After three weeks (assuming no new contents are allowed to fall into the tray) the material in the tray is very dry compost that can be put right on top of the ground outside. The only real problem with this unit is that if the above tasks of adding composting additives, tumbling and back tumbling are not executed properly; the material that is dumped onto the ground outside is "rich" and unacceptable for surface use. This means it would have to be buried and authorities can't count on people dealing with this problem adequately on a regular basis. Since there is this potential, these units are not being accepted in any area that is, or has the chance of being, highly developed. The bottom line is the Excel-NE works very well if you know how to use it, but chances are you won't get it approved in a reasonably populated area. It is great for remote home sites and responsible people.

For those who can't be that close to "fecal matter", the low flush toilet with the Centrex-NE model can work well under certain conditions. It also must have a DC fan going all the time. If horizontal runs are used from the low flush toilet to the composter, an occasional flush out of the lines with scalding hot water is necessary. We advise short or no horizontal runs if possible.

This SunMar remote composting unit (Centrex-NE) used in conjunction with the Sealand low flush toilet (discussed in Volume II) has some drawbacks. If the composting unit is placed <u>directly below</u> the toilet so there is a direct drop into the composting unit, it works well with the same procedures as the Excel-NE. Obviously, it has the same potential for misuse.

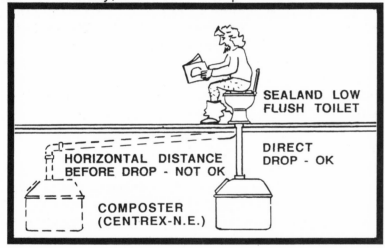

It does take very little water to flush in this circumstance. However, the addition of any water seems to retard the composting process. Furthermore, if too much water is used (and there is a tendency to do this) the overflow is forced into action. It clogs very easily and simply does not work well. If there is any horizontal distance required to get to the composting unit, too much water is required to carry the solids to the unit. This results in more use of the easily clogging overflow. This can cause overflow into the tray which is supposed to remain undisturbed and dry. When you empty the tray it can be filled with some pretty foul stuff. What you end up with is wet, soggy, partially composted stuff that should be buried into the ground rather than dumped on the surface. *The mixing of water with human excrement is simply a mistake.* The plumbing and remote space required to use the composter with the Sealand low-flush toilet results in an expensive situation. In that the remote unit requires a two story building, it is automatically not feasible in many Earthship situations. *We absolutely do not recommend this set up if you have any substantial horizontal distance to "travel" between toilet and composting unit.*

In a <u>direct drop situation</u> it can work if you treat it like a rabbit and feed it kitchen compost, peat moss, leaves or straw daily. Also, it is imperative to keep water to a minimum. The more water you use, the more additives (compost, peat moss etc.) you need. Most Earthships are one story and this unit is not worth the expense of trying to create a direct drop situation. However, a knowlegable, responsible person with the right architectural circumstances can successfully use this unit.

The problem that environmental authorities and codes have with compost toilets is that if used in large numbers in dense urban areas and if not used properly we could have a big problem. (There have also been some complaints of flies and gnats with both units.) We recommend intelligent use of the SunMar compost toilets in rural areas but we respect the fears of the authorities in urban areas. The fact that compost toilets aren't allowed in urban areas means that we still have a problem.

We need a solution that will work for both rural and urban areas, and something that is impossible to misuse.

SOLUTION
We found ourselves looking for a dry toilet situation that required less effort and that produced a more acceptable "product" to put back on the land. We were also looking for a fool proof process that was not as tedious as taking care of a rabbit. The bottom line is, at best, the SunMar units require too much care for the average busy twentieth century human to want to deal with.

The ultimate unit must do everything itself and leave you with a truly transformed product that no building inspector or environmental authority would have a problem with. The reason compost toilets are not acceptable in many areas is that the final product is often too rich and the widespread production of this product could create an undesirable situation. The final product must be something so benign that you could hold it in your hand and would want to put it in your yard or hallway planters.

Many people have seen and/or heard about solar ovens. They are a well insulated black box with tempered glass on the front. They really work. You can boil water and cook turkeys in them.

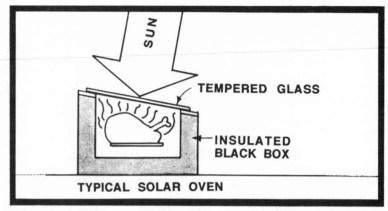

We tried using a large solar oven with a toilet seat built into the top side. The results blew us away. Have you ever left a casserole in the oven on "warm" over night. What you end up with is ash - crackling ash.

THE SOLAR TOILET CONCEPT
The concept of this toilet is a cross between a solar oven and a compost toilet. It uses no water and no electricity. It uses sun. The excrement goes into a basket that holds the solids and lets the liquids drip through. This basket is placed against the solar front face of the Earthship (or south side of any house) in a black insulated space similar to a solar oven. Extreme temperatures (200 to 400 degrees) and direct sun simply fry the solids and evaporate the liquids. The fried solids turn to black ash and fall through the basket into a pull-out tray where it almost turns to dust. This tray is emptied once a month. This black ash is not going to scare anyone. It can even be put on an interior planter. We have put this black ash/powder into water and had the water tested. _The test showed no bacteria in the water._

96

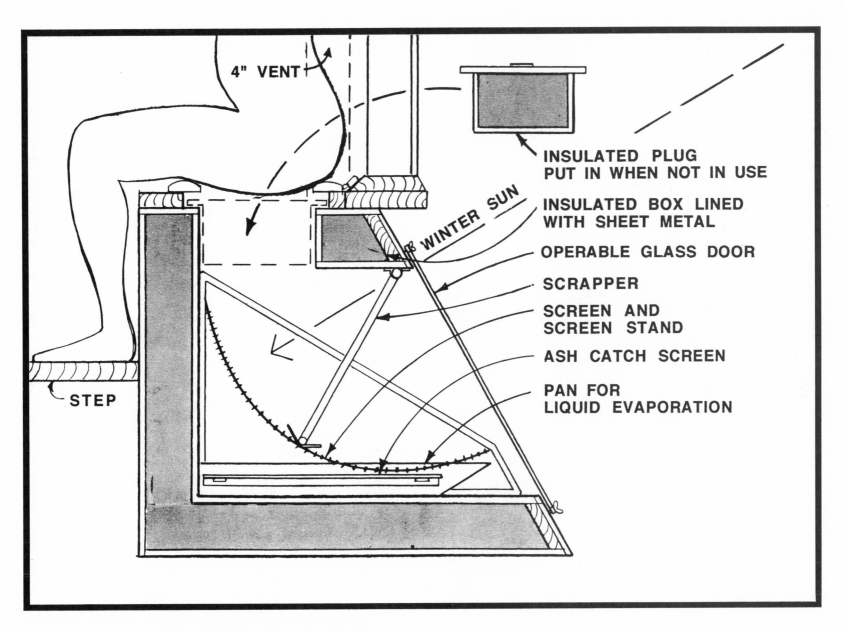

4" VENT

INSULATED PLUG
PUT IN WHEN NOT IN USE

INSULATED BOX LINED
WITH SHEET METAL

WINTER SUN

OPERABLE GLASS DOOR

SCRAPPER

SCREEN AND
SCREEN STAND

ASH CATCH SCREEN

PAN FOR
LIQUID EVAPORATION

STEP

SECTION OF SCRAPER MODEL SOLAR TOILET

The volume of fried ash that is emptied out once a month is remarkably small. The ashes from two people using a solar toilet for one month will half fill a quart container.

Regular toilet paper can be used. It simply dries up and turns to flakes, then dust. You can drop a match in and burn it for instant disappearance in the scraper model. This unit can be totally built in with the architecture <u>with no plumbing</u>. It essentially costs no more then the Excel-NE. It vents like a wood stove and requires a scraper to be moved back and forth once a day. The following picture illustrates the final product - fried ash.

Our first working prototype, (the scraper model) worked great but had one drawback - you could see the fecal matter through the glass. Obviously, many people couldn't handle this. We have since evolved a tumbler model which is more expensive, but contains the contents in a steel tumbler drum. In this circumstance, you can see nothing through the glass nor through the seat. Yes, tampons can be put in. On this tumbler model we have moved the door opening that allows the tray to be removed to the inside. This pull out plug is easier to operate (inside the building) and cheaper to build than the "glass door" on the front.

Both units require a D.C. fan similar to the SunMar units. An important factor here is that the electric fan is *only turned on during use* and kept off the rest of the time in order to maintain high temperatures in the "oven". It is not on all the time like the fans in the Sun Mar units. We have a set of construction drawings available for the scraper model. The tumbler model is more involved and we simply manufacture it. Both units are designed to fit into the front face of an EARTHSHIP.

The tumbler model works much the same as the SunMar composter when the sun is not out. Then when the sun comes out it fries the back tumbled compost. Thus the tumbler model extends the use of the concept to cloudier areas and minimizes the visual contact with the compost.

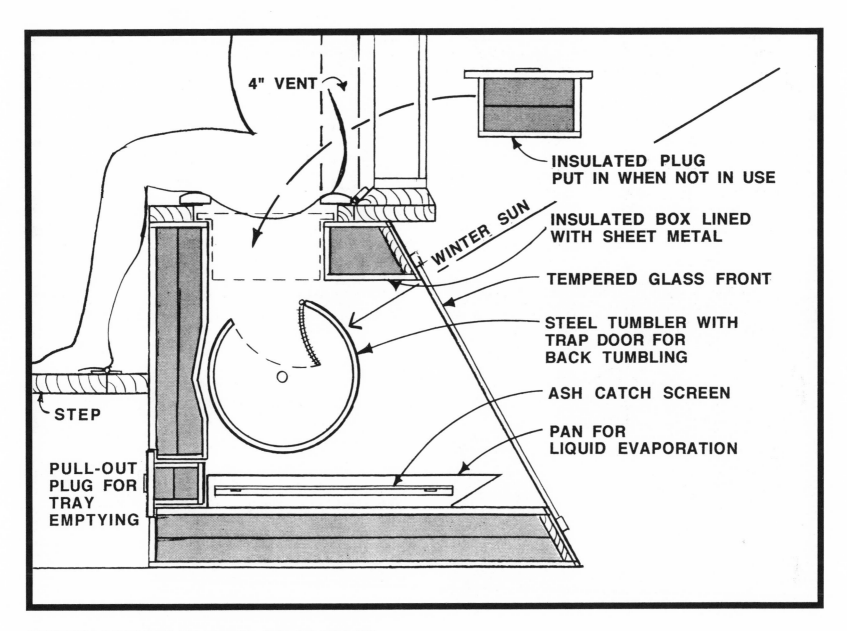

4" VENT

**INSULATED PLUG
PUT IN WHEN NOT IN USE**

WINTER SUN

**INSULATED BOX LINED
WITH SHEET METAL**

TEMPERED GLASS FRONT

**STEEL TUMBLER WITH
TRAP DOOR FOR
BACK TUMBLING**

ASH CATCH SCREEN

**PAN FOR
LIQUID EVAPORATION**

STEP

**PULL-OUT
PLUG FOR
TRAY
EMPTYING**

SECTION OF TUMBLER MODEL SOLAR TOILET

OUTSIDE OF SOLAR TOILET PROTOTYPE

INSIDE OF SOLAR TOILET PROTOTYPE

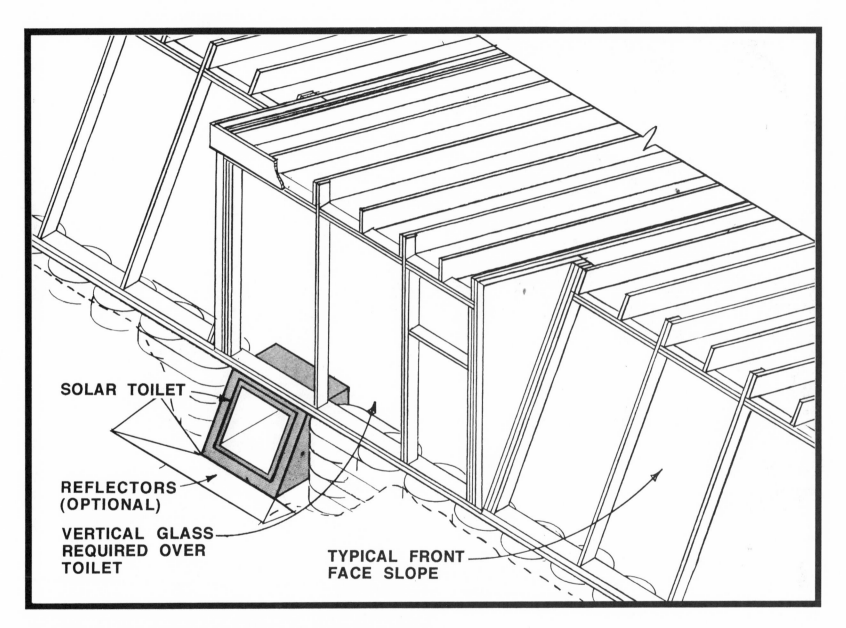

SOLAR TOILET

REFLECTORS (OPTIONAL)

VERTICAL GLASS REQUIRED OVER TOILET

TYPICAL FRONT FACE SLOPE

FRAMING FOR GENERIC SOLAR TOILET INSTALLATION

101

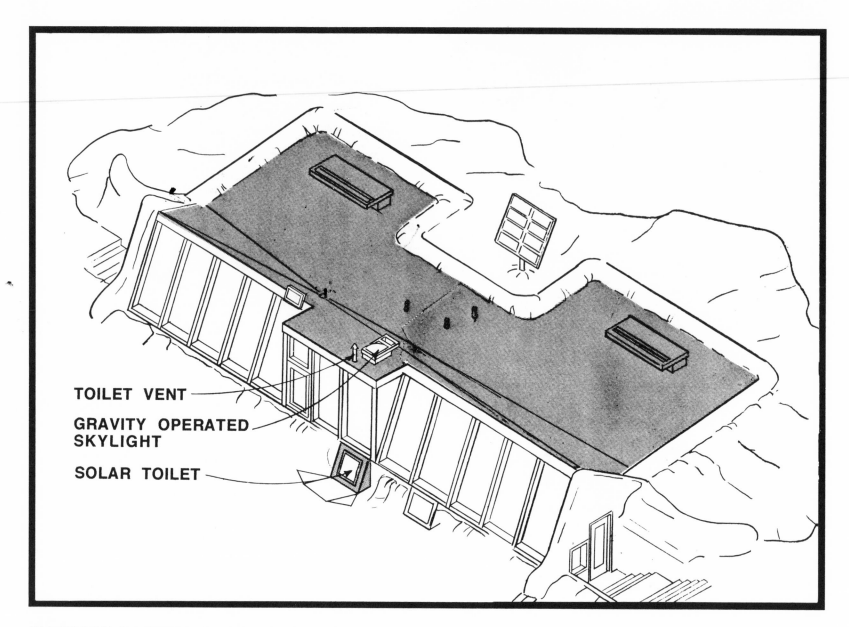

TOILET VENT

GRAVITY OPERATED SKYLIGHT

SOLAR TOILET

OVERVIEW OF GENERIC EARTHSHIP SHOWING SOLAR TOILET

102

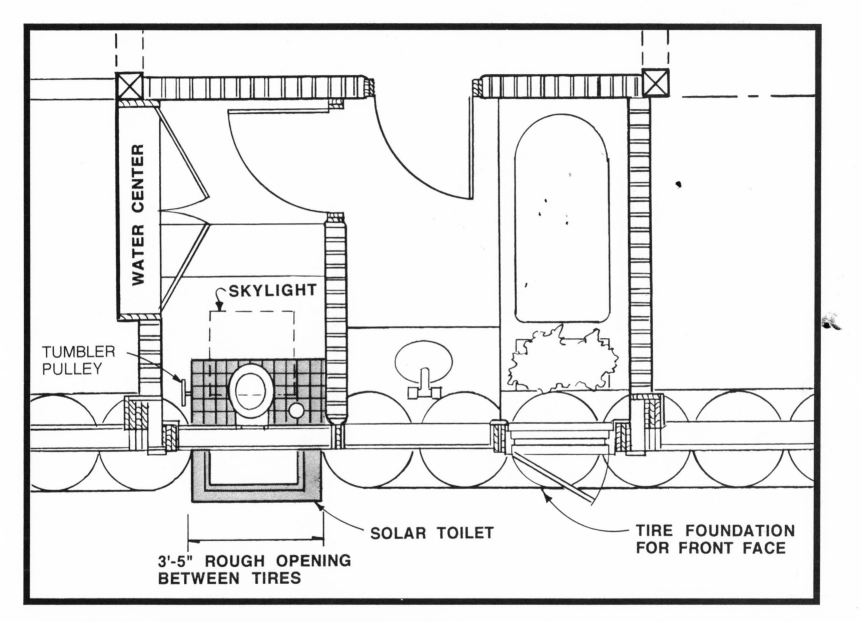

WATER CENTER

SKYLIGHT

TUMBLER
PULLEY

SOLAR TOILET

**3'-5" ROUGH OPENING
BETWEEN TIRES**

**TIRE FOUNDATION
FOR FRONT FACE**

FLOOR PLAN OF GENERIC SOLAR TOILET INSTALLATION

These units can be installed in any building whether it is an Earthship or not. They must however, be placed on the south side of the structure (in the northern hemisphere), as the sun is what makes them work.

We still recommend a little closed off room for the toilet (see previous page) with a small gravity operated skylight (see Chapter 8, Vol. II). Different geographic locations would require different glass angles similar to the EARTHSHIP itself. Either model will work as a composter during cloudy weather. For extremely cloudy weather the tumbler model is the only choice. At this point the scraper model is great for areas with 200 or more sun days per year and the tumbler model will extend the use to areas with only 150 sun days per year. You need one for every 4 people in sunny areas and one for every 2 people in areas down around 200 sun days per year. Optional reflectors will enhance the performance of either model.

Both units are available through SSA. The DC fans and construction drawings for the scraper model are also available through SSA.

INSTRUCTIONS FOR USE ARE AS FOLLOWS:
1. Turn on fan
2. Open damper
3. Lift toilet seat and pull plug then reposition toilet seat
4. Use toilet (optional - drop match in and burn paper-scraper model only)
5. Install plug and close toilet seat
6. Turn off fan
7. Close damper
8T. Tumble 2 turns (on tumbler model only)
8S. Move scraper back and forth a few times at the end of each day (scraper model only)
9. The back tumbling operation (described on page 100) must happen once a month on the tumbler model

PRODUCT LIST:

DC Fan	$50.00
Solar Toilet Scraper Model	$1500.00 plus freight
Solar Toilet Tumbler Model	$1700.00 plus freight
Construction Drawings and Procedures For Scraper Model	$100.00
Sunmar Excel-NE	$999.00 plus freight
Sunmar Centrex-NE	$999.00 plus freight
Sealand 910 Traveler	$161.00 plus freight

Prices subject to change after the printing of this book

ORDER FROM:

Solar Survival Sales
P.O. Box 1041
Taos, New Mexico 87571
(505) 751-0462

5. SOLAR OVEN / DISTILLER AND ELECTRIC COOK TOP

MOST EARTHSHIPS, UP UNTIL NOW, HAVE BEEN USING GAS FOR COOKING. THIS IS BECAUSE ELECTRIC OVENS USE TOO MUCH POWER TO RUN OFF OF A SOLAR ELECTRIC SYSTEM. WE ARE CONSTANTLY TRYING TO ELIMINATE USES OF FOSSIL FUEL IN EARTHSHIPS FOR MANY ENVIRONMENTAL, ECONOMIC, AND PHILOSOPHICAL REASONS. WE HAVE, THEREFORE, DEVELOPED A SOLAR OVEN THAT IS THE SAME BASIC CONFIGURATION AS THE SOLAR TOILET. THIS LEAVES US WITH ONLY THE COOK TOP TO POWER WITH SOLAR ELECTRICITY AND THAT CAN BE DONE. SINCE (BEING SOLAR) THE SOLAR OVEN IS "ON" ALL DAY LONG AND ONE DOES NOT COOK ALL DAY LONG, WE HAVE DETAILED IT TO DOUBLE AS A SOLAR DISTILLER. DISTILLED WATER IS NEEDED FOR THE BATTERIES IN THE SOLAR POWER SYSTEMS IN ADDITION TO ITS USE AS FOOL PROOF, SAFE DRINKING WATER.   OUR SOLAR OVEN/DISTILLER IS A WELCOME ADDITION TO THE VARIOUS EARTHSHIP APPLIANCES THAT FREE US FROM THE BONDAGE OF TWENTIETH CENTURY DOGMA.

Graphics by   Tom Drugan
Photographs by   Chris Simpson

THE OVEN

Since the solar toilet is basically a solar oven that can reach temperatures of up to 400 degrees Fahrenheit, we have used the same basic unit as a point of departure for manufacturing the solar oven/distiller. We have simply replaced the toilet seat with an oven door.

There is no vent pipe necessary in the oven and it is always light on the inside during use because of the sun. The unit is somewhat larger than a regular gas or electric oven but this better facilitates the distilling aspect. The unit must be installed on the solar front face of the Earthship. It can also be used in a regular house as long as it is built in to the south face (in the northern hemisphere).

The solar toilet has a 5/8" sheetrock liner under the metal liner. This sheet rock liner acts as thermal mass and helps the toilet hold its heat when the sun goes behind a cloud. In the solar oven we are allowing for a brick liner that will hold heat thus creating a very slow cool down situation. This allows a dinner dish to be cooked in the late afternoon and remain "on warm" until dinner time. Standard fire brick (painted black) would be used and they would be placed in the oven by the home owner after the oven is installed into the home. The opposite page illustrates a detailed section of this unit with the fire brick in place.

This oven used in conjunction with a standard AC electric cook top will provide a total cooking system that uses no gas. Most two burner electric cook tops work perfectly on the inverter that comes with the

Power Organizer Module discussed on page 51. The wattage of any appliance is usually given in the accompanying literature or on the device. Electric cook tops usually have one 1000 watt burner and one 700 watt burner. The maximum on the small POM inverter is 1700 watts. The maximum on the large POM inverter is 2500 watts. Look for these wattages when purchasing an AC two burner cook top. If you can find a DC electric cook top, you can use four burners as there is no inverter to relate to for DC. This will require that you have the appliance on a circuit by itself with wire to the POM sized correctly for the distance involved.

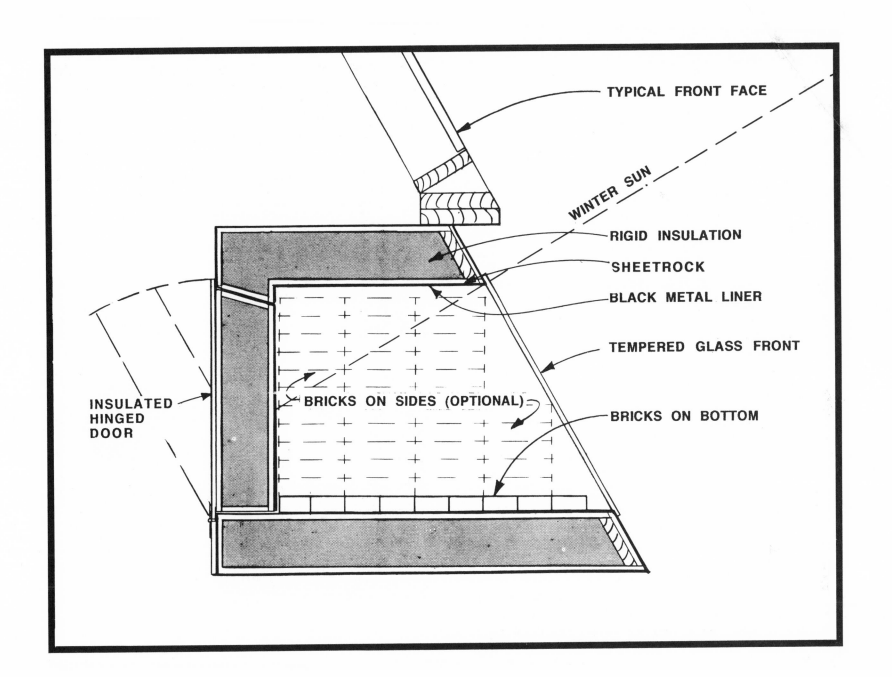

TYPICAL FRONT FACE

WINTER SUN

RIGID INSULATION

SHEETROCK

BLACK METAL LINER

TEMPERED GLASS FRONT

INSULATED
HINGED
DOOR

BRICKS ON SIDES (OPTIONAL)

BRICKS ON BOTTOM

The solar oven has to be built in to the south face. A typical kitchen layout sympathetic to this is shown below.

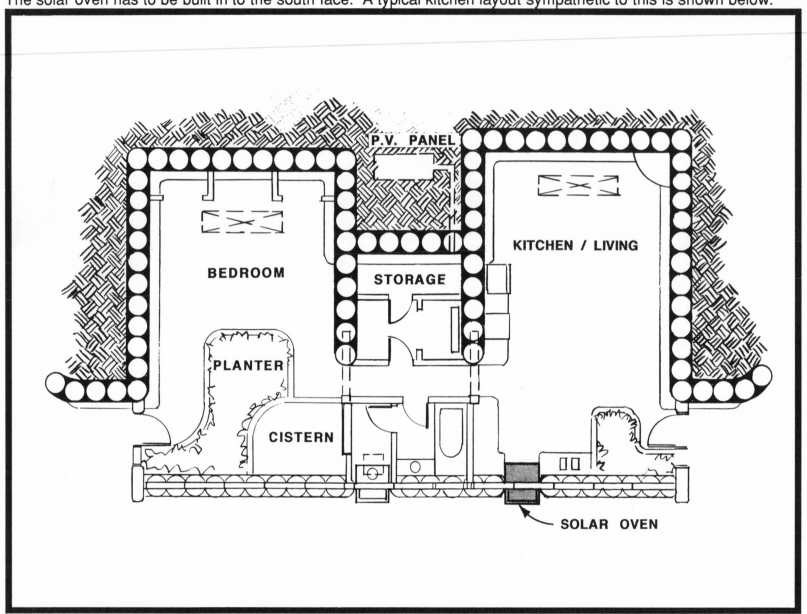

P.V. PANEL

BEDROOM

KITCHEN / LIVING

STORAGE

PLANTER

CISTERN

SOLAR OVEN

108

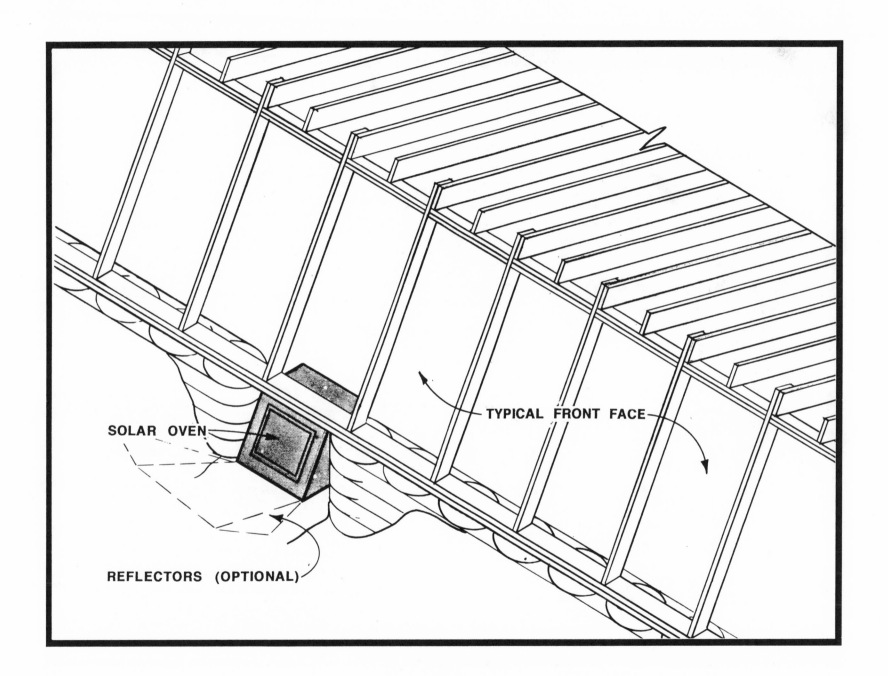

SOLAR OVEN

TYPICAL FRONT FACE

REFLECTORS (OPTIONAL)

SOLAR OVEN AND TOILET INSTALLATION UNDER CONSTRUCTION

THE DISTILLER

The water distilling aspect of this unit is simply a device that is placed in the oven when it is not used for cooking. Since the oven will be well over 200 degrees Fahrenheit for most of all the sunny days, there will be plenty of time for distilling water when cooking is not going on. The distiller/oven comes with a drain pipe on the side.

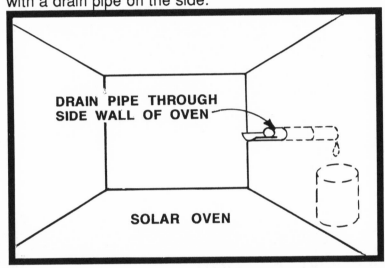

The distilling unit fits on to the opening to this pipe. Water evaporates up from the water chamber, hits the stainless steel plate and runs into the collection tube. This tube directs the distilled water to the drain pipe. You set your own container under this pipe outlet and watch the distilled water fill your container on a sunny day.

This unit is obviously only effective in or near the sunbelt. Two hundred or more sun days a year would make this unit a feasible appliance for your Earthship. Research is going on right now for a gas

backup aspect of this unit. This would increase its range of use and allow free cooking and distilling whenever there is sun.

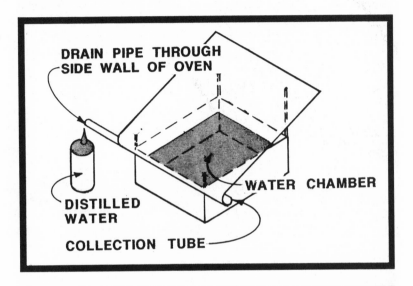

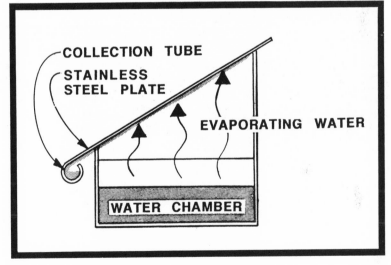

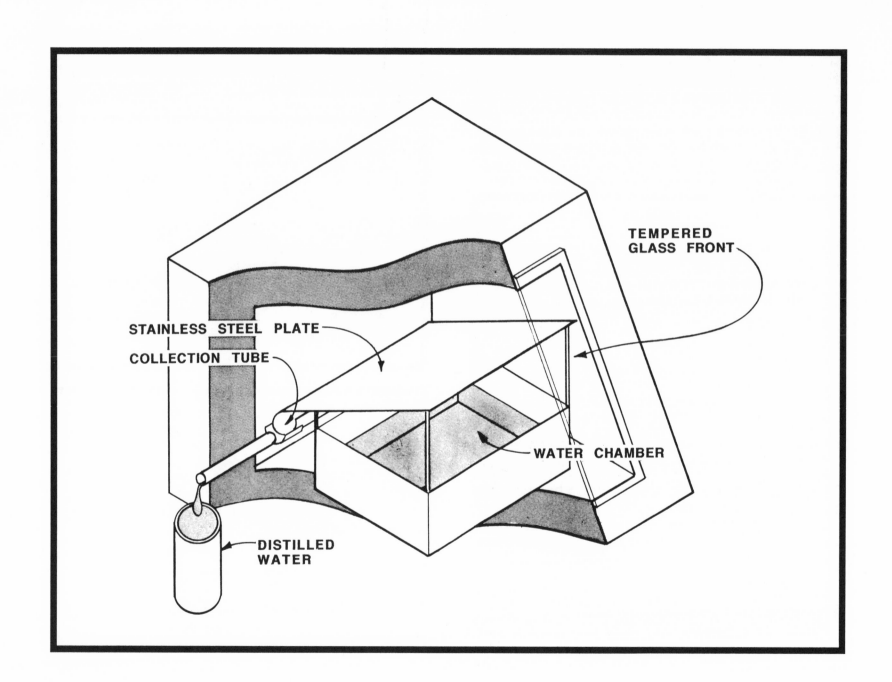

TEMPERED
GLASS FRONT

STAINLESS STEEL PLATE

COLLECTION TUBE

WATER CHAMBER

DISTILLED
WATER

SOLAR OVEN UNDER CONSTRUCTION

Drawings for solar oven $150.00

Solar oven $ plus freight

Distiller unit $ plus freight

Prices subject to change after the printing of this book.

ORDER FROM: Solar Survival Sales
               Box 1041
               Taos, NM 87571
               (505) 751-0462

6. STRAW BALE - TEMPORARY STRUCTURE

ONE MAJOR BURDEN PEOPLE HAVE WHEN TRYING TO BUILD THEIR HOME IS PAYING RENT OR A MORTGAGE WHILE THEY ARE BUILDING. THIS CONDITION USUALLY PUSHES THEM FARTHER FROM THE POSSIBILITY OF BUILDING OUT OF POCKET AND INTO THE BANK LOAN NIGHTMARE. SOME PEOPLE HAVE ATTEMPTED TO SOLVE THIS PROBLEM BY LIVING IN TENTS, TEEPEES, SCHOOL BUSES, OR MOBILE HOMES WHILE BUILDING THEIR EARTHSHIP. A GOOD TEEPEE COSTS $800 OR MORE TO GET SET UP. SCHOOL BUSES GO FROM $1000 AND UP AND MOBILE HOMES OR CAMPERS ARE EVEN MORE EXPENSIVE. NONE OF THESE CAN REALLY BE INCORPORATED IN TO THE ULTIMATE PLAN OF THE HOME, I.E. THEY ARE TEMPORARY SITUATIONS. SCHOOL BUSES AND MOBILE HOMES ARE NOT ALLOWED ON SOME PARCELS OF LAND AND TENTS AND TEEPEES ARE REALLY LIKE CAMPING OUT AND PROVE TO BE DIFFICULT FOR LONG TERM LIVING THROUGH COLD, WIND AND RAIN. **THERE IS THEREFORE A NEED FOR A CHEAP, DURABLE, COMFORTABLE, QUICKLY ERECTED, LOW VISUAL IMPACT, TEMPORARY STRUCTURE FOR HUMANS TO USE WHILE BUILDING A MORE SUBSTANTIAL AND CODE APPROVED EARTHSHIP.** IF THIS STRUCTURE WERE SUBSTANTIAL AND VISUALLY PLEASING ENOUGH THAT IT COULD LATER BE USED AS A PERMANENT PART OF THE EVENTUAL BUILDING (TOOL SHED, UTILITY ROOM ETC.) IT WOULD BE EVEN MORE JUSTIFIED. AS WE BEGAN THE **STAR** COMMUNITY, WE FOUND OURSELVES IN THE IMMEDIATE, TEMPORARY STRUCTURE DILEMMA. PEOPLE WANTED TO USE MOBILE HOMES, SHEDS, AND OTHER QUICK, RELATIVELY CHEAP TEMPORARY STRUCTURES TO AVOID PAYING RENT AND HAVE AN IMMEDIATE, TEMPORARY SHELTER. IN A COMMUNITY PROJECT THIS COULD RESULT IN A VERY "JUNKED OUT" LOOK ON THE LAND. POTENTIAL PROBLEMS WITH ENFORCING TIME LIMITS FOR TEMPORARY STRUCTURES AND KEEPING A LESS OFFENSIVE COMMUNITY "LOOK" ON THE LAND WOULD ALWAYS BE LOOMING IF UNCONTROLLED TEMPORARY STRUCTURES WERE ALLOWED. YET THE CONCEPT OF TEMPORARY STRUCTURES IS NECESSARY AND *NECESSITY IS THE MOTHER OF INVENTION.*

Graphics by   Claire Blanchard
Photographs by   Pam Freund

"Life is what happens to you while you are making other plans", John Lennon.

Many people in the real world opt to use mobile homes just while they get their lives together. This always turns out to be forever because we all know that *no one gets their life together*. There is, however, something to learn from the **temporary** approach to life. Alas, **life is temporary**. So why have a permanent home? The price of **temporary** *anything* is much less than the price of permanent *anything*. Many of us spend our entire lives building and paying for a permanent home - *then we die*.

With the Earthship concept we have plucked the conventional house off the various grids, built it out of materials indigenous to the twentieth century, and made it possible for anyone to do it. *We have changed the concept of housing into a vessel which* <u>*independently*</u> *takes us on a voyage the rest of our lives.* We have seen that the traditional concept of housing can be budged from its place in our reality. Let's go little further, "if you can move it an inch, you can move it a mile."

This chapter will explore some thinking from the **temporary** concept and blend that with the Earthship concept in an effort to:

1. Come up with something more aligned with the environment both in terms of aesthetics and independent performance than any of the existing temporary types of shelter.

2. Match or beat the square footage price paid for existing temporary type shelters.

3. Provide (in a temporary shelter) most of the amenities that any permanent home would have.

There is a great advantage to this **temporary** concept. It allows us to escape our permanent *dream home* dogma and get in position emotionally to accept the alternative because *we know it is temporary*.

THE FIVE DAY HOME EXPERIMENT

Five people work for free for five days to build a 300 square foot space for one of the five to live in. The design of this space (available from SSA) will be identical for everyone involved. The nature of the design will be such that more identical space and a solar greenhouse, hallway, heating duct (see Earthship Volume I., p.) could be added. Functional shelter, comfortable winter and summer, will exist after five days. This five day program will provide 300 S.F. of warm/cool space finished on the exterior with south facing glazed doors. The owner of each space will provide approximately $1,200 worth of materials delivered to the site and staged in an organized position for the five day event. This materials list can be compiled from drawings provided by SSA and will include straw bales, plastic sheeting, concrete and some lumber. The staging for each project and acquisition of materials would be executed by each individual owner. $1,200 and five days work with five people will provide very comfortable temporary shelter that can have interior finishes, details and systems added at the owners leisure. Other than the $1,200 materials price, each of the five persons involved will have to commit to 4 more five day work *events to repay each of the four people for helping him/her. All involved will be considered as equals regardless of race, sex, or personal status.*

A model of this straw bale structure was built on office grounds by SSA. The physical net result is that after $1,200 per person and a total of 25 work days five people will be inside their own "homes" in spaces that will take care of them comfortably through all kinds of weather.

The intellectual net result is that possibly, from placing ourselves in this *temporary plateau*, we will see that we don't really need all that we thought we did in a *dream home*. If every member of our family had their own "five day space" (that they helped to build) maybe that would be enough. Imagine having the rest of your life to yourself, helping others and learning more about the earth that supports us.

Cloaking this unit with the title **temporary** gives us freedom. We are simply using this freedom to explore an approach to living not allowed before, by banks, codes and our own preconceived ideas of housing and life. New approaches to living will not be found *within* our own existing dogma. We must trick ourselves and the prevailing enforced dogmas (codes, traditions, etc.) with a "false I.D." to allow us out of existing dogma long enough to look around. We might be amazed at what we find.

DESIGN FACTORS
The structure should be made from an insulative material easy and cheap to acquire anywhere, preferably organic in nature. Straw bales which are already being looked at for cheaper permanent housing have a major advantage - they can be very quickly assembled into a temporary structure. Our objective is to create a quick, cheap temporary structure "engineered" well enough that it could possibly be incorporated into the eventual permanent Earthship.

In order to hold temperature with minimal auxiliary heating or cooling the structure should have some thermal mass. This can be achieved by sinking the structure into the ground with earth cliffs, similar to the Earthship concept.

The temporary structure should require a minimal amount of exterior finishing with a maximum of protection from the elements. Solution - bury it.

For codes or engineers to even consider accepting a straw bale structure, the design should evenly distribute a minimal amount of weight to very short straw bale walls. The weight is simply meant to stabilize these walls, not load them. The majority of the weight should go to post and beam structure as straw bales are inconsistent and can't be safely rated for large loads. Shorter and curved walls increase what little bearing potential the straw walls have. A circular shape will also resist burial around the circumference.

The roof should be of a slope that will allow collection of water and should be south sloped to facilitate collection of water from snow.

The appearance should be as soft and camouflaged as possible. The structure should have solar gain and have permanent or temporary green house potential. This achieves the possibility for the temporary structure to be worked in to eventual Earthship design as a tool room, utility room, etc. Accordingly it should have adequate ventilation and egress. Material costs and manifestation time should relate to other temporary structures.

Throughout design, construction, and use the thought must be entertained of long term use of this temporary structure and possible evolution toward code requirements in structure and safety.

With the above needs and thoughts in mind we offer the following straw bale temporary structure with step by step construction procedures.

119

The first step in the construction of the temporary straw bale structure is to dig the "keyhole" shaped excavation into the earth. This hole should be 14' in diameter and 4' deep with a sloped opening for the doorway.

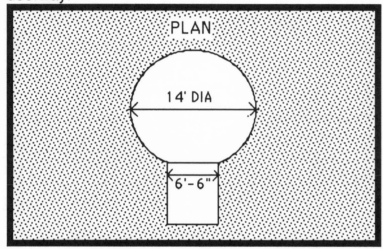

PLAN

14' DIA

6'-6"

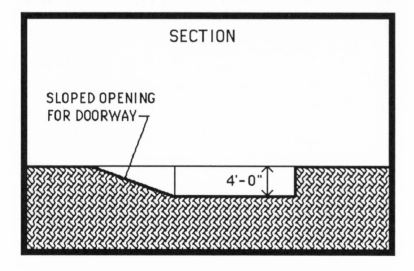

SECTION

SLOPED OPENING
FOR DOORWAY

4'-0"

The next step before stacking the straw bales is to install the door frame, which doubles as two columns. The door frame is a 6'-0" by 6'-8" clear opening. This width will allow a reasonable amount of solar gain through glass doors even without a greenhouse. The frame is constructed of 2"x12" lumber as shown in the next diagram. Be sure to use pressure treated lumber for the bottom piece and the two outside pieces as the frame will be in contact with the earth and weather. Brace the door frame in a square position as shown.

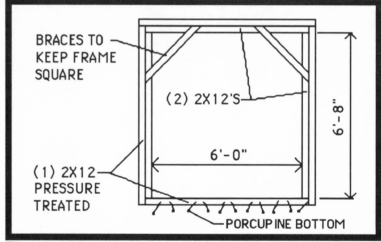

BRACES TO
KEEP FRAME
SQUARE

(2) 2X12'S

(1) 2X12
PRESSURE
TREATED

6'-8"

6'-0"

PORCUPINE BOTTOM

The door frame is then placed in the opening of the circle, trimming the earth around it for a tight fit. It will be placed on a 10" thick concrete footing with (2) 1/2" rebar as shown. The bottom piece of pressure treated lumber will be porcupined (Volume I pp. 157-7) to attach it to the footing. The footing is necessary as the door frame will be acting as a column and to minimize contraction and expansion of materials by going below the frost line..

120

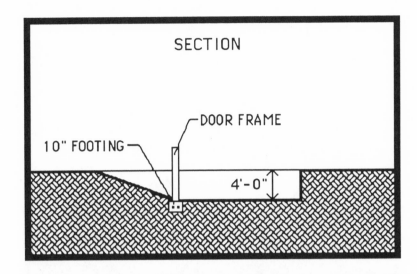

SECTION

DOOR FRAME

10" FOOTING

4'-0"

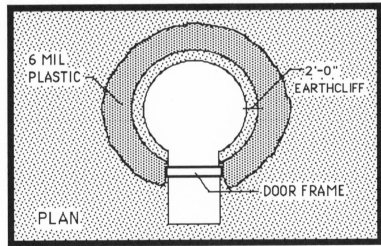

6 MIL PLASTIC

2'-0" EARTHCLIFF

DOOR FRAME

PLAN

6 mil plastic is then placed around the excavation in the path of the straw bales. Notice the path of the straw bales allows for a 2'-0" earth cliff to be carved later, similar to the Earthship "U". The plastic protects the bottom of the bales from contact with any ground moisture.

Before the bales are stacked, additional blocking is attached to the part of the door frame that is above grade. This blocking, made of a 2x4 and a 2x12, is angled to receive the straw bales. Screw these members to the door frame as nailing could knock it out of square.

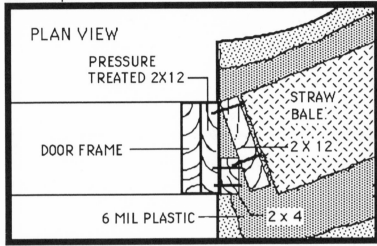

PLAN VIEW

PRESSURE TREATED 2X12

STRAW BALE

DOOR FRAME

2 X 12

6 MIL PLASTIC

2 x 4

Before continuing with the walls, a footing must be poured in the floor to receive the column which supports the major part of the roof. Because the construction of the building is so quick it is best to pour the footing now to give it time to set up. Dig a hole 10" deep and 2'-6" diameter. The column will be centrally located but near the rear to allow as much uninterrupted open space as possible.

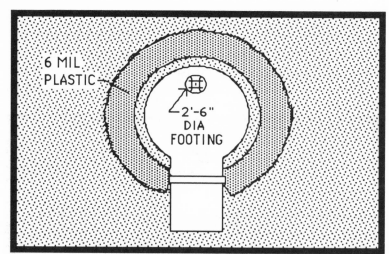

Lay in a grid of (4) 1/2" rebars. Place one piece of 1/2" rebar vertically in the center leaving 5" sticking out above the top of the footing to receive the column. The concrete can now be poured in.

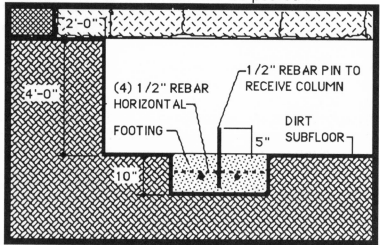

The straw bales are laid in a circle around the hole like bricks leaving a 2'-0" shelf that will later be

carved to 12". Each of the three courses is staggered from the one below..

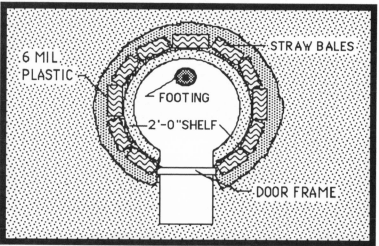

Drive a 1/2" rebar pin into every bale on the first two courses. All pins should go into the ground at least 18".

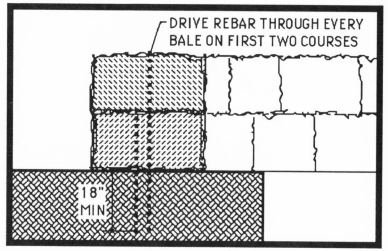

122

When all three courses are done, plastic is draped over the top and outside of the bale wall and the wood bond beam plates are placed. The first layer of the wood bond beam plate, made of 2x12 pressure treated lumber, is laid in sections around the circle.

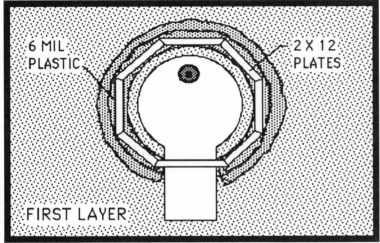

6 MIL PLASTIC

2 X 12 PLATES

FIRST LAYER

A second layer of wood plate is laid, overlapping joints and nailing both layers together (see Volume I, p).

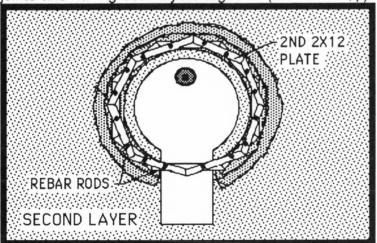

2ND 2X12 PLATE

REBAR RODS

SECOND LAYER

Holes are drilled in the plates and rebar rods are then hammered through all three courses and 18" into the ground to anchor the plates. Leave about 6" of rebar sticking up above the plate so you can bend it over with a steel pipe. This anchors the plates to the straw bales

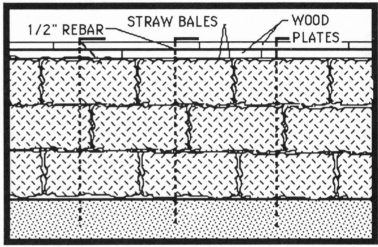

1/2" REBAR   STRAW BALES   WOOD PLATES

Now the roof structure begins by first placing an 8" round wood column towards the back of the straw bale room on the footing poured earlier. Add a double bearing plate made of 2"x12" lumber. This plate is a 2'-0" octagon and is placed 12" above the bond beam plates.

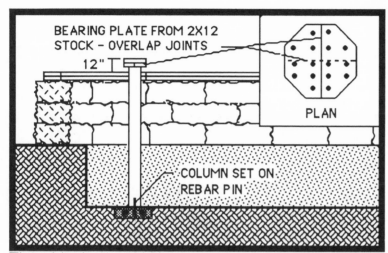

BEARING PLATE FROM 2X12 STOCK – OVERLAP JOINTS

12"

PLAN

COLUMN SET ON REBAR PIN

Then blocks or shims are added to the bond beam plates to create a slope from north to south. The front by the door is 0" and the back near the column is 16".

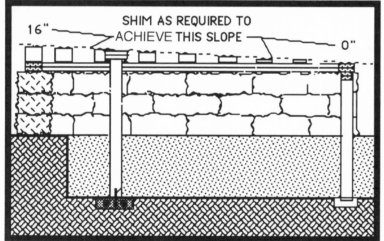

SHIM AS REQUIRED TO ACHIEVE THIS SLOPE

16"

0"

These shims should be made of scrap lumber. Use whatever thickness will achieve the desired height. These pieces should be securely nailed to the plate with 16d nails. Now the beams can be placed as shown opposite.

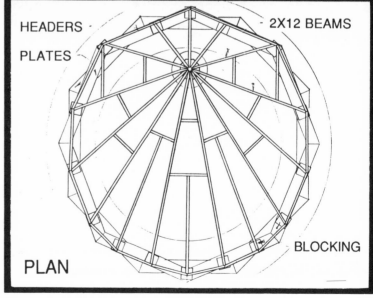

HEADERS

2X12 BEAMS

PLATES

BLOCKING

PLAN

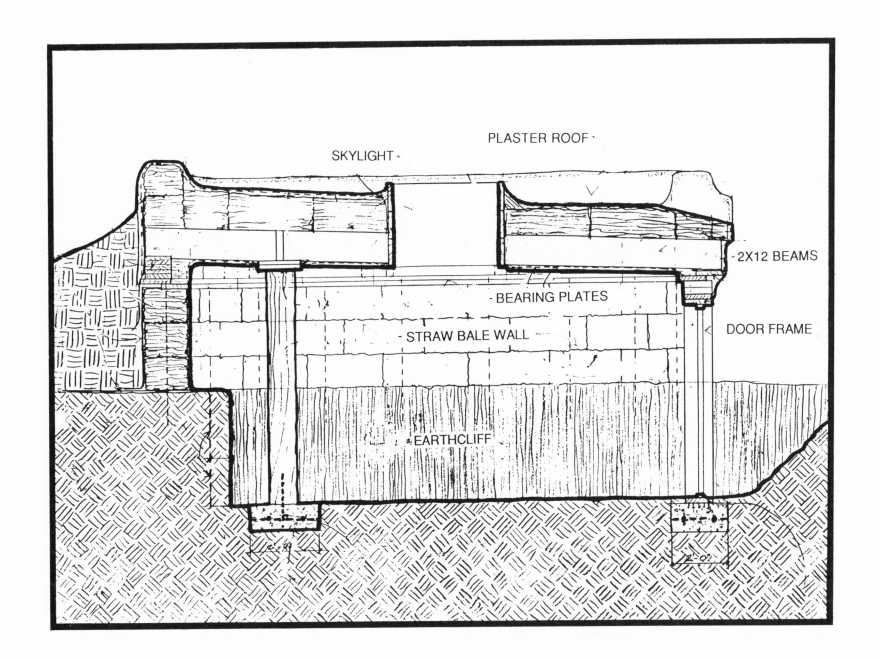

SKYLIGHT

PLASTER ROOF

2X12 BEAMS

BEARING PLATES

DOOR FRAME

STRAW BALE WALL

EARTHCLIFF

125

Beams are attached to the plate by toenailing with 16d nails.

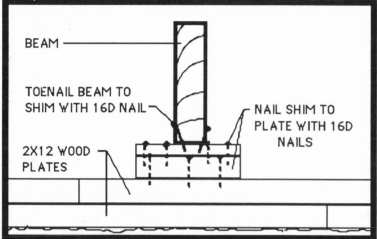

Once the beams are all set in place, the skylight box should be framed out with two more layers of 2x12 stock added vertically. This will later receive the skylight lid. (See Earthship Vol II, Chapter 8)

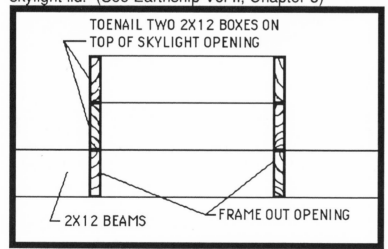

Now a plastic vapor barrier and chicken wire are

nailed to the underside of the beams (leave the skylight hole open), which then can be filled with loose straw.

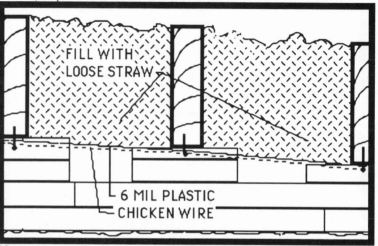

Now cover the beams with plastic as shown. Drape plastic down and cover the outside of straw bale wall.

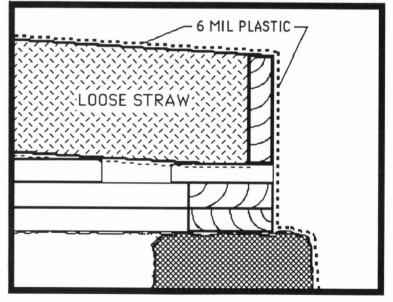

Now bury up to this level.

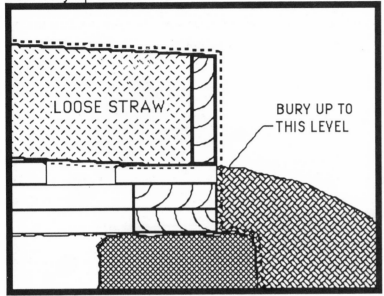

LOOSE STRAW

BURY UP TO
THIS LEVEL

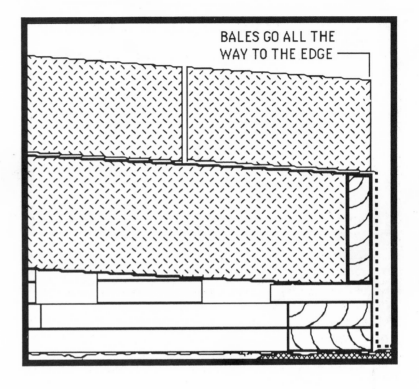

BALES GO ALL THE
WAY TO THE EDGE

On top of the beams and loose straw, bales of straw are laid side by side (or in a circular pattern) to provide an additional 14" of insulation. These bales cover the entire roof and should go all the way to the outside edge of the plates. This results in about 26" of straw insulation, approximately R50-60. Be sure you use straw - not hay as it can spontaneously combust and result in fire. Also be very sure that your straw bales amd loose straw are dry. Do these insulating operations all in one day to avoid getting caught in a rain and having wet straw. You will end up with compost if you have wet straw.

Then a second layer of bales is laid in a ring at the edge to provide a parapet wall to contain rainfall. A space approximately 24" wide should be left in the parapet at the lowest point of the roof. This will serve as the drain for the water runoff (see overview page 120).

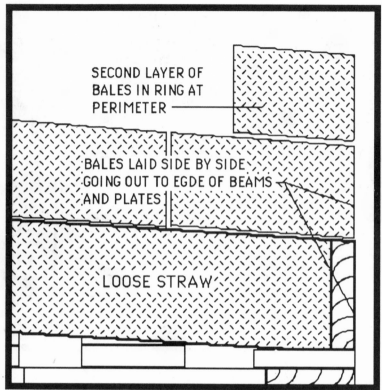

SECOND LAYER OF
BALES IN RING AT
PERIMETER

BALES LAID SIDE BY SIDE
GOING OUT TO EGDE OF BEAMS
AND PLATES

LOOSE STRAW

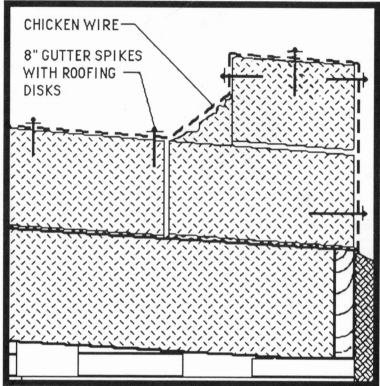

CHICKEN WIRE

8" GUTTER SPIKES
WITH ROOFING
DISKS

Now you can begin to seal the exterior of the structure. First, using loose straw, make a cant where the parapet joins the roof. Then cover the entire roof and parapet with chicken wire. To keep the chicken wire secured onto the straw use 8" gutter spikes with roofing disks.

Finally the whole roof is covered with 3 coats of scratched cement plaster. This plaster mixture is one part portland cement to three parts sand with a good handful of engineering fibers with every wheelbarrow or cement mixer load. The plaster can be applied with a trowel or with your hands. Remember to always wear rubber gloves when working with cement. A final coat of smooth troweled plaster is added for a finish. This cement roof can be sealed with an acrylic coating available from SSA.

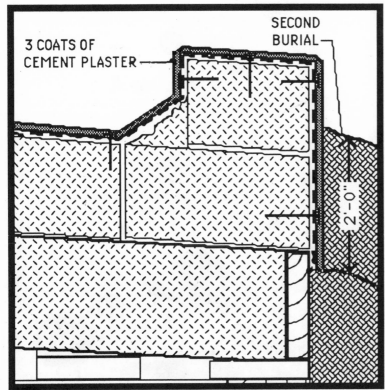

3 COATS OF
CEMENT PLASTER

SECOND
BURIAL

2'-0"

Now the exterior of the building is sealed. The final burial can come up another 2'-0".

To finish the interior of the building, the ceiling can be finished with wood, fabric or plaster. The walls and floor can be finished with mud. The procedure for mudding walls and floors is explained in Chapter One of Volume III.

A spout for water runoff can be formed with metal lath and plastered. A gutter will have to be rigged up to take this water to an outside cistern or tank.

A straw bale unit can be incorporated into a future Earthship

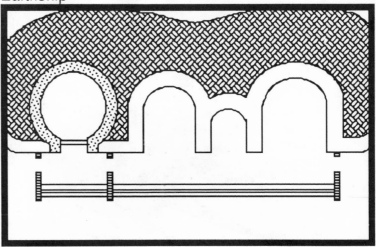

An entire home can be built out of straw units where codes allow.

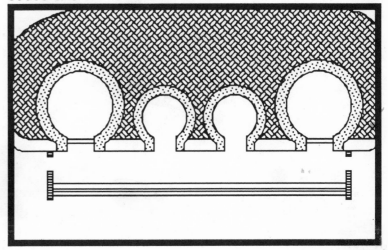

Straw bale construction drawings $150.00

129

130

...TAIN BUILDING SUPPLY

1291 YOUNG HARRIS HWY.
P.O. BOX 1299
BLAIRSVILLE, GEORGIA 30512

TEL. (706) 745-5200

THANK YOU FOR YOUR BUSINESS!!

CUSTOMER NO.	JOB NO.	PURCHASE ORDER NO.	REFERENCE	TERMS
*5				CASH/CHECK/BANKL...

SOLD TO

**** CASH ****

*Heather Smith
No Phone*

SHIP TO

6258 No Reynolds-

SLSPR: 05
TAX : GF

ALL MERCHANDISE MUST BE RETURNED WITHIN 60 DAYS OF PURCHASE. NO RETURNS ON SPECIAL ORDERS.

SHIPPED	ORDERED	UM	SKU	DESCRIPTION	SUGG
8		EA	R1915	R19 6 X 15 INS (77.50 SF)	
2		RL	R1923	R19 6 X 23 INS (122.67 SF)	
2		PK	4122685	505 OF 5000 STAPLES 5/16	
1		EA	6122493	JT21M ARROW STAPLE GUN	
1		EA	MH	KWIKSET KEYED ENTRY	

129-10 — Potfecs — 10...

3rd (Sign Freedem Grph...

1st Rd. av Rt. to c...

** PAYMENT RECEIVED **
** CHANGE GIVEN **

X

RECEIVED BY

CASH PAYMENT

7. RETROFIT A CRACKER BOX

WE ARE ASKED OFTEN ABOUT ADDING AN EARTHSHIP TYPE ADDITION TO A REGULAR CRACKER BOX HOUSE. AT FIRST IT SEEMED RIDICULOUS BUT THERE ARE SO MANY OF THESE BUILDINGS OUT THERE THAT WE DECIDED TO PUT SOME ENERGY INTO IT. IT IS ACTUALLY A VERY GOOD IDEA BECAUSE IF YOU ALREADY LIVE IN AN INEFFICIENT CRACKER BOX YOU AT LEAST HAVE A PLACE TO LIVE WHILE YOU BUILD YOUR EARTHSHIP ADDITION. THE ONLY REQUIREMENT IS THAT THE HOUSE SHOULD HAVE A SIDE FACING SOUTH OR CLOSE TO SOUTH. IF YOU HAVE THIS SITUATION YOU CAN VIRTUALLY TURN YOUR CRACKER BOX INTO AN EARTHSHIP.

Graphics by Claire Blanchard

Let's look at a typical cracker box.

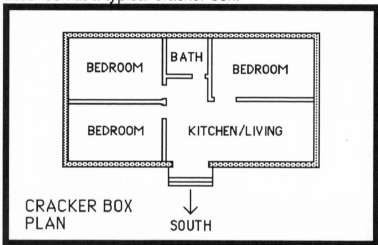

CRACKER BOX
PLAN

SOUTH

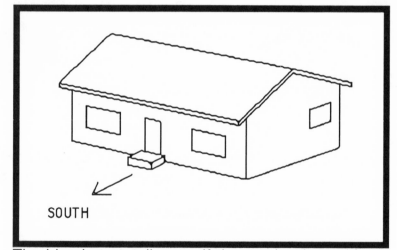

SOUTH

The idea is to totally engulf the cracker box with an Earthship. Start by adding a "U" to the east or west. It must be **totally structurally independent** of the original structure. Let it extend out beyond the south face of the house by the diameter of one tire.

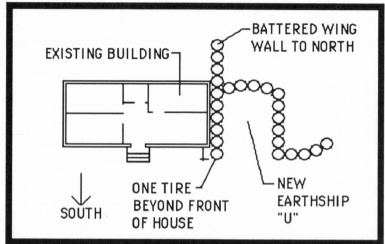

EXISTING BUILDING

BATTERED WING WALL TO NORTH

ONE TIRE BEYOND FRONT OF HOUSE

SOUTH

NEW EARTHSHIP "U"

It can be right up against the original building. Leave a battered wing wall (see Chapter 1) extending out to the north to retain the burial of the new "U". Now do the same thing on the other end of the house. Original east-west egress windows in bedrooms will have to punch in the north or south walls of the original frame building.

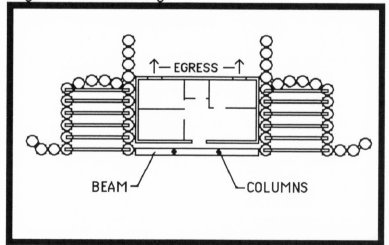

↑—EGRESS—↑

BEAM

COLUMNS

Now add a typical Earthship greenhouse. You will have to install some columns and a beam in front of the original structure to lean the greenhouse against.

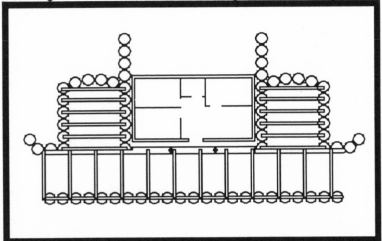

The typical Earthship greenhouse (see Earthship Volume I, Ch. 7) covers the entire south face of the original structure and the new "U"'s. Some form of thermal mass (stone, rock, water, adobe bricks, small tires plastered) can be added to the south side of the original structure if you desire to add thermal storage.

You may wish to increase the size of openings on the south side of the original building in order to draw warm air from the greenhouse into the house

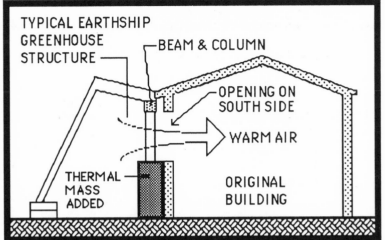

The new "U"'s are then buried as per the typical Earthship details (Volume I, p. 121-128).

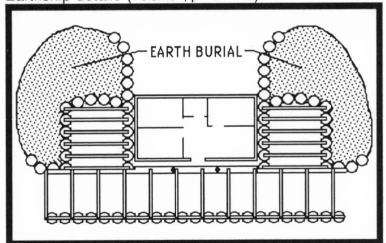

The protected patio created on the north can now be covered and enclosed for more northern protection.

133

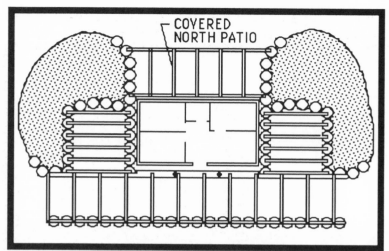

COVERED
NORTH PATIO

This leaves you completely snuggled in a cracker box that can function much like an Earthship.

If you want to catch water, the roof of the existing structure can be coated with Earthship roofing materials over appropriate cricketing (see page 49-50 for cricketing).

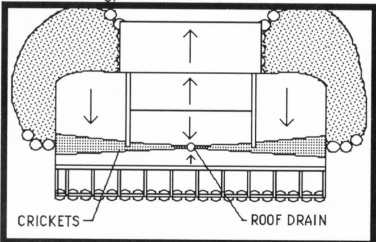

CRICKETS

ROOF DRAIN

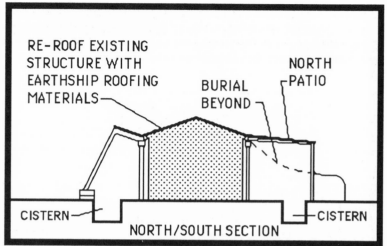

RE-ROOF EXISTING STRUCTURE WITH EARTHSHIP ROOFING MATERIALS

BURIAL BEYOND

NORTH PATIO

CISTERN

CISTERN

NORTH/SOUTH SECTION

Your property dimensions are your only limitations on how far you can go with this concept. The new generics (see Chapter 13) can be applied with variations of the "U"'s and "mU"s placed where necessary. The catch water and grey water jungle systems as well as the solar toilets and solar ovens can all be used.

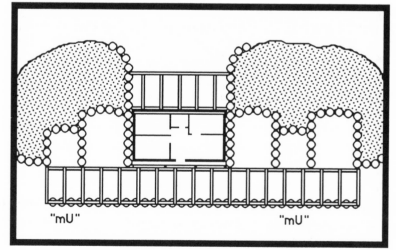

"mU"

"mU"

So if the real world dealt you a cracker box - be a magician - turn it into an Earthship. We do suggest that you get some consultation from Solar Survival Architecture on specific details, egress, systems, permits, etc.

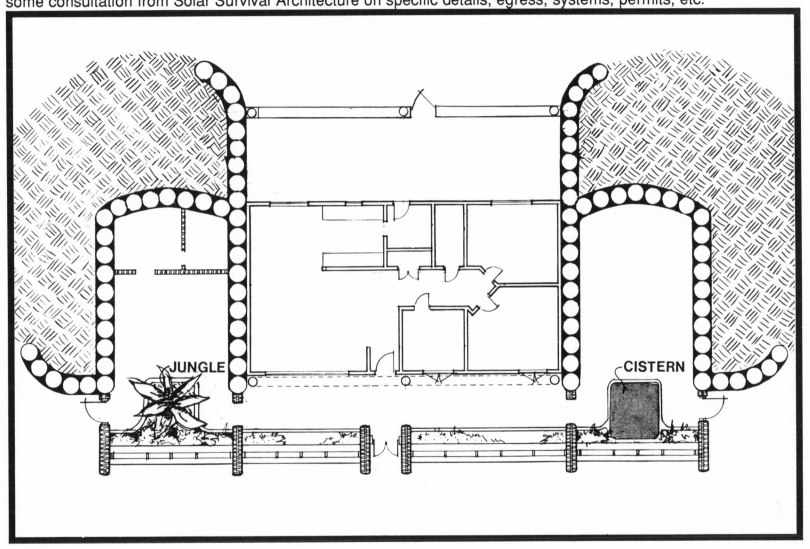

JUNGLE

CISTERN

FLOOR PLAN

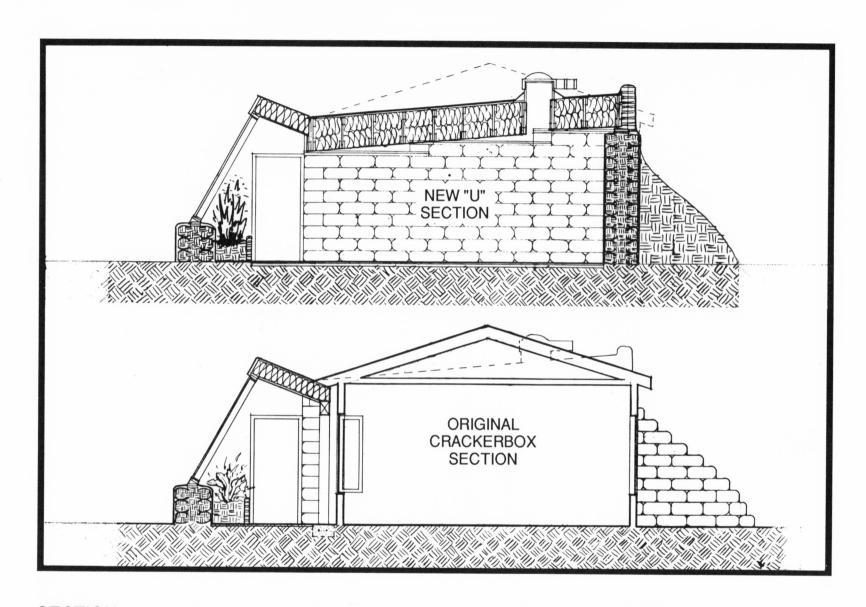

NEW "U" SECTION

ORIGINAL CRACKERBOX SECTION

SECTION

136

PART THREE
COMMUNITY AND URBAN CONCEPTS

EARTHSHIP COLONY

STAR LOG 3/7/93

WE HAVE SEEN AN INTERESTING PHENOMENON IN THE EVOLVING EARTHSHIP COMMUNITIES. AS WITH ANY GROUP OF HUMANS, THERE WAS (IN A CERTAIN EARTHSHIP COMMUNITY) THE USUAL INTRIGUE THAT CONCERNS ITSELF WITH ONE PERSON WHO DOES NOT PARTICULARLY MIX WELL WITH SOME OF THE OTHERS SOCIALLY. THEN THERE ARE AGE AND RACIAL DIFFERENCES WHICH TEND TO FORM SUB GROUPS WITHIN A COMMUNITY. IN GENERAL THERE ARE ALWAYS SEEMS TO BE CERTAIN BARRIERS WHICH DETER CERTAIN PEOPLE FROM SPENDING MUCH TIME WITH OTHER PEOPLE. THESE BARRIERS RELATE TO PERSONALITY, IDEALS, AGE, RACE, SEX, ETC. THESE BARRIERS ARE TYPICAL OF HUMAN NATURE AND WHILE THEY SELDOM BRING ABOUT REAL CONFLICT, THEY DO INHIBIT UNRESTRAINED COMMUNITY BONDING. OFTEN A RELIGIOUS OR POLITICAL DOCTRINE WILL TRY TO OVERCOME THESE BARRIERS BUT EVEN IN THE MOST ARDENTLY DEFINED GROUPS THIS "INTERNAL INTRIGUE" STILL EXISTS. RARELY DOES SOMETHING COME ALONG SO POWERFUL THAT IT MELTS THE SOMETIMES NOT SO SUBTLE PERSONAL BARRIERS BETWEEN INDIVIDUALS WITHIN A GROUP.

WE OBSERVED ABOUT A DOZEN VARIED INDIVIDUALS OF VARIOUS AGES, RACES, SEXES, IDEALS AND HABITS THAT DID HAVE ONE (ALMOST RELIGIOUS) COMMON GROUND. THEY WERE ALL TRYING TO BUILD THEIR OWN EARTHSHIP "OUT OF POCKET" WITH NO MORTGAGE PAYMENT. NONE OF THEM HAD MUCH MONEY BUT THEY WERE ALL FAMILIAR WITH VARIOUS EARTHSHIP TECHNIQUES. SOME WERE PLASTERERS, SOME CARPENTERS, SOME STRONG, SOME WEAKER, SOME MORE INTELLECTUAL, OTHERS MORE BASIC WORKERS BUT THEY WERE ALL ATTEMPTING THE SAME THING (BUILDING AN EARTHSHIP) UNDER SIMILAR CIRCUMSTANCES IN THE SAME COMMUNITY.

A FEW BEGAN TRADING FOR WORK AND ONE THING LED TO ANOTHER AND LO WE SAW A BAND OF PEOPLE (WHO NORMALLY WOULD NOT BE PARTYING TOGETHER) ALL PLASTERING ONE PERSONS HOME. THEN WE WOULD SEE THEM ALL POUNDING TIRES ON ANOTHER PERSONS EARTHSHIP. THEN, DOING A FRONT FACE ON SOMEONE ELSE'S PROJECT. THEY SAW (WITHOUT SUPERVISION OR DIRECTION FROM ANY LEADER OR DOCTRINE) THAT HANDS ARE HANDS, WORK IS WORK, HELP IS HELP NO MATTER WHO IT IS FROM. THEY ALL NEEDED A HOME WHICH MEANT THEY ALL NEEDED EACH OTHER. THIS NEED DISINTEGRATED THE BARRIERS AND THE RESULT WAS A BAND OF BUILDERS - ONE FOR ALL AND ALL FOR ONE. THIS INITIAL BONDING WEAVES A LASTING COMMUNITY FABRIC.

8. COMMUNITIES

HERE IN THE LATE 20TH CENTURY, MANY PEOPLE ARE ATTEMPTING TO BAND TOGETHER AND START COMMUNITIES. THIS IS PROBABLY FROM A FEELING OF ABANDONMENT BY ALL EXISTING DOGMA, I.E. THE *AMERICAN DREAM*. THEIR EFFORTS TO PROVIDE FOR THEMSELVES AMENITIES THAT OUR BUREAUCRACY LADEN DEMOCRACY CAN'T, ARE ADMIRABLE BUT OFTEN FUTILE. SOLAR SURVIVAL ARCHITECTURE HAS THE EXPERIENCE OF FAILED ATTEMPTS AT COMMUNITY AS WELL AS TWO SUCCESSFUL COMMUNITY BIRTHS. IN THIS CHAPTER WE WOULD LIKE TO MAP OUT OUR UNIQUE APPROACH TO LAUNCHING A COMMUNITY VIA THE EARTHSHIP CONCEPT.

We cannot "build" a tree that has life.
A beautiful tree grows from rich, fertile soil.

We cannot build a community that has life.
A community also grows from a rich, fertile soil.

We have to create fertile soil if we want to grow a good garden,
a beautiful tree, or a flourishing, healthy, community.

Photographs by   Pam Freund

139

Modern approaches to community living have tried to *physically create* the community. It has been hard for humans to achieve this just in terms of the actual structures. (Few of them, if any, have been really earth or human friendly.) The thread of collective human energy in a specific locale has rarely, if ever, been *consciously* woven into a tapestry of unbroken continuity. This thread must grow as the fibers of a tree are formed year after year in rich soil with lots of sun and water. We can create the *conditions* for a tree to grow, but a force beyond us grows the tree. It is the same for a community. We can create the *conditions* for the community - not the community itself. This knowledge alone increases the chances for a successful community manyfold.

The Earthship concept (as presented in Volumes I, II, and III) **is a method of creating a fertile soil from which a community can grow**. We should not try to structure or build the community either physically, spiritually or emotionally any more than we should try to build a live tree. We can, however create the ideal conditions from which a community can grow and flourish. We are makers of soil. An unarguable phenomenon (some call it GOD) makes trees and communities.

Imagine hundreds of people in a certain area building their own earth friendly homes out of pocket. If these people all end up with an **independent** home that grows food year round with **no mortgage payment or utility bill**, they are going to experience a richer existence because much stress has been removed from their lives. This richer existence becomes a rich *psychic soil* from which a healthy community fabric can grow. Absence of survival stress would result in more *time*. More time for people to experience the earth and each other. They would not be struggling so hard for survival. The state of mind and being of these people would be softer and richer than the hard edged shallow state of mind and being that stress from mere survival leaves us with. This is similar to hard, dry, dead soil as compared to rich fertile soil for growing plants. The hard dry soil is going to produce, at best, some thorny weeds. (we've got some pretty thorny humans out there.) The rich fertile soil will produce blossoms and fruit. All we need to do is create the proper psychic soil for a community - *not the community itself*. We are not capable of this. This is why we have not succeeded.

A typical development requires not only a land purchase but thousands and thousands of dollars up front to install sewer lines, power lines and water lines. This is called an *infrastructure*. Since an Earthship makes its own power and water and deals with its own sewage, an Earthship community requires no infrastructure. This immediately lowers the physical cost and stress to both humans and planet of "planting" a community. We encourage (with books and videos) people to build their own Earthships. We continue to evolve basic mechanical components and to simplify structural details toward this goal. This is beginning to work. We are seeing people build their own Earthships out of pocket. It is happening. This means that the actual physical development of a community of Earthships that needs no infrastructure could happen "by the people".

Conventional real estate developments can be regulated by local governing bodies. Development projects are limited relative to the amount of electricity, water or sewage facilities that local governing bodies can afford to provide for that property. Earthship communities do not have this problem as the Earthship itself provides its own utilities. Conventional developments (subdivisions) also require an amazing amount of paper and legal work meant to protect potential home owners from greedy, careless developers. These limitations and legal bogs from the conventional approach to community make it almost impossible for a group of well meaning people (who just want a nice place to live) to put their own project together. When a group of people wanting to form a community face the legal bog and *infrastructure* on top of their own inner bureaucracy and disagreement, failure is often the result.

Our "REACH" type communities are set up to avoid these pitfalls. There is still paperwork but it deals with the important issues about how we want to live together and not about how we intend to tangle ourselves up in public utilities and protect ourselves from each other. Conventional stress breeds these entanglements. Self sufficient, independent Earthship dwellings can individually provide for needs it usually takes a corporation to tackle. Although our "model communities" are still in the formative stages, we are describing our methods for setting them up as these methods have already ventured where "wise men fear to tread".

We have observed people building their own Earthships out of pocket with no mortgage - *for the home.* They did, however, have to get a mortgage to buy the land. The price of decent land has gotten out of control thanks to the realtors and developers in quest of money. In response to this we have developed the REACH (Rural Earthship Alternative Community Habitat) concept. This is a method of acquiring land together as a "club". Any club or organization has pitfalls in that a bureaucracy is inherent and we all know what a bureaucracy can do to us. I have talked to groups of 12 to 30 people who have been trying to start a community for years but can't all agree on the land, the rules, etc. The trick is for just one or two people to start it.

First the land is selected. If you have a climate with a winter you must select flat or south facing land preferably not in a valley with a water table close to the surface and definitely not the north slope of a mountain. You would want to choose an area that has at least eight or nine total inches of precipitation per year and over 250 sun days per year if possible. Beyond tnis there are no limits because you do not need to be close to power, sewers or a water source. In most cases this means you can go a little farther out from towns and get much cheaper and more beautiful land. Another financial stumbling block is that remote land usually means bad roads. People seem to worry about this more than they need to. Todays four wheel drive vehicles can go just about anywhere. We have launched two communities and both have extremely "bad" access but this has not hindered membership. **If you create someplace worth going to, a way to get there (a road) will happen.** The Earthship doesn't require a cement truck for foundations so a mere dirt path is the beginning. The idea is to get started with n o expenses up front.

The price of the land is then divided by the number of people the land can accommodate to arrive at a membership price taking into account the various density levels and costs which will be required to cut roads and otherwise make it possible for people to build there. The initiators fee is also built into this.

Communities evolve as a result of the people who live in them so it is possible for each community to take a very different form. The nature of the land has a significant bearing on the evolution of the community. For the "REACH" project we found a piece of steep mountain property backing onto national forest. It was beyond the reach of utility lines and steep enough to be considered unbuildable and in an area where nearby "usable" property sold for $15,000 an acre. We got 55 acres for only $1000 an acre because there were no utilities, no water, and steep terrain. Probably only 50 % of the 55 acres was buildable for south facing Earthships. This instantly determined "green belt" or park areas and building areas.

In the REACH community we now have crew members building their own homes near the Earthships they built for clients. Owner residents range in age from 21 to 70 and have such diverse occupations as artists, doctors, actors, builders, therapists, architects and even a realtor.

When we had generated enough interest in the concept to risk a down payment on the land, we bought it under the initiators name but filed the property description, Treatise, Land Users Code, Articles of Association, and By Laws under the REACH Land Users Association at the county court house. This in itself presents the intentions of the association to the public and to the court to assure that members will be treated as per these documents. The initiator would yield to the association in a matter of years. We found this method easier and faster than getting a large group of people to agree on a piece of land and a set of documents. One person with some advisors and consultants sets up the framework allowing for the association to evolve it as they choose after a certain period of time. For the first five to seven years, however, the initiator makes the decisions.

At REACH we began construction of Earthships the day we closed on the land - no infrastructure - no waiting. This brought tears to the eyes of some developers who had spent hundreds of thousands of dollars and many years putting in infrastructures for similar projects. People who had doubted the feasibility of the REACH project changed their minds and bought in. As news spread, the waiting list grew. If a spot became available (we also want to control growth) many people wanted it. It became evident that 55 acres on a mountainside would not be enough. When the waiting list reached 100 we started looking for more land.

LEVEL "A" AT R.E.A.C.H. NEAR TAOS, NEW MEXICO CIRCA 1993

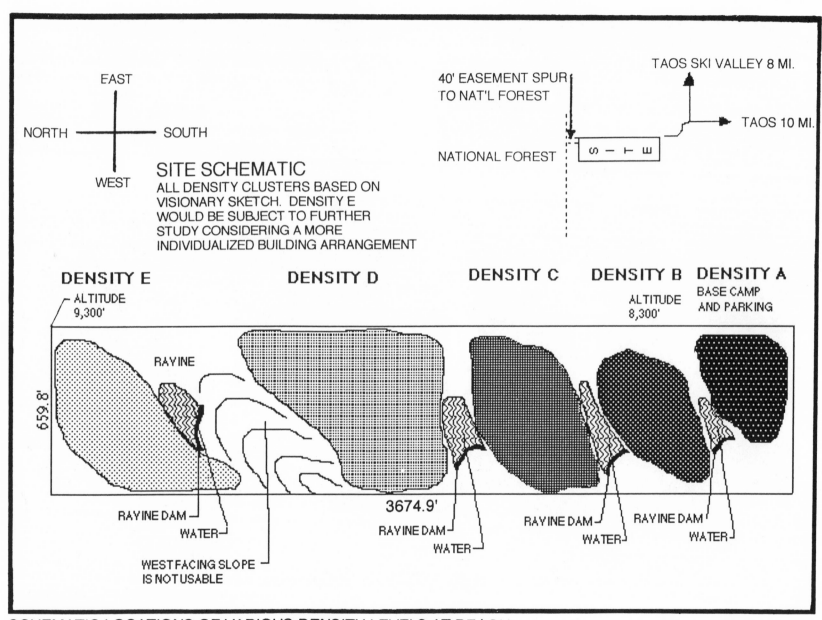

EAST

NORTH ——————— SOUTH

WEST

SITE SCHEMATIC
ALL DENSITY CLUSTERS BASED ON
VISIONARY SKETCH. DENSITY E
WOULD BE SUBJECT TO FURTHER
STUDY CONSIDERING A MORE
INDIVIDUALIZED BUILDING ARRANGEMENT

TAOS SKI VALLEY 8 MI.

40' EASEMENT SPUR
TO NAT'L FOREST

TAOS 10 MI.

NATIONAL FOREST   S I T E

DENSITY E   DENSITY D   DENSITY C   DENSITY B   DENSITY A

ALTITUDE   BASE CAMP
9,300'   ALTITUDE   AND PARKING
                                                                 8,300'

RAVINE

659.8'

RAVINE DAM
WATER   RAVINE DAM   RAVINE DAM   RAVINE DAM
                                       WATER   WATER   WATER

                        3674.9'

WEST FACING SLOPE
IS NOT USABLE

SCHEMATIC LOCATIONS OF VARIOUS DENSITY LEVELS AT REACH.

Energized by the seeming success of the Earthships at REACH - (on an extremely difficult site which taught us all kinds of new skills) and the hopes of a 100 more people on our side, we found 1000 acres of rolling mesa land for only $150.00 an acre. This price was based on purchasing 1000 acres at a time. The land we chose for our star community had been abandoned in the 40's when a dam built by the army corps of engineers failed to make the over grazed property farmable.

It is bordered by national forest and two private interests, and once again, out of reach of public utilities. The east boundary is Tres Orejas mountain and a miniature gorge runs through it. Being mesa land it will be much easier to build on than our mountainside and with 1000 acres we have the opportunity to create a full scale community with parks, schools, shops and restaurants. It all depends on who lives there....

OVERVIEW OF S.T.A.R. NEAR CARSON, NEW MEXICO

145

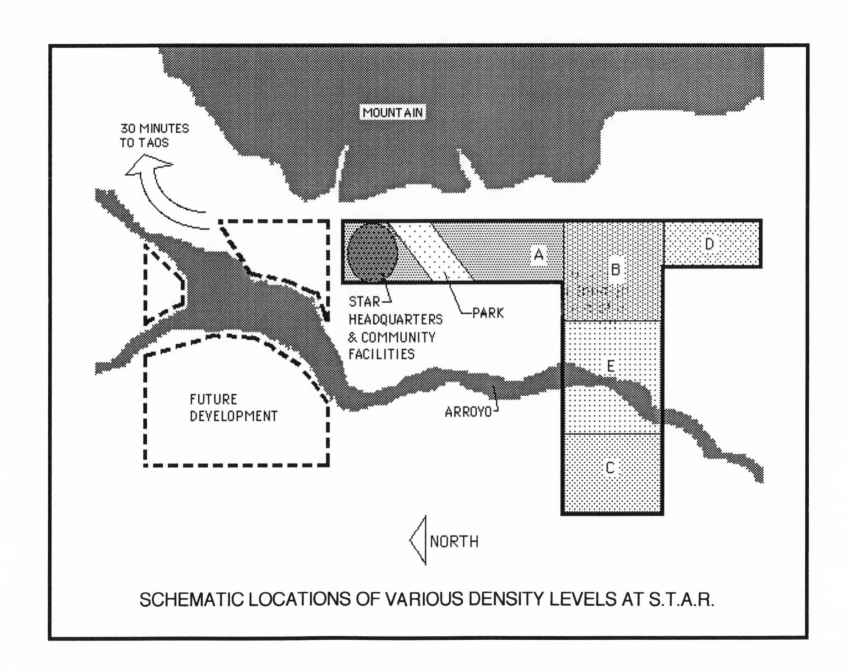

MOUNTAIN

30 MINUTES
TO TAOS

A

B

D

STAR
HEADQUARTERS
& COMMUNITY
FACILITIES

PARK

E

ARROYO

FUTURE
DEVELOPMENT

C

NORTH

SCHEMATIC LOCATIONS OF VARIOUS DENSITY LEVELS AT S.T.A.R.

Most raw land can be purchased on contract. Depending on acreage, a typical down payment can range from $10,000 to $50,000. We have seen many individuals pay this much for *one lot*. This down payment does have to be fronted by one person who will also sign for the payments which should be set up as annual installments. These payments (over the next few years) are paid by the membership fees. The person who takes the risk by fronting the money for the down payment and signing for the installments is the *initiator*. This person is basically "lord of the land" until the land is paid off and a board of directors takes over. The initiator puts in much more than money. It takes a lot of time and energy to do this. The initiator can build in payment for this work by calculating membership funds to pay for the land, do some road work, and pay the initiator a fee for initiating the project. This fee is a salary for time invested - not a profit. **There is no sale of or profit from the land.** This fact coupled with the fact that there is no infrastructure gives the project a buoyancy that launches it into orbit almost immediately. The dead weight of infrastructure expenses and greedy investors looking for profit demands a "Titan rocket" (thousands of dollars and stress) just to get off the ground.

It is an important point to remember that no land is sold. The land is owned by the Association and the members <u>are</u> the association. Memberships are priced relative to square footage of dwelling and variable density areas. These density areas were established in order to make the property affordable and appealing to different types of people. The areas of highest density were established as those with the lowest membership fee.

Example: 1000 square foot home in the *high density* area would be $2.00 per square foot for a membership fee of $2000. Homes can be as close as 50 feet.

1000 square foot home in the *low density* area would be $10.00 per square foot for a membership fee of $10,000. Homes can't be closer than 400 feet.

The next step is to form an **unincorporated land users association**. It must have a purpose. The following treatise is an example of the purpose of our R.E.A.C.H. (Rural Earthship Alternative Community Habitat) and STAR (Social Transformation Alternative Republic) communities.

RURAL EARTHSHIP ALTERNATIVE COMMUNITY HABITATS

TREATISE

OVER THE LAST TWENTY TWO YEARS SOLAR SURVIVAL ARCHITECTURE HAS DEVELOPED A MODULAR/CELLULAR METHOD OF BUILDING TOTALLY SELF-SUFFICIENT DWELLINGS USING BY-PRODUCTS OF TWENTIETH CENTURY CIVILIZATION AND NON-FOSSIL FORMS OF ENERGY. WE CALL THESE UNITS **EARTHSHIPS.** THEY HAVE PROVEN TO BE ACCESSIBLE AND DESIRABLE TO BOTH ENDS OF THE FINANCIAL STRATA. TWO BOOKS, <u>EARTHSHIP VOLUME I</u> AND <u>EARTHSHIP VOLUME II</u>, ON HOW TO BUILD THESE UNITS HAVE BEEN WRITTEN AND A SMALL GROWING SCHOOL HAS BEEN FORMED FOR TEACHING THE TECHNIQUES TO ARCHITECTURAL STUDENTS, OWNER BUILDERS AND PROFESSIONAL BUILDERS. AN ARCHITECTURAL FIRM, A BUILDING COMPANY AND A PUBLISHING COMPANY HAVE ALSO EMERGED AROUND THE EARTHSHIP CONCEPT.

WE ARE NOW ESTABLISHING PROTOTYPE COMMUNITIES FOR THE PURPOSE OF DEMONSTRATING, EVOLVING AND PROMOTING A NONDESTRUCTIVE AND MORE INSPIRATIONAL METHOD OF LIVING THAT IS LESS STRESSFUL TO BOTH THE PEOPLE AND THE PLANET.

MAJOR OBJECTIVES ARE AS FOLLOWS:
* TO **REDUCE** THE ECONOMIC AND INSTITUTIONAL BARRIERS BETWEEN HUMANS AND THEIR HABITAT.
* TO BEGIN **REVERSING** THE OVERALL NEGATIVE EFFECT THAT CONVENTIONAL HUMAN HOUSING HAS ON THIS PLANET.
* TO **CREATE** A LESS STRESSFUL PLANE OF EXISTENCE FOR HUMANS IN AN EFFORT TO REDUCE THE STRESS THAT THEY IN TURN PLACE ON THE PLANET AND EACH OTHER.
* TO **INTERFACE** ECONOMICS AND ECOLOGY IN A WAY THAT IMMEDIATELY AND TANGIBLY AFFECTS CURRENT PRESSING PROBLEMS WITH LIFE ON EARTH.
* TO **PROVIDE** A DIRECTION FOR THOSE WHO WANT TO LIVE IN PEACE WITH EACH OTHER AND THEIR ENVIRONMENT.
* TO **EMPOWER** INDIVIDUALS WITH THE UNARGUABLE FORCES OF NATURE AS OPPOSED TO INCAPACITATING THEM WITH THE SMOTHERING FORCES OF POLITICS AND BUREAUCRACY.
* TO **FIND AND DISTRIBUTE** THE APPROPRIATE SOIL FROM WHICH THE FLOWER OF HUMANITY CAN BLOSSOM.
* TO **EVOLVE** HUMANITY INTO AN EARTHEN HARMONY ALREADY EXEMPLIFIED BY MORE EVOLVED STRUCTURES SUCH AS PLANTS, ANIMALS AND WATER.

We find it best not to have any spiritual, political, class, race or age overtones. The thing the members all have in common is the Earthship concept. This, in its own way, is both a spiritual and political cause and will in itself be the structure, common ground and fertile soil for the community to grow from.

Just as a grapevine is most effective if it has a trellis to guide its growth and lift its fruit up off the ground, so must a community have guidance for evolution. We have developed a **Land Users Code** for members of the community to follow. This code must first be developed by the initiator and must be allowed to evolve as members grow. It must respond to the members and the specific site, climate, and planet. This code should not get too detailed. It should basically address environmental and structure type issues. We set the initiator up as full director for a period of 5 to 7 years - usually until the land is paid off This code simply makes clear to all members the intentions of the initiator. After 5 to 7 years (or when the land is paid off) the initiator appoints a board of directors made up of members of the community. The Land Users Code can be evolved both during the initiators reign and later by the board of directors. Many issues such as recycling efforts, grounds keeping efforts, animals, noise, etc., will come up and must be democratically handled by all. These issues and their solutions unfold themselves as the community unfolds. Problems should be observed, then addressed. Different associations will deal with the same issues differently but all solutions will be coming from humans with a softer, less stressful state of mind. This state of mind is continuously nurtured by the Earthship concept.

Eventually community networks will form and ideas and mistakes will be shared. *The Land Users Code allows this evolution.* This saves on up front paperwork. Just as a farmer cannot predetermine every twist and turn of a grapevine, there is no way an initiator can come up with all the potential problems of a community *not to mention the solutions.* A basic direction is all that is required. A basic trellis - "just elevate and decide in the air". Following is the Star Land Users Code.

Star Land Users Code

APRIL 1993 EDITION

EXHIBIT F

MEMBERSHIP

Members will be provided with a membership certificate which will allow, define and locate the members lodging site. The price of a membership will be as per the current membership purchase form which is adjusted periodically by the initiator and/or the board of directors. Memberships are paid for in two payments. Half of the membership price is paid upon submitting of the membership application form. The final half of the membership fee will be due when members receive their certificates. Members cannot build until the membership fee is paid in full. *Members cannot build any more actual interior floor space than the square footage described on the membership certificate.* Members will then occupy thirty feet beyond the outside of the outside wall of their lodging due to typical burial of the Earthship design. Beyond this 30 feet, the member must get Association approval for any land use. Lodging site location and size will be defined by the membership certificate with a legal description of the STAR land for purposes of securing the member's investment.

All members accepted into the association are assumed to understand and be in agreement with the experimental nature of the **STAR** program. All members are also assumed to understand and be in agreement with the enforcements of these restrictions described in another paragraph of this document.

BUILDINGS

All permanent buildings of any kind will be based on the Earthship "U" module concept as described in the books Earthship Volume I, Earthship Volume II, and Earthship Volume III and while financed by the individual members, will be subject to the codes, articles, and bylaws of **STAR**. Variations will be subject to **STAR** approval specifically by the initiator or current board of directors. **No "Out Buildings" allowed.** If storage buildings are desired by members, they must acquire a membership with enough building square footage to accommodate such. Building square footage that is separate from the dwelling and used strictly for storage can be acquired at half the membership square footage price for the specific density area in question. The architectural nature of storage buildings must conform to the "Earthship" concept or approved building variations described in another paragraph of this document. Storage buildings can be unfinished on the inside. Open carports can be attached to the lodging or incorporated into the berm and will not affect membership price. Carports must be contained within 20'-0" of a non - buried exterior wall of lodging. Enclosed automobile garages count as storage space and are subject to the same definitions, restrictions and prices.

TWO STORY

Two story buildings are generally discouraged. Certain building locations however, may lend themselves to two story construction, based on the Earthship "U" module concept. Two story construction will be approved by **STAR** on request and on a limited basis. In no case shall more than 30% of floor space delineated on membership certificate be two story construction.

BUILDING VARIATIONS

STAR is not a forum for individual experimental projects. It is intended as a demonstration of concepts already tested and proven by SSA. SSA is working in cooperation with the New Mexico Construction Industries Division and will strictly enforce the uniform building code and the New Mexico tire building code as well as mechanical systems discussed in another portion of this document.

BUILDING PERMITS

No dwellings will be built without building permits from the New Mexico Construction Industries Division. At this time, the State of New Mexico requires an architect's and an engineer's stamp of approval on all tire construction. Solar Survival Architecture can be commissioned to provide these services and will advise members as to the most economical method to obtain permit drawings. **No building will be started without proof that a building permit has been applied for at the New Mexico Construction Industries Division. All buildings must be built exactly as per permitted drawings.**

CONSTRUCTION

STAR Architectural Staff will inspect buildings under construction to enforce restrictions of this document at their own discretion. Owners may secure supervision, consultation or guidance from SSA. Fees will be assessed as per the SSA fee schedule.

MECHANICAL SYSTEMS

No mechanical systems of any kind (power, water, or sewage) shall be started without a mechanical permit from STAR. As at the REACH project, **STAR** will apply for mechanical variances from the state of New Mexico. It is possible that **STAR** will be allowed certain variances from the State of New Mexico for purposes of research and development.

These variances are a privilege and **STAR** will fully cooperate with the State. Therefore, all power, sewage and water systems must either be designed by SSA or submitted to SSA for approval. All mechanical systems must be built exactly as per permitted and approved drawings.

POWER

No power grid electricity shall run on this land. All energy will be solar or wind produced independently by members under supervision of STAR and in accordance with New Mexico Building Codes. All electrical wiring shall be done by licensed electricians with appropriate electrical permits and inspections by local state officials.

SEWAGE

All sewage will be split into "grey" water and "black" water (see Earthship Volume II). Members will reuse grey water with guidance and approval of all systems from SSA and **STAR.** Compost or solar toilets will be required and will produce no "black" water. Dry Toilet systems must be certified by SSA. All decisions relative to sewage will be made and enforced by **STAR.** The idea is that there will be no sewage.

WATER

Roof water catches will be built into each dwelling by owners. These catches will feed individual cisterns from which the water will be pressurized for household use by solar pumps. Design of these catches must be approved by **STAR.** Members will install their individual catches and cisterns at their own expense under supervision of **STAR.** These catches will be designed so the catch water will be suitable for drinking. No wells will be allowed on the property at the time of this edition of the Star Land Users Code.

BUILDING APPEARANCE

All exterior finishes shall be color coded to **blend with surrounding foliage and/or earth** for purposes of lowering the overall impact of the architecture on the property. Earth and foliage colored stuccos are required. ALL other finishes are subject to **STAR** approval. Exterior Tire work shall not remain exposed for more than 2 years.

SITE APPEARANCE

All construction sites and home sites must be kept organized, neat and free from blowing debris, stacks of junk, garbage, etc. All construction sites are subject to **STAR** standards of neatness and organization. Once buildings are complete, storage must be kept inside. Members are advised to allow sufficient storage space in their original square foot delineation on their membership certificate to allow for projected storage, since **no exterior storage will be permitted.** Members are advised to allow a "U" module specifically for storage. This paragraph will be strictly enforced.

GARBAGE

STAR will immediately provide areas for tires and aluminum cans and bottles. All other garbage is the member's responsibility for removal to local dumps. **STAR** will eventually provide for total on site garbage disposal and reuse, however this is not an immediate priority for phase one activity.

PARKING

Parking at lodging sites will be permitted for 1 (only) vehicle per 500 s.f. of building space. No junk or dead cars permitted on STAR land.

SITE TRANSPORTATION

After buildings have been built and occupied the construction access roads will be retired and used only for maintenance and service access. Ground transportation around the **STAR** property and to dwellings will be designed in the future for minimum impact.

ROADS

No paved roads will be provided by **STAR** at this time. **STAR** will provide limited dirt road access to each building area for construction and moving in. These roads will be maintained by the members who use them. Consider the roads to be primitive for the first few years and select your vehicles accordingly. **Automobile use will be restricted and**

enforced to defined roadways.

TREES AND LANDSCAPING

No tree shall be cut or moved without approval by **STAR** and the member who moves trees and seedlings is responsible for their replanting elsewhere. No trees or landscaping will be permitted that cannot survive from catch water and/or swale systems.

ANIMALS

No livestock will be permitted in high density areas. Small livestock (chickens, geese, ducks etc) will be permitted in designated areas. Large livestock will be confined to one or more common livestock areas. Only one dog is allowed per membership under 2000 S.F. Memberships over 2000 S.F. can have 2 dogs. All A level memberships are limited to one dog. All dogs are the responsibility of their owners and are subject to community eviction if necessary. Any dog caught killing sheep from the neighboring ranch is subject to being shot.

ILLEGAL SUBSTANCES

Because the STAR property is land owned in common by all the members, any and all members of the association can be held responsible for any illegal activity on the property. There will be no growing of illegal substances on STAR land.

Therefore, STAR members are encouraged to dispose of any and all illegal substances found on common land which might incriminate the Members of the Association. STAR will not tolerate a member whose activities put the other members at risk.

ENFORCEMENT

Members, upon signing their membership acceptance form, document that they agree to and accept these restrictions and definitions presented as exhibit "F on membership certificate.

The STAR Land Users Code will evolve as per the conditions we encounter in the first 5 to seven years. Members will be required to validate their Agreement to the SLUC updates by signing addendum's as they are issued. Refusal to sign a SLUC Update can result in membership nullification as noted below.

Failure to follow the restrictions and definitions of the SLUC will result in a notice by certified mail or courier. If the specific member still fails to respond to the satisfaction of STAR within two weeks, another certified notice will be sent. Failure to respond to this within two weeks will be met with an unbiased real estate appraisal of the member's lodging, and proceedings will begin for STAR to reimburse and remove the member in question based on current architectural value. Any member who has received a certified warning letter shall not be allowed on the board of directors for 4 years from the date of the certified letter. All members understand and agree to the above possibility with signing of the membership acceptance form. The purchase of a STAR membership is subject to the above restrictions and enforcements. STAR members fully understand and agree to these procedures upon signing of the membership acceptance form.

Upon presentation of evidence of two certified letters two weeks apart, and with evidence of failure by said member to respond to the satisfaction of STAR ----- STAR can reimburse and remove the member without the member's signature as the members signature and acceptance of this removal condition is already on the acceptance form. In this event the

members certificate will be rendered nullified and void. The member's signature on the membership acceptance form stands toward the potential end described above. If this potential situation occurs, the member in question will be sent a membership nullification document and lodging reimbursement check by certified mail.

Clarification of STAR Obligations

The object of this endeavor is to make land available for **STAR** members to participate in the research and development of architectural, mechanical, environmental, sociological, economic, spiritual and ecological ideas as put forth in the books published by Solar Survival Press by Michael Reynolds - EARTHSHIP VOLUME I, EARTHSHIP VOLUME II, EARTHSHIP VOLUME III, and A COMING OF WIZARDS without a major real estate investment. This is not a condominium project nor a co-op nor a subdivision. It is a **non-profit unincorporated association.** The price of membership and resulting opportunity to build a lodging is very small. STAR is therefore not a maintenance agency or a care taker of the land. The people care for the land. STAR is simply an association formed so that many people can use the land to pursue a more mentally, physically, spiritually and ecologically healthy way of life on this planet Earth (as a family or club) under the direction of the STAR Land Users Codes.

In order to allow many to use the property, we set up Articles of Association and Bylaws exhibited on the following pages. We used these same Articles and Bylaws for both the REACH and STAR communities.

OVERVIEW OF THE R.E.A.C.H. COMMUNITY CIRCA 1993

ARTICLES OF ASSOCIATION

In compliance with the requirements of Section 53-10-1-8 N.M.S.A. (1978), as amended, the undersigned, this day voluntarily forms a **non-profit unincorporated association** and does hereby certify:

ARTICLE I

The name of the association is SOCIAL TRANSFORMATION ALTERNATIVE REPUBLIC, hereafter called "Association" or "STAR."

ARTICLE II

The mailing address of the Association is in care of Michael Reynolds, at P.O. Box 1041, Taos NM 87571.

ARTICLE III

PURPOSES AND POWERS OF THE ASSOCIATION

This association does not contemplate financial gain or profit to the members thereof. The specific purposes for which it is formed are to:

A. Provide a "real life" setting for the research and development of architectural, mechanical, environmental, sociological, economic, spiritual and ecological ideas as put forth in the books by Michael Reynolds - EARTHSHIP VOLUME I, EARTHSHIP VOLUME II, EARTHSHIP VOLUME III and A COMING OF WIZARDS. This setting is to be contained in that certain real estate in Taos County, New Mexico, shown on Exhibits "A" & "B" attached hereto and incorporated herein by reference and to demonstrate a more mentally, physically, spiritually and ecologically healthy way of life on this planet within the above described property.

B. Pursue a method of making human lodging less stressful to acquire and operate with the goal of reducing the stress that current survival methods place on people and the planet. This method will involve teaching people to build absolutely self-sustaining Earthships (dwellings as described in the books EARTHSHIP VOLUME I, VOLUME II, and VOLUME III) for themselves. These dwellings will require no electrical power lines as they will make their own electricity. They will have no sewers as they will use composting or solar toilets and recycled grey-water systems. They will have no wells as they will have catch water systems from roof run-off. They will capture (with no outside energy) an interior space suitable for growing food year round. Code variances will be granted by the State of New Mexico to allow research and development in these directions on this project.

C. Demonstrate that eliminating mortgage payments and utility bills for people and discontinuing the extraction of fossils fuels from the planet will promote peace on and *with* the Earth. The long range effects of this on a larger scale could have a positive effect on crime, drug abuse, ecology, energy, homelessness, child abuse, and war. It is the opinion of this association that the current fundamental approach to living by modern society is at the root of all of these problems and that the efforts of this association could shed light in the direction of change.

D.   Evolve and demonstrate a legal model for the non-profit acquisition and/or distribution of real estate for environmentally friendly, owner built housing as the marketing of real estate for financial gain has driven the cost of decent land out of reach for most citizens and thus rendered them at the mercy of mortgage companies, realtors and profit seeking conventional developers *to acquire a place to build a home*. In most cases conventional restrictions imparted by mortgage companies, realtors and developers whose concerns are resale and profit further the dilemma of expense and control and the citizens are channeled into a method of living that is extremely stressful to both them and the planet.

E.   Present an alternative approach to human habitat that puts housing back within the grasp of the average citizen.

ARTICLE IV

POWERS OF THE ASSOCIATION

One membership in this Association shall be issued for each lodging site created within the real property described in Exhibits "A" & "B". It shall be mandatory for a land user to be a member of the Association. A copy of these Articles of Association and the Bylaws and the Star Land User's Code,"Exhibit F", shall be provided to land users at the time of membership. The Association shall have responsibility for maintenance of the following aspects of the development. The only assessments to be levied on the members will be real estate taxes and liability insurance. The Association shall have the power and authority to levy these assessments on the members and referred to herein all as is or will be more fully set forth in the Bylaws. And to:

Section A: Fix, levy, collect and enforce payment by any lawful means, charges or assessments necessary to cover the cost of real estate taxes and insurance on the property; pay all expenses in connection therewith, and pay all office and other expenses incident to the conduct of the business of the Association related to the collection and payment of real estate taxes and insurance, including all or any governmental charges levied or imposed against the property of the Association;

Section B: Acquire (by gift, purchase or otherwise), hold, improve, build upon, operate, maintain, convey, dedicate for public use or otherwise dispose of real or personal property in connections with affairs of the Association;

Section C: Have and to exercise all powers, rights and privileges which an association organized under the unincorporated association law of the State of New Mexico by law may now or hereafter have or exercise, except as otherwise provided herein.

ARTICLE V

MEMBERSHIP

Every person or entity who pays the then prevailing membership initiation fees shall be a member of the Association. Membership shall be appurtenant to and may not be separated from the use of any lodging site. Each member shall be entitled to one vote per membership certificate.

ARTICLE VI

BOARD OF DIRECTORS

After the first seven (7) years, the affairs of the Association shall be managed by a board of five (5) co-directors, who shall be members of the Association. The number of directors may be changed by amendment of the Bylaws of the Association. The name and address of the person who is to act in the capacity of director and initiator for the first seven years is:

Michael Reynolds   PO Box 1041 Taos, NM 87571
NAME   ADDRESS

At the seventh year of existence, the initiator shall appoint five (5) directors with terms of 5 years, 4 years, 3 years, 2 years, 1 year respectively; and at every year thereafter, the members of the association shall elect one (1) director for a term of five (5) years as their terms shall expire. This is meant to allow a new director every year.

ARTICLE VII

DISSOLUTION

The Association may be dissolved only with the assent given in writing and signed by all members. Upon dissolution of the Association, other than incident to a merger or consolidation, the assets of the Association shall be distributed among the members in good standing proportionate to their original membership certificate as it relates to the sum of all the other membership certificates issued before the date of written assent of dissolution by all members.

ARTICLE VIII

DURATION

The Association shall exist for a period of thirty (30) years. The Association may be renewed thereafter under then similar statutory provisions as now pertain upon the written consent of seventy-five (75) percent of it's then members in good standing.

IN WITNESS WHEREOF, I the undersigned, have executed these Articles of Association, this _____ day of _____ 1993.

STATE OF NEW MEXICO)
) ss.
COUNTY OF TAOS)
    The foregoing instrument was acknowledged before me this _____ day of
_____, 1993, by _____.

                                    _____
                                              Notary Public

(SEAL)
My commission expires: _____

BY-LAWS
OF
STAR LAND USER'S ASSOCIATION

ARTICLE I

NAME AND LOCATION

The name of the association is STAR LAND USER'S ASSOCIATION, here in after referred to as the "Association." It's mailing address is:

PO Box 1041, Taos, New Mexico 87571

but meetings of the members and directors may be held at such places within the County of Taos, State of New Mexico, as may be designated by the Board of Directors.

ARTICLE II

DEFINITIONS

Section 1. "Association" shall mean and refer to STAR LAND USER'S ASSOCIATION.

Section 2. "Properties" shall mean and refer to that certain real property described on Exhibits "A" & "B" attached to the Articles of Association.

Section 3. "Lodging Site" shall mean and refer to any portion of land created from within the real property described on Exhibits "A" & "B" hereof, the use of which shall be governed by and subject to those terms contained in the STAR Land Users Code as it may be from time to time amended by the initiator or the Board of Directors. Use of a lodging site shall include membership in the Association and rights appurtenant thereto.

Section 4. "Member" shall mean and refer to the holder, whether one or more persons or entities, of a membership certificate to any lodging site created and described for use within the real property.

Section 5. "Members" shall mean and refer to every person or entity holding a membership in the Association.

ARTICLE III

MEMBERSHIP

Section 1. Every person or entity who is an owner of a Membership Certificate for the use of a lodging site within the real property shall be a member of the Association. The Association is the sole entity that owns the "properties" described in Article II Section 2. The members own their lodgings and other personal affects on the "properties".Membership shall be appurtenant to and may not be separated from the use of any lodging site. Use of a lodging site and ownership of a Membership Certificate shall be the sole qualification for membership. In absence of a contrary agreement, voting rights shall be exercised by the named owner/owners of the Membership Certificate. A single Membership Certificate shall entitle the holder/holders to a single vote. One person may hold more than one Membership Certificate, thus entitling said person to more than one vote.

ARTICLE IV

MEETINGS OF MEMBERS

Section 1. Annual Meeting. The first annual meeting of the members shall be held within one (1) year from the date of filing the statement required by S 1 of the Uniform Association Act, and each subsequent regular annual meeting of the members shall be held within the same month of each year thereafter, on a set date, time and place to be fixed by the director with notices mailed to the members, at least thirty (30) days in advance.

Section 2. Special Meetings. Special meetings of the members may be called at any time by the initiator or by the director/directors, or upon written request of members who are entitled to vote.

Section 3. Quorum. The presence at the meeting of members entitled to cast, or of proxies entitled to cast, two-thirds (2/3) of the votes of membership shall constitute a quorum for any action except as otherwise provided in the Articles of Association, or these Bylaws. If, however, such quorum shall not be present or represented at any meeting, the members entitled to vote thereat shall have power to adjourn the meeting from time to time without notice other than announcement at the meeting, until a quorum as aforesaid shall be present or be represented.

Section 4. Proxies. At all meetings of members, each member may vote in person or by proxy. All proxies shall be in writing and filed with the board twenty-four (24) hours prior to the meeting. Every proxy shall be revocable and shall automatically cease upon elimination of the member from the association, as is possible, as described in the October 1992 edition of the STAR Land User's Code.

ARTICLE V

SELECTION OF TERM OF OFFICE OF DIRECTOR / CO-DIRECTORS

Section 1. The affairs of this association shall be managed by a single initiator/director, Michael Reynolds, the designer and founder of the concept, for the first seven years following the filing of this association.

Section 2. In the event of this director's death prior to the end of the seven (7) year term, a board of five directors shall be elected by the members as per Section 4.

Section 3. Number. Following the seven (7) year term of the single director, the affairs of this Association shall be managed by a board of Five (5) co-directors who shall be members of the Association.

Section 4. Term of Office. The initiator shall appoint or (if necessary because of death) the members shall elect <u>Five</u> (5) co-directors for a term of <u>Five</u> (5) years, Four (4) years, Three (3) years, Two (2) years and One (1) year respectively and at every annual meeting thereafter, the members shall elect a director for a term of Five (5) years in order to provide a new director every year.

Section 5. Removal. Any co-director may be removed from the board, with or without cause, by a majority vote of the members of the Association. In the event of death, resignation or removal of a co-director, his successor shall be selected by the remaining members of the board and shall serve for the unexpired term of his predecessor.

Section 6. Compensation. No director or co-director shall receive compensation for any service he may render to the Association. However, any co-director may be reimbursed for his actual expenses incurred in the performance of his duties, or members may, by a two-thirds (2/3) vote, decide to reimburse director(s) or co-directors for exceptional services.

Section 7. Action Taken Without a Meeting. The director or co-directors shall have the right to take any action in the absence of a meeting which they could take at a meeting by obtaining the written approval of all the co-directors. Any action so approved shall have the same effect as though taken at a meeting of the co-directors.

Section 8. Indemnification. The initiator/director or members of the board of co-directors shall not be liable to the members for any mistake of judgment, negligence, or otherwise except in the event of willful misconduct or malfeasance. The Association shall indemnify and hold harmless the initiator/director and each of the members of the board of co-directors against all contractual liabilities to others arising out of contracts made by the director or board of co-directors on behalf of the Association and it's members, and in connection with any acts performed pursuant to the Declaration of Covenants hereinbefore referred to unless such director or co-directors are adjudged guilty of willful misconduct or malfeasance in the performance of their duties as directors.

ARTICLE VI

POWERS AND DUTIES OF INITIATOR/DIRECTOR AND CO-DIRECTORS

Section 1. During the first seven years the single initiator/director will evolve and refine all aspects of this association including but not limited to bylaws, codes, architecture, mechanical systems, ground transportation, and legal model.

Section 2. Powers. The initiator/director and eventually the board of co-directors shall have the power to:

a.   Adopt and publish rules and regulations governing the use of the lodging sites in all aspects inclusive of regulation of design and construction of buildings, and inclusive of dimension, materials, design, systems, provisions of water, sewage and trash disposal, and of the entire tract of real property, parking, access and tree removal and the personal conduct of the members and their guests on roadways and easements;

b. Fix, levy, collect and enforce payment of the tax and insurance assessments of the members of the Association. A distinction may be made in the assessments to be charged for an improved lodging Site or an unimproved lodging site; Taxes and insurance and related costs thereof are the only assessments placed on the members.

c. Remove a member as described in the current STAR Land User's Code;

d. Procure and maintain adequate liability and hazard insurance on property owned by the Association;

e. Cause the members' solid waste to be collected;

f. Cause the roadways and easements to be maintained; and

g. Cause all taxes and insurance of the Association to be paid from assessment funds.

h. Issue Membership Certificates;

i. The initial director, by his signature hereby adopts the following :

    1. The STAR Land User's Code, as it now stands, and may evolve from time to time.

    2. Each member is responsible for the maintenance of his own lodging site.

ARTICLE VII

BOOKS AND RECORDS

After the initiator steps down and the board of directors is appointed, the books and records and papers of the Association shall at all times, during reasonable business hours, be subject to inspection by any member. The Articles of Association and the Bylaws of the Association shall be available for inspection by any member at the principal office of the Association, where copies may be purchased at a reasonable cost.

ARTICLE VIII

MISCELLANEOUS

Section 1.   The fiscal year of the Association shall begin on the first day of January and end on the thirty-first day of December of every year, except that the first fiscal year shall begin on the date of filing of the statement required by S1 of the Uniform Association Act.

IN WITNESS THEREOF, I being the director of the STAR LAND USER'S ASSOCIATION, have hereunto set my hand this day of _____ 199___

A bunny rabbit is a soft, almost defenseless, non aggressive creature. However, if you trap it in a corner, fear and stress will make it attempt to claw and bite you. We believe human nature is basically (designed to be) soft and nonaggressive. This is evident from the physical structure and characteristics of the human body. However, fear and stress brought on by modern day living conditions can and has (the gun business will testify to this) turned human beings into clawing, biting creatures. This is why we have so many laws and policed enforcements necessary in our world today. **Remove the stress and survival related fear from the human and you have a soft, rather cosmic, adaptable being capable of enhancing the planet it lives on.**

A community structure will evolve much the same as the structure of a tree evolves as it grows. Since no one in the modern world has ever lived without stress of survival we do not know what conditions will arise. Any attempt at a preconceived community structure would simply inhibit *natural manifestation* much the same as nailing limbs onto a tree would inhibit the growth of real limbs. The emergence of the community is an adventure - not without problems and dilemmas. Questions and directions in this adventure are dealt with as they come up. To try to predict and solve every problem in advance is futile, impossible, and ridiculous. We must only create a more whole, broader scoped, softer state of mind from which to deal with inevitable suburban and urban type dilemmas. The *fertile soil* concept provides a general direction of community evolution that will produce more of the *blossoms and fruit of humanity* than current, conventional clusters of human habitat allow.

"Just elevate and decide in the air".

The above is a phrase used by basketball players like Michael Jordan, who is famous for his "air born" tactics. The idea is just to get up in the air - then decide what to do after you get up there. Your options and view are both extremely enhanced from the "elevation". There are some wide scale problems we have on this planet. Rather than trying to solve the problems now, we must *elevate* our existence to a higher psychic plane, then try to solve problems after the enhancement of our options and views. This "elevation" has been attempted with drugs, meditation, magic, and religion but all of these seem to only have a temporary effect. *The method of living itself must also be the method of elevation.*

An independent Earthship community has the potential to elevate the overall general existence of its inhabitants.

The Earthship is a vessel that will allow us to explore new worlds. New worlds on our own planet. Imagine a hard packed, dry vacant lot. This is the "soil of stress" on which our current community and political concepts are built. Our views and options are reflected from this condition. Imagine that same vacant lot with rich tilled soil and lots of water. It would be a forest, a wonderland. This is the soil of *conscious evolution* from which our future community and political dreams can grow. The Earthship concept creates this soil. It allows us to *"decide in the air".*

165

CARE AND MAINTENANCE OF NATURE BY HUMANS IN THE LATE 20TH CENTURY

9. URBAN EARTHSHIPS - CITY APPLICATION

THE EARTHSHIP CONCEPT IS MATURING INTO A VERY REALISTIC METHOD OF ACQUIRING APPROPRIATE AND INSPIRATIONAL SHELTER ON THIS PLANET IN THE LATE 20TH CENTURY. WE HAVE TAKEN IT TO EUROPE, BOLIVIA, JAPAN AND CANADA AND WILL SOON BE GOING TO AUSTRALIA, NEW ZEALAND AND RUSSIA. IT WORKS FOR RURAL DWELLINGS EVERYWHERE. HOWEVER, HALF OF THE PEOPLE ALL OVER THE WORLD LIVE IN CITIES. WE HAVE CONSEQUENTLY HAD MANY REQUESTS FOR AN URBAN APPLICATION OF THESE CONCEPTS. EVEN THOUGH THE U.S. DOES HAVE ABUNDANT LANDS FOR EARTHSHIP DEVELOPMENT IN RURAL AREAS, WE HAVE CITIES THAT ARE DYING DUE TO SUBURBAN DEVELOPMENT BEING SO REMOVED FROM THE CITY CORE. THE "WASTELANDS" BETWEEN THE CITY CORE AND THE FARTHER AND FARTHER AWAY SUBURBS ARE PRIME AREAS FOR AN URBAN APPLICATION OF THE EARTHSHIP CONCEPT. THIS WOULD BRING DWELLINGS BACK CLOSER TO THE DYING CITY CORES AND REVITALIZE OUR EXISTING CITY GRIDS BEFORE THEY BECOME GHOST TOWNS OR ASPHALT JUNGLES. *CAN ONE BUILD ONES OWN EARTHSHIP IN A MAJOR CITY USING SOLAR ELECTRICITY, CATCH WATER, SOLAR TOILETS, RECYCLED AUTOMOBILE TIRE BUILDING BLOCKS, ETC?* THE ANSWER IS YES. THIS CHAPTER WILL EXPLORE HOW.

Graphics by Marty Remaly, Jonah Reynolds

In that there is not available land in urban areas (especially in Europe) for large amounts of Earthship developments, we must first devise a method of creating the "land" within the existing city fabric for such a concept. Think of a flower pot in a window. The typical city apartment has no yard to grow flowers, herbs, or vegetables because everything is paved. Consequently, people in the city get large and small flower pots and fill them with earth to grow things. *Earthships also need "earth" to enable them to "grow" in the city.* We must conceptually and physically find a way of creating land/space for the Earthship concept. It must be accommodated exactly like it is in rural areas. Cans, bottles, tires, etc. are more easily available in the cities than the rural areas. All of the utility systems in most cities are in trouble. Water is sometimes rationed in many major cities and is often bad. Electricity is expensive and usually a step away from "black out". Sewers are the worst and usually end up in what was once a river. Yet people still come to cities for jobs, opportunities, culture, etc. The materials for the Earthship concept are more available in the cities and the need for the independent vessel is also more explicit in the city. Imagine living in the city with your own independent power, water and sewage. Imagine low income housing projects; warm and well lit (at no cost to the tenant) and full of plants that produce food. **Imagine the city fathers getting an additional tax base with no additional utilities needed to support it.** The key issue here is the land - the *flower pot*. What kind of " flower pot " will allow Earthships to grow in the city?

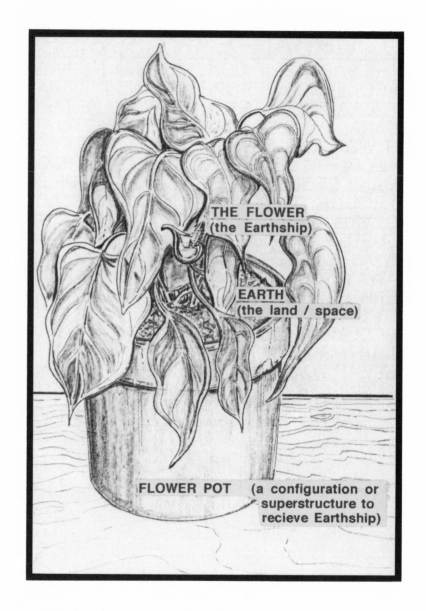

THE FLOWER
(the Earthship)

EARTH
(the land / space)

FLOWER POT   (a configuration or
superstructure to
recieve Earthship)

The REACH community illustrates a dense application of Earthships on a very steep slope of a mountain.

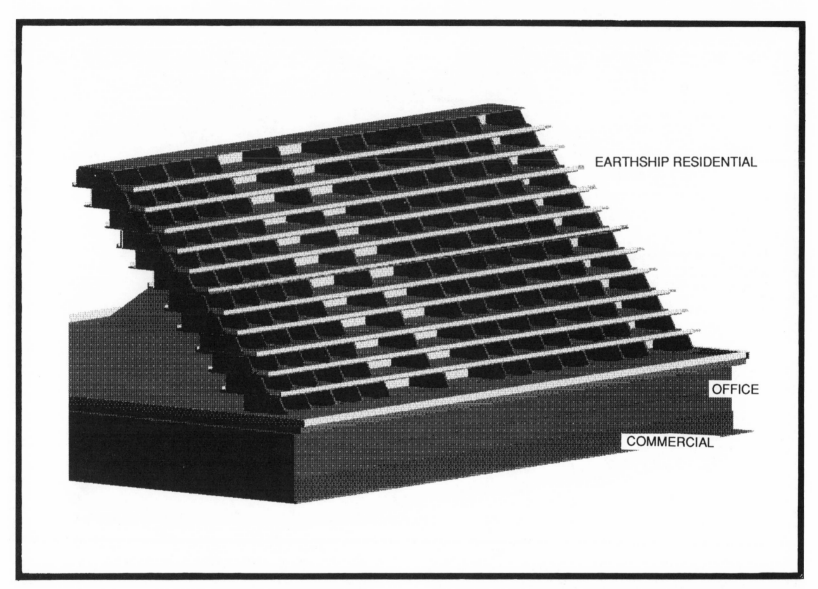

EARTHSHIP RESIDENTIAL

OFFICE

COMMERCIAL

A city application can be modeled after the already existing successful rural mountain application. The idea would be to *create the "mountain"* as a **super-** **structure** built of concrete much the same way a conventional parking garage is built. This concept would apply to the areas close to the city core.

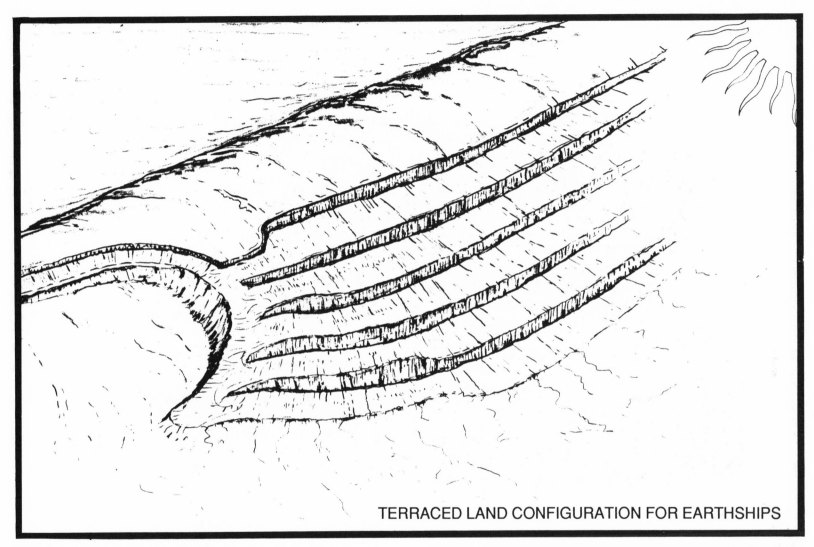

TERRACED LAND CONFIGURATION FOR EARTHSHIPS

Another approach is to *create a mountain* (or hill) out of compacted earth thus creating a south facing slope on which to build Earthships. Practical application of this method would involve less density and slope than the previously suggested concrete super structure and would therefore be used a little farther from the city core. Either of these "man made mountain slopes" (south facing of course) can be developed with the Earthship concept very similar to a real mountain slope such as at REACH (page 165).

171

Potential home owners in such a project would purchase the use of a volume of square footage in the super structure or man made hill and build (or fill in) their own Earthship type home with its own electrical system, water system, sewage system, etc. Existing city systems are all over taxed and antiquated anyway so this self sufficient housing concept should be welcomed in any existing city. The concrete superstructure approach would involve one or many existing city blocks. The "man made hill" could also be fit into the existing city grid.

*Solar Survival Architecture has been working for almost a quarter of a century toward developing a self sufficient, earth friendly housing concept that is easily accessible (in terms of skill, money and materials) to the majority of the people on the planet. After many years of prototypes, the **Earthship** concept was born in the late 1980's and has proven and continues to prove itself as a vessel that will sail independent of existing housing dogma. The **Earthship** is built from used automobile tires rammed with earth and laid into load bearing thermal mass walls. Because these walls are close to 3'-0" thick, they are already wider than the required foundation for such a wall. Thus the walls are a monolith which is foundation, load bearing structure, and temperature control through tremendous mass. These walls can be built by unskilled people with earth from their own construction site and free used automobile tires from their community. These structural and thermal concepts have been in use now for over twenty years. Solar Survival Architecture has produced a "how to" manual on this subject - Earthship Volume I. A more thorough*

presentation of these building concepts is presented in Chapters 1-4 of that book.

*After the structural and thermal aspects of the **Earthship** were evolved enough to be used on a wide scale globally, Solar Survival Architecture challenged every aspect of the mechanical systems in conventional housing. The result was Earthship Vol. II and Earthship Vol. III. Through these manuals, water, power, and sewage were all approached from different perspectives. At this point, the **Earthship** home built anywhere on the planet out of automobile tires rammed with earth can stand alone and independent of all centralized utility systems. These buildings heat and cool themselves. They provide their own water and electricity and deal with their own sewage. They grow significant quantities of food and can be built by relatively unskilled people on an "out of pocket" basis. They have become (and continue to become) more available to people all over the planet. For those who want to have their homes built for them, SSA has trained licensee's to spread out over the planet and guide people through the process or completely do it for them. Generic architectural drawings have been developed for building permits, bank loans, and construction. **The Earthship movement is in place and growing at many levels.** The **Earthship** program not only effectively uses large quantities of automobile tires but also uses aluminum cans and bottles (see Earthship Vol. I) and seriously effects other major global problems such as energy, housing, recycling, water, sewage, etc. We feel that if all inhabitants of the planet, both urban and rural, were to have access to **inspirational, earth friendly accommodations,** the world would be a better place.*

THE "LAND BUILD" CONCEPT

The automobile makers began seriously making automobiles in the early 1900's. At some point automobiles were recognized as a "fact" of our age and tax dollars and political input were directed toward highways to further enhance the usefulness of the *automobile concept*.. We see a parallel here. **Just as the highways have "paved the way" for automobile evolution - there is a method of "paving the way" for the Earthship evolution.** Highways for automobiles require tremendous tax dollar allotments, i.e. budgets for

their emergence into our world. The "pathways" for **Earthships** also require a budget. This budget already exists in every community, in every state. The **Earthship** "pathways" would simply require the *redirection of this existing budget*.. This redirection would both fulfill the the original use of the particular budget and create (in the process) "pathways" or ideal conditions for **Earthship** development. There is a perfect site for the construction of a High Performance Generic **Earthship**. There is also a perfect site for a whole complex of them. In section that perfect site would be as follows.

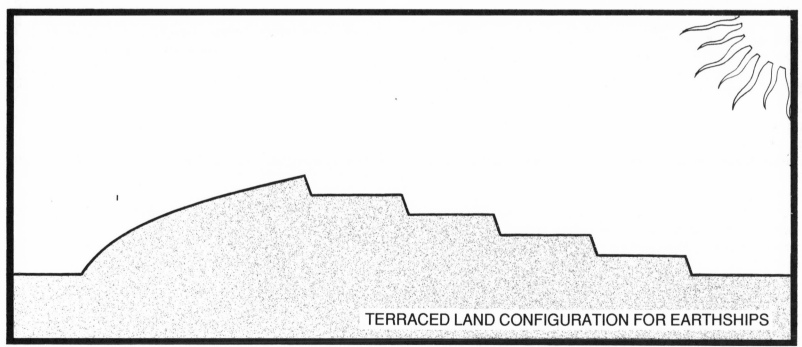

TERRACED LAND CONFIGURATION FOR EARTHSHIPS

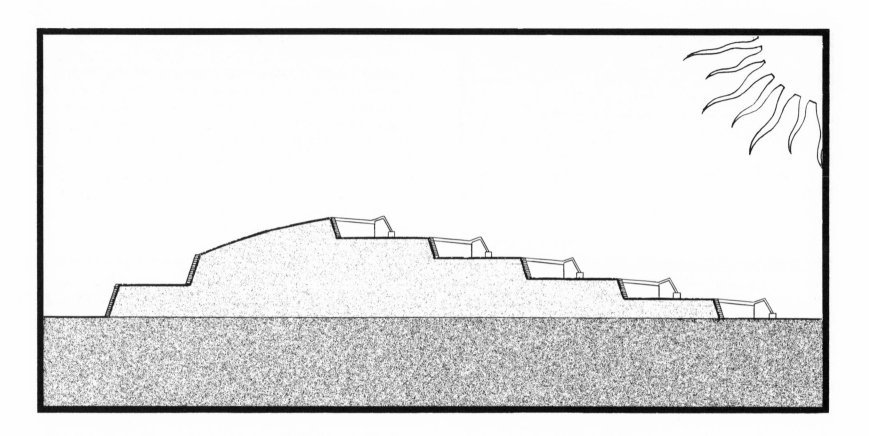

This configuration would accommodate a colony of **Earthships** that step up the hill as shown above. If this land configuration were available in urban areas it would invite the application of urban **Earthships** by both individuals and developers.

174

The configuration above makes it much easier to drive an automobile. As a matter of fact, this configuration has influenced the very development and evolution of the automobile. Now, how do we cause the ideal **Earthship** land configuration to "happen" in every city and town like highways and roads have happened?

In these times trying to get a new budget for anything with the tax payers money is difficult. Too much money has to be used to support the bureaucratic dinosaur. Thus trying to get government funding for building an Earthship land configuration would be futile. However, what if the redirection of an *already existing budget* were to produce this configuration *while at the same time still doing what the budget was originally intended to do?* This is the kind of "force finding" it will take to get us through the future.

There are many inefficient forces in our "civilized" world that can be "sharpened" and "focused" better to yield more. Our pompous traditions and dogmas are really the things that inhibit our natural evolution. *Tradition and dogma are products of intelligence. When looked at with a broad scope through a large window of time, intelligence begins to look like an "adolescent type" phase that humankind must go through to evolve. Let's hope we make it through this phase soon. The trees and the plants have been able to maneuver **beyond intelligence** on their way to unity with the planet. Imagine if trees and plants had dogmas and egos, there would be **war in every garden.***

Every town and city has a budget for a land fill or other method of garbage disposal. Any independent company can bid for the disposal of the garbage from that municipality. The "budget" is the amount of money the city currently spends on waste management at a specific land fill site not including the actual pick up and transportation of the garbage. Based on existing "phenomena", this is apparently enough to purchase or lease land, dig monstrous holes and bury the garbage with heavy equipment and labor. Now let us say that we use this existing phenomenon to create a "land build" rather than a "land fill". A normal land fill involves a giant pit filled with layers of garbage and layers of earth as shown on the following page.

Land fill description of next two diagrams:
1. Perforated pipes collect leachate that has percolated through the trash and chanels it to a treatment center
2. Unloaded and pushed into place and covered daily
3. Pipes collect methane gas
4. Impermeable clay seals landfill after it has reached capacity
5. Structures can eventually be built on top of the final layer of soil

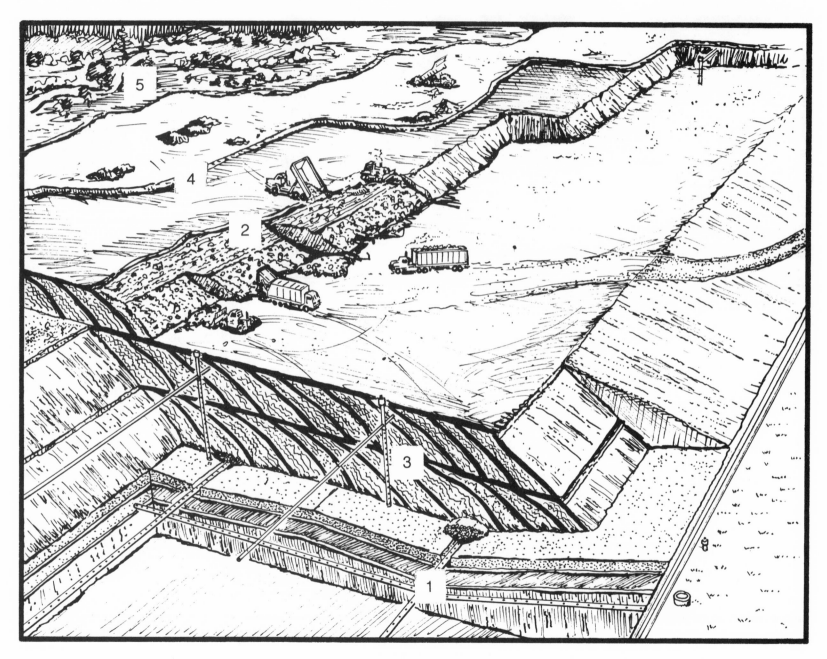

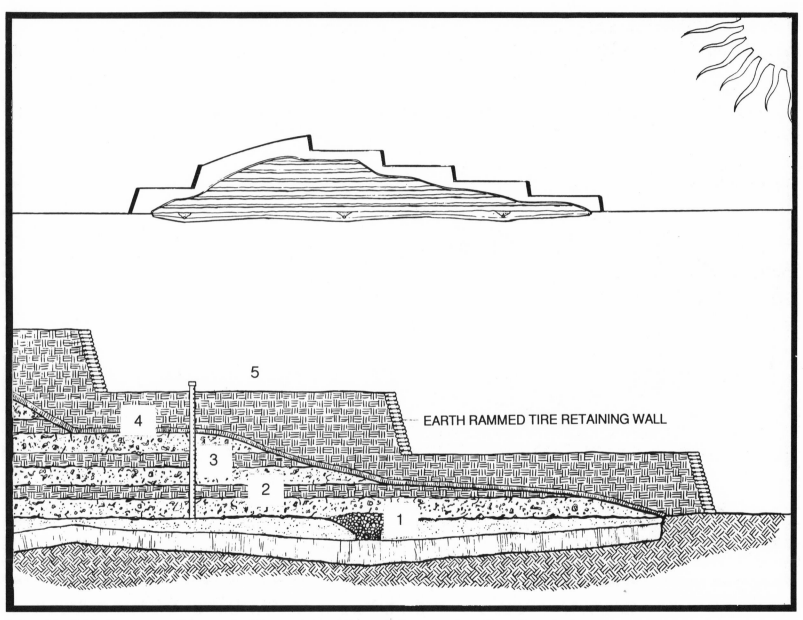

EARTH RAMMED TIRE RETAINING WALL

A land build is the same thing only it is on top of the existing grade rather than below.

177

The south side of the **land build** could be used for **Earthship** lodgings. An example of a **land build** in use is shown above.

This is an over view of a land build Earthship colony.

Land builds can spawn colonies of Earthships built into the perfect land configuration

Whole cities can be shaped out of flat lands. We could shape the terrain to suit the needs of the future in an effort to align with existing human influenced and natural phenomenon. Below an example- a land build city created in the flat lands of Texas from El Paso's garbage.

Garbage is a phenomenon of our age. We can't change that overnight, yet we need an overnight solution. *We must therefore use a force that is already at hand - we only need to redirect it.* **Use the existing garbage force, budgets, and economics to make a "land build".** In the northern hemisphere we could manifest south facing terrain for ideal **Earthship** developments via the waste management avenues that already exist. Soon, cities grow from their own garbage.

Let us dream here for a moment on how this "land build" could emerge.

The first occupants are workers on the site; i.e as soon as Earthship shelter of any kind is available, it is used by the construction workers for temporary offices, workshops and bunk type housing. This reduces construction costs and co-ordination. On site temporary housing is a good attraction for student and learner types and free housing is trade for lower cash pay. We have already begun to use this approach in our REACH and STAR communities and it works. Now, low income housing evolves out of this situation. The main reason the lodgings are low income is because we expect a psychological garbage stigma or "vibe" to be present initially which will discourage higher income tenants from initiating this type of project at first. We have experience at this because **we have been building with garbage for over twenty years.** *Of course, we have millionaires building garbage houses now so we know the garbage "vibe" fades quickly when performance and livability set in. As the "garbage vibe" fades and the strong, durable, embracing architecture begins to prevail, a softness begins to*

emerge as plants and human input do their part. Then low income people suddenly realize they have a higher income market for their homes. The Earthship neighborhood evolves into a very desirable place. It blooms. This results in the lower income people (who actually "wore out" the garbage vibe from the land build) having the opportunity to capitalize on a "buy low - sell high" situation. They in effect would be the pioneers of this new frontier in human habitat thus creating opportunity for themselves and a harmonious earth friendly future for others.

After more than twenty years of design and development evolving the **Earthship** we always have in mind the "easiest" terrain for an **Earthship** development.

If a "land build" were to create this terrain, it would be like paving the way for a community of **Earthships** much the same way as a highway paves the way for motorists to travel on. This would mean that the garbage management budget (a significant one) for any

182

metropolitan area would (with the same stroke) be the budget for zone preparation for off the grid **Earthship** housing. The generic **Earthship** design would fit into this **land build** perfectly. ***We are talking about a living system which is the by product of our present condition.*** We would be like the trees dropping leaves that rot and make soil for the baby trees to grow in. We drop our garbage (and our dogma) and a new breed of housing springs forth from the environment. This housing changes the face of the earth both physically and spiritually.

Now lets look at the more dense urban application near the city core.

LAND ASSEMBLAGE SUPER STRUCTURE

The cities must accommodate half of the housing units for the next decade. Many city cores in America are decaying while their suburbs are flourishing and devouring vast quantities of energy, water and what is left of the countrysides. We could contribute to the retardation of suburban sprawl and the conservation of remaining lands by taking advantage of the great potential of the city core for human housing.

This can be done by means of planned dwelling increases within the city providing Earth friendly accommodations attractive to all human beings.

Physically attractive - it must provide physical comfort and pleasure for the human body. This must include comfortable exposure to the elements as well as shelter from them.

Mentally attractive - It must not impose a way of thinking or reacting on an individual. It must allow his/her mind to function freely and individually. It must be an asset to mental health rather than a detriment to it. Housing can and has effected the mental attitude of whole communities.

Financially attractive - it must be capable of adapting to the poor person's pocketbook as well as allowing the wealthy people to utilize theirs.

Environmentally attractive - it must accommodate the Earthship concept in the city as fully as it is used in rural areas. If the rural Earthship vessel were compared to an environmentally friendly automobile - an urban superstructure would be a "parking lot" for environmentally friendly vessels.

PROPOSALS

1.   We are proposing a lodging scheme that will provide the suburban amenities such as: an exterior yard, auto parking near the unit, freedom to individualize one's own unit, psychological distance from the city and community identity. These *suburban amenities* would be coupled with proximity to and involvement in the *amenities of the existing central business district* such as: central business district entertainment, shopping, employment, cultural activities, religious centers, and civic activities. This concept would bring together the best of both types of life (urban & rural) in a city housing scheme that is totally an expression of the people and planet - **green architecture in the city**.

2.   We are proposing a lodging scheme that could be placed in the heart of a city without interrupting the commercial conduct of that city. The commercial potential of an existing square block near the city core is too valuable to be replaced with

183

a residential complex. At the same time, however, the commercial potential of a city core would be greatly increased if a residential complex were there to make use of it. As with the land build this would create a tax base with no new utility obligation on the municipality.

As it is now, the existing residential areas are providing their own commercial facilities in our suburbs. These suburban "cities" compete with and weaken our existing city cores. As a result our city cores are losing their strength symbolically and physically. This is especially true in medium sized cities such as Albuquerque, Louisville and Indianapolis. For this reason we are proposing a **"residential blanket"** over a typically structured commercial complex in the city core. This commercial complex would be of a similar concept to that of existing city floor commercial facilities, thus aligning with the existing fabric of the city core and at the same time providing the people needed to make it prosper. The dwellers within the **residential blanket** would be within arms reach of the central business district amenities. The concept of the **residential blanket** would be such that it would provide individual dwelling amenities heretofore found only in the suburbs.

3.   We are proposing a lodging scheme that is adaptable to any income bracket in any city. The scheme would be capable of providing for many different income brackets simultaneously in mass or singularly. All classes of people must be considered in order to fully revitalize our cities.

Even though incomes vary, the basic needs for physically and mentally healthy, inspirational accommodations are the same for all human beings. These needs would become the conceptual foundation for a framework into which low, medium and high income dwelling types could be injected. **Inspirational accommodations should be available to all.** This will do more toward changing our planet than any platform of any political party.

4.   We are proposing a lodging scheme that would use the <u>same</u> concept to produce a <u>different</u> type of complex in every city. The people (and the climate) would be the variables which bring about this difference.

The ideas and attitudes of people vary in different parts of the country. Climate varies in different parts of the country. Lodging should reflect these ideas attitudes, and climatic differences. Lodging should be an expression of people and planet. As it is today people are becoming an expression of their poor quality housing and the planet is tragically not even being considered.

In most high density lodging schemes today the total design of the complex is so tied down by the architect and investors that their ideas, attitudes and financial motives are imposed upon the tenants and the environment. To solve the large-scale urban housing problems of today, **an environmentally functional and humanely aesthetic "breed" of inspirational dwelling accommodations must be developed. These accommodations must allow for the financial, psychological, and**

physical differences in human beings with the existing activities of the planet being their common denominator. A super structure would supply the physical and functional needs (building sites, vehicular and pedestrian access ways, etc.) for a residential community in a way which advocates a peaceful coexistence of all races, creeds and classes in the same intra-city community in harmony with the planet. Thus the super structure would accommodate any approach to **Earthship** dwellings be it owner-builder or developer produced. It should be capable of handling many types (high/low income) of housing simultaneously or individually depending on the need of the city. We have found in our rural communities (REACH and STAR) that a community needs both high and low income people to conveniently function. The high income people usually need the wage workers to build, maintain and caretake their units for them. The lower income wage workers usually need higher income people to provide these jobs for them. An example of how this could work in an urban higher density community is as follows: *A "high roller" buys a volume of building space in the "urban mountain". The high roller buys enough for his own unit plus some rental or investment units. He then builds for and rents to the wage workers or better still subsidizes their building of their own units near him. This way the high roller has a hand in selecting the wage worker types to help maintain and caretake his/her compound. This same scenario can also happen by chance. We have seen this happen in the REACH and STAR communities.*

5. We are proposing a super structure within the city that simply increases the usable land area by creating land areas stacked or overlapped above ground. They would be assembled in such a way so they would still receive sunlight, rain, breezes, etc. The super structure would provide the necessary auto/pedestrian access ways as the suburban developments do. Into this super structure low, medium, or high income dwelling types could be injected. The potential to build an Earthship independent of existing over-taxed utilities would now exist in the city. They could be singularly built, totally individual homes with the same freedoms of building that a rural or suburban site offers. However, If the need be to meet a demand and provide for the poor, mass produced economy units could be injected. These would be required to meet certain specifications but would still allow individual freedom within and without. This is similar to the same highway providing for a BMW or a Chevy Nova.

This structure would be a **"land assemblage"** superstructure and could be re-used by different "vessels" in the same way as land itself or highways. The superstructure would be designed with the permanence of raw land.

185

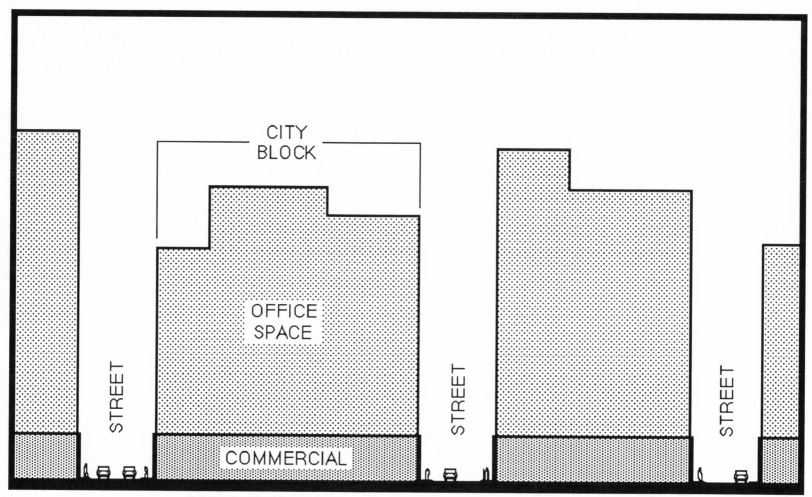

CITY
BLOCK

OFFICE
SPACE

STREET

STREET

STREET

COMMERCIAL

EXISTING CITY STRUCTURE

Where in the city can people live without interrupting the existing city structure? The existing city structure has a cohesive and commercial value to the city; it can not be conveniently interrupted.

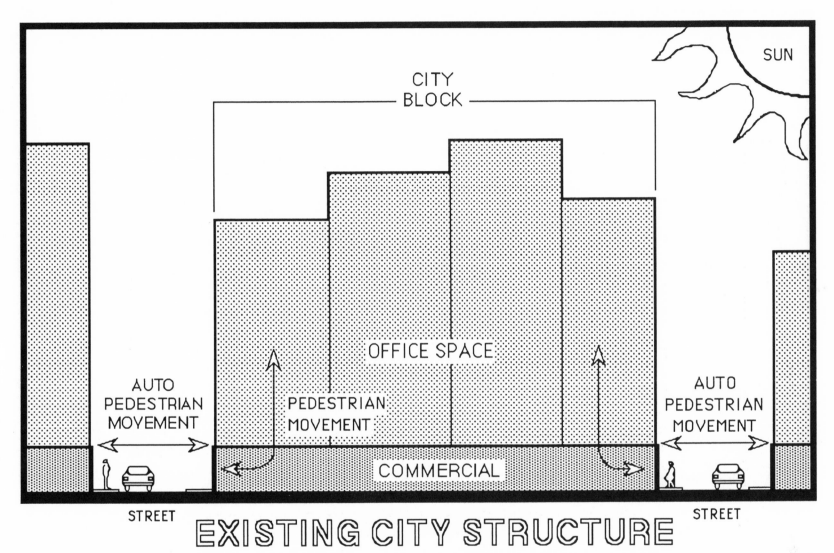

SUN

CITY
BLOCK

OFFICE SPACE

AUTO
PEDESTRIAN
MOVEMENT

PEDESTRIAN
MOVEMENT

AUTO
PEDESTRIAN
MOVEMENT

COMMERCIAL

STREET

STREET

EXISTING CITY STRUCTURE

What part of the city has the most to offer toward a pleasant residential environment for people? One part of the city answers both questions.

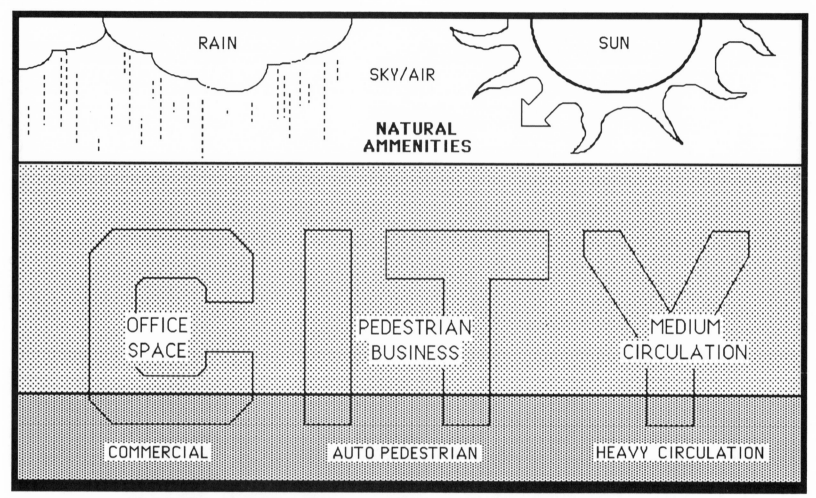

CITY STRUCTURE ABSTRACTION

An abstract view of the city emphasizes the part of the city that is wasted - the part of the city that offers more usable area than the entire city floor - the part of the city that could be utilized without affecting the existing conduct of the city - the part of the city that has potential for a pleasant and healthy residential environment.

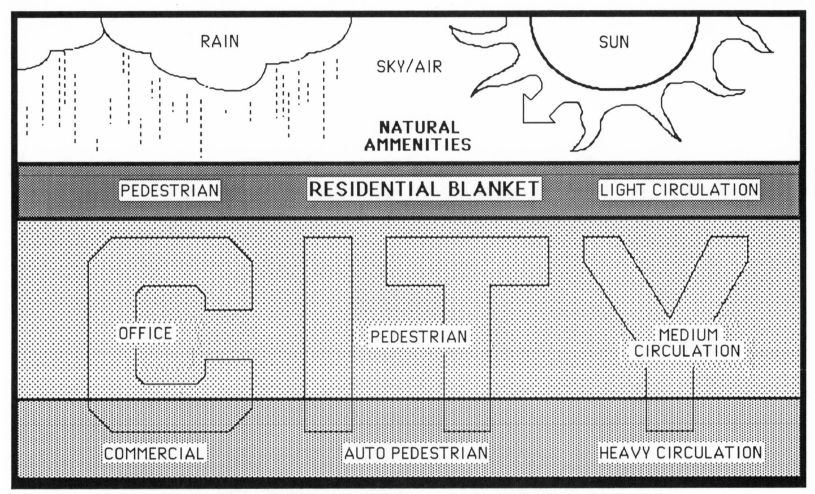

RAIN
SKY/AIR
SUN

NATURAL
AMMENITIES

PEDESTRIAN   RESIDENTIAL BLANKET   LIGHT CIRCULATION

OFFICE   PEDESTRIAN   MEDIUM CIRCULATION

COMMERCIAL   AUTO PEDESTRIAN   HEAVY CIRCULATION

CITY STRUCTURE ABSTRACTION
WITH APPLICATION OF RESIDENTIAL BLANKET

People belong on top of the city: to take advantage of exposure to the natural amenities, to be removed from the intense activity of the city floor, and to take advantage of the view, sky, sun and air. The **residential blanket** does not interrupt the existing conduct of the city.

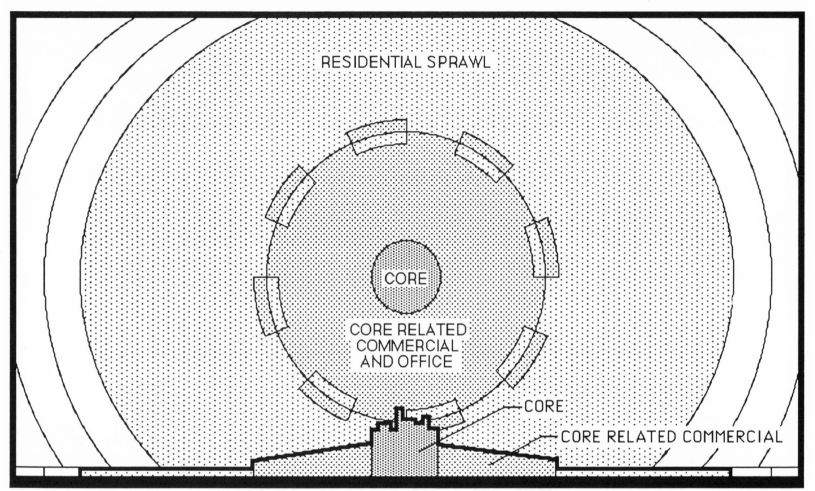

RESIDENTIAL SPRAWL

CORE

CORE RELATED
COMMERCIAL
AND OFFICE

CORE

CORE RELATED COMMERCIAL

CITY ABSTRACTION
PLAN AND SECTION OF TYPICAL CITY

Because of the sprawling structure of existing residential areas around our cities, almost as much land is eaten up by suburban streets as by housing. This consumes much more land and consequently puts people farther from the city core.

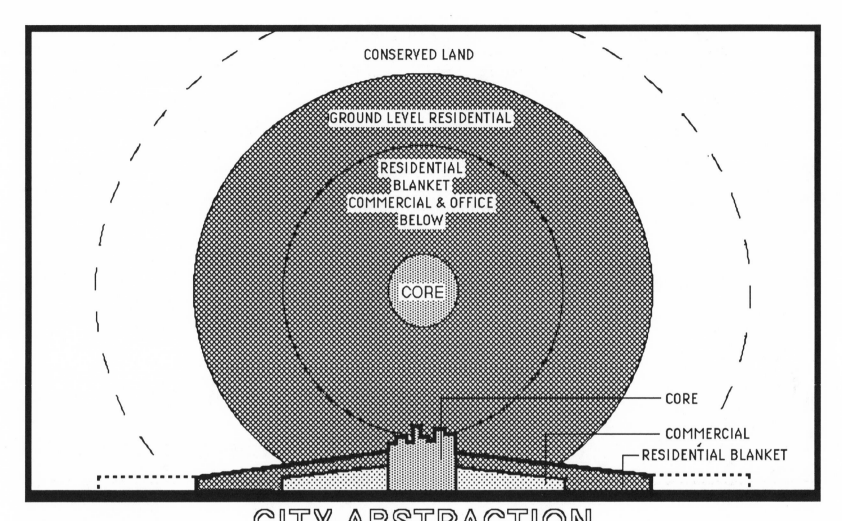

CONSERVED LAND

GROUND LEVEL RESIDENTIAL

RESIDENTIAL
BLANKET
COMMERCIAL & OFFICE
BELOW

CORE

CORE

COMMERCIAL

RESIDENTIAL BLANKET

CITY ABSTRACTION
PLAN AND SECTION SHOWING CONSERVING EFFECTS OF RESIDENTIAL BLANKET

The same amount of housing units offering the same amenities can be blanketed *over* the commercial and office space. The stepped and overlapped system which can be used has a condensing affect. With this type of blanket system, a great amount of land can be conserved which would otherwise be used for suburban sprawl. The city is revitalized as people are able to live closer to and make use of the existing facilities of the city core.

The previous proposals would constitute a concept for a <u>land assemblage super structure</u> right in the heart of the city, into which independent **Earthship** type dwellings would be injected.

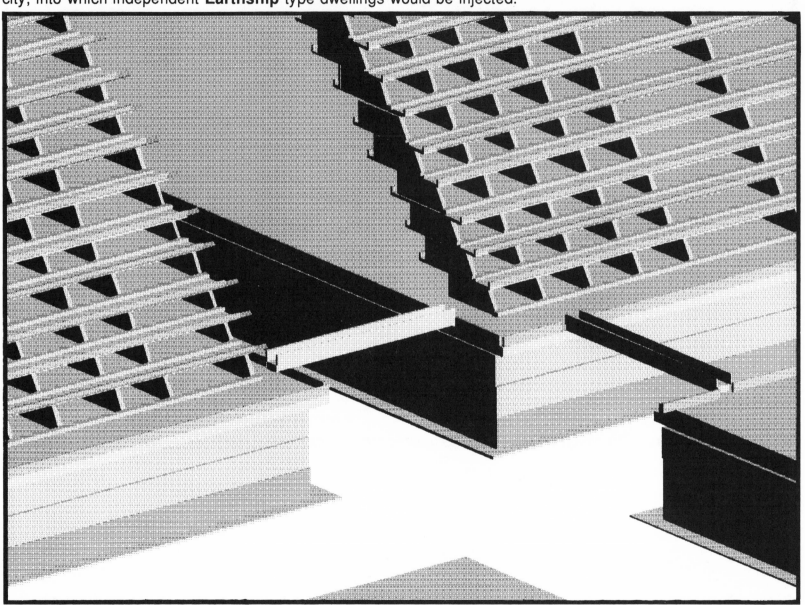

The super structure would be placed in the city but its nature would be such that it would offer the coveted amenities of suburban life. It would simplify the initial construction of units in that two surfaces of volume would already be present (top and bottom). Structural support and auto/pedestrian access would be immediately available at each site. The definition of the unit itself (based on rural Earthship systems, components and technique) would be all that is required. If this scheme were used on a large-scale in several cities the *original superstructure* or various forms of it could be identically repeated in every city without being monotonous or stereotyped as the Earthship dwelling infill would make each superstructure one of a kind.

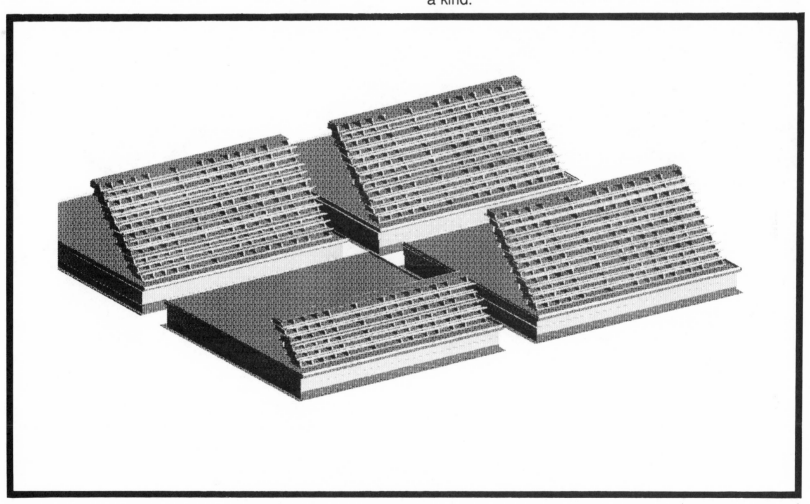

193

The type and character of the dwellings that are injected into the residential blanket would determine the final appearance of each intra-city community.

Thus every city could have its own identical series of "land assemblage" plans and specifications. The construction of the "land assemblage" would become as common as highway construction.

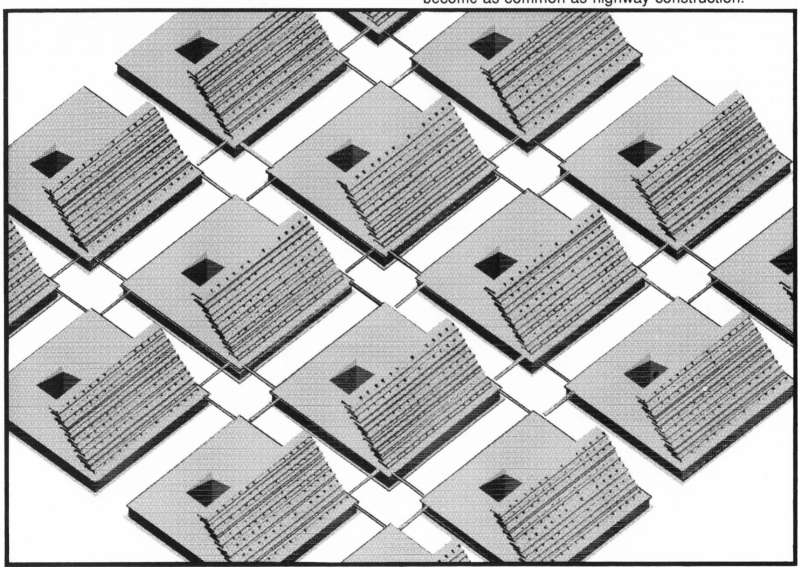

Earthship dwelling elements or components would be mass produced to specifications relating to the "land assemblage" superstructure just as autos are mass produced to specifications relating to our highways. Techniques would evolve unique to this situation but the results would be the same as rural Earthships - independent earth and user friendly dwellings.

In addition to residential sites being sold or leased individually, "land parcels" from the residential blanket (or the commercial volumes below) could be sold or leased in any quantity to private developers. This concept simply increases the permanent re-usable land area available to sell or lease to the public in an existing city block. The permanent and re-usable qualities of the "land assemblage" would insure its eventual cost return.

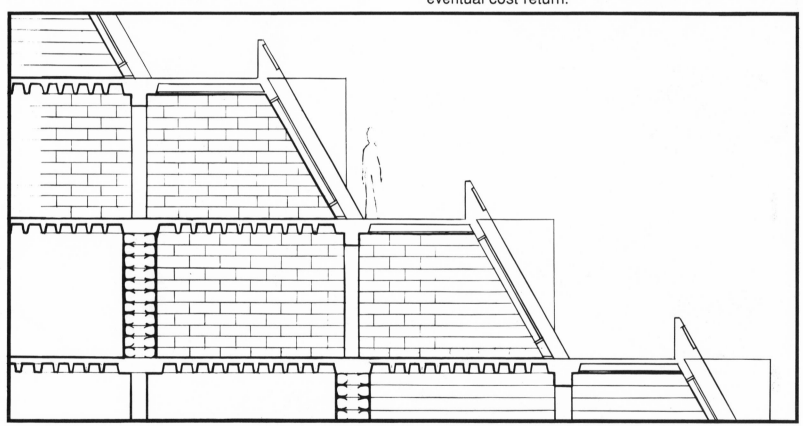

195

EARTHSHIP SUPER-STRUCTURE NEAR CITY CORE.

PART FOUR
1993 NEW DIRECTIONS

10. A BUILDING CODE FOR BEARING AND RETAINING WALLS MADE FROM EARTH-RAMMED TIRES

IN EARTHSHIP VOLUME I WE PRESENTED A METHOD OF BUILDING LIVING MODULES FROM DISCARDED AUTOMOBILE TIRES RAMMED WITH EARTH. OVER THE TWENTY TWO YEARS OF DEVELOPMENT AND RESEARCH, WE HAVE COME TO THE OPINION THAT THIS METHOD FAR EXCEEDS ANY OTHER KNOWN BUILDING TECHNIQUE WITH REGARD TO THERMAL, STRUCTURAL, ENVIRONMENTAL, AND AVAILABILITY ASPECTS. OUR BOOKS ARE AIMED AT MAKING THIS CONCEPT PHYSICALLY AVAILABLE TO OWNER BUILDERS. IF THE METHODS PUT FORTH IN THESE BOOKS ARE FOLLOWED, THE RESULT IS A VERY "SUBSTANTIAL LIVING MODULE".   HOWEVER, IF THE CONCEPT IS USED BUT NOT EXECUTED COMPETENTLY WITH APPROPRIATE RESPECT FOR AND UNDERSTANDING OF THE NATURE OF THE MATERIAL, AN UNSAFE BUILDING CAN BE THE RESULT. THIS IS TRUE OF ANY BUILDING TECHNIQUE. THIS IS WHY WE HAVE BUILDING INSPECTORS. THESE BUILDING INSPECTORS HAVE A CODE (THE UNIFORM BUILDING CODE - UBC) TO FOLLOW. THIS CODE PROVIDES CRITERIA FOR AN INSPECTOR TO RELATE TO IN DETERMINING WHETHER A PARTICULAR BUILDING TECHNIQUE IS BEING EXECUTED SAFELY OR NOT. THE PURPOSE OF THIS BUILDING CODE FOR BEARING AND RETAINING WALLS MADE FROM EARTH-RAMMED TIRES IS TO PROVIDE THAT SAME KIND OF CRITERIA FOR AN INSPECTOR TO RELATE TO IN DETERMINING WHETHER A TIRE BUILDING IS BEING EXECUTED SAFELY OR NOT. ANY BUILDING TECHNIQUE CAN BE EXECUTED IN A COMPETENT MANNER OR AN INCOMPETENT MANNER. TIRE BEARING WALLS AND THE PERIPHERAL DETAILS ARE NO EXCEPTION. THIS CODE WILL BE AIMED AT BOTH THE INSPECTOR AND THE BUILDERS AS A CLEAR SIMPLE PRESENTATION OF TIRE CONSTRUCTION STANDARDS ("DOS AND DON'TS") THAT MUST BE FOLLOWED TO INSURE A SUCCESSFUL, SAFE, COMFORTABLE BUILDING. IT IS OUR HOPE THAT VARIOUS STATES WILL ADOPT THIS CODE AS THEY MOVE INTO THE ERA OF THE USE OF AUTOMOBILE TIRE CASINGS FOR THE CONSTRUCTION OF BUILDINGS HERE IN THE LATER PART OF THE TWENTIETH CENTURY.

The walls are really the only aspect of a tire building that is significantly unconventional. The roof and floors use conventional materials and are covered by the existing Uniform Building Code. Therefore a thorough presentation of the **standards for bearing and retaining walls made from automobile tire casings rammed with earth** will be used as a guide to those whose job it is to inspect tire buildings for structural integrity, safety and quality.

1. TIRE SIZES USED IN BEARING AND RETAINING WALLS

Automobile tires come in sizes called 13, 14, 15 and 16. These sizes relate to the radius of the tire in inches, #13 tires being the smallest tires used in a bearing or a retaining wall and #16 tires being the largest. These sizes will be specified in different parts of the structure as such.

2. TIRE WALL AS FOUNDATION

In that a tire wall is already wider than its required foundation, it becomes a monolith which is both wall and foundation (see EARTHSHIP VOL. 1 pp. 65-66).

A. The first course of tires of any tire wall must be leveled and dug into undisturbed soil free of organic surface matter such as plants, tree roots or other bio-degradable substances.

B. The first course of tires must be as large in diameter or larger in diameter than any other tire in the wall. No tire may appear in a wall that is larger in diameter than the tires on the ground course of that wall.

C. Tire walls over six courses high must have a ground course of tires #15 or larger exclusively.

3. COURSING

A. All tire walls must use staggered running bond coursing.

B. Joints between tires on any given course must be aligned with the central area of all tires on courses above and below. No joint between tires on any given course may align with any joint on the courses above or below.

C. Half tire techniques as outlined in article 4 must be used to maintain running bond coursing.

4. HALF TIRE TECHNIQUES

A. WOOD HALF TIRES

Wood half tires are outlined in EARTHSHIP VOL. I pp. 95-97. Wood half tires must be treated with two coats of wood preservative and wrapped in two layers of six mill plastic when they occur on outside walls. Breather slits must be slashed into the <u>inside surface</u> of all wrapped wood half tires occuring in exterior tire walls. Wood half tires must be treated with two coats of wood preservative with no plastic wrapping when used on inside walls. Wood half tires must be wired to the adjacent tires in their particular course as per EARTHSHIP VOL I pp. 95-97.

B. CONCRETE HALF TIRES

Concrete half tires must use a mix of 3 parts cement-4 parts sand-5 parts gravel with engineering fibers. All tires adjacent to concrete half blocks must be porcupined (see EARTHSHIP VOL III pp. 2-4) with 16d nails to lock concrete to tires. In that concrete half tires are the most substantial half tire method, they will be specified in some situations by the architect. All two story tire wall applications will use concrete half tires.

C. RAMMED EARTH HALF TIRES
Rammed earth half tires are described in EARTHSHIP VOL III p. 5. Rammed earth half tires can be used only in tire walls five courses high or less and never at the end of a wall.

5.   BEARING WALLS
A. Bearing walls built from earth rammed automobile tire casings must follow articles 1 through 4 of this code.

B.   All bearing walls built from earth rammed automobile tire casings must have a continuous bond beam of wood or concrete as described in EARTHSHIP VOL I pp. 101-103 or EARTHSHIP VOL III pp. 6-9.

C. All bearing walls eight courses or higher for their entire length built from earth rammed automobile tire casings must have a continuous bond beam that connects to a continuous bond beam on adjacent non bearing tire walls.

6.   RETAINING WALLS
A.   All retaining walls built from earth rammed automobile tires must follow articles 1 through 4 of this code.

B. All retaining walls built from earth rammed automobile tire casings must be stepped back or lean into the earth they are retaining.

C. Specifications and construction drawings certified by a licensed architect must appear in the stamped construction drawings for the permitted building for all retaining walls built from earth rammed automobile tire casings.

7.   FREE STANDING WALLS
DEFINITION - Any wall not tied into the roof structure of a building.

A. All free standing walls built from earth rammed automobile tire casings must follow articles 1 through 4 of this code.

B. All free standing walls over 2 courses high built from earth rammed automobile tire casings must have continuous arcs built into the design of the wall. These walls cannot be straight for any distance.

C.   Free standing walls built of earth rammed automobile tire casings cannot be over 5 courses high unless designed by an architect and certified specifications and construction drawings are provided for that wall.

8.   PLATES AND BOND BEAMS
A. All tire walls that are an integral part of the roofed building shall have a **continuous** wood or concrete bond beam. This bond beam shall be anchored to the tire wall with 1/2" anchor bolts set in concrete every other tire or 1/2" rebar driven down through

three courses of tires and bent over the top of the wood plate or set in the concrete bond beam.

B. Wood bond beam plates shall be no less than four inches thick and twelve inches wide. Wood bond beam plates can be made up of (2) 2 x 12 's with 6 mil plastic between the rammed earth tire wall and the wood bond beam plate. The bottom bond beam plate must be treated lumber. Joints in the lower layer of lumber shall never be closer than 2'-0" away from joints in the upper layer of lumber. Upper and lower layers of lumber shall be laminated with (6) 16d nails per running foot.

C. Concrete bond beams shall be a minimum of 8"deep x 8"wide and have two pieces of 1/2" rebar continuous.

9. OPENINGS IN WALLS
A. All openings in walls made of earth rammed automobile tires shall have concrete half blocks on either side of the opening.

B. The wood or concrete bond beam spanning the opening shall be increased in thickness by a minimum of 8". This additional thickness shall extend on either side of the opening a minimum of 2'-4" and shall set on and be anchored to a concrete bearing block equivalent in thickness to the tire coursing height.

10. TWO STORY
A. All two story earth rammed tire structures shall be designed by a licensed architect or engineer.

B. A continuous 9" deep x 2'-0" wide concrete bond beam must occur at each floor level.

C. All tires on the first level must be #15 or larger.

D. All tires on the second level must be #14 or smaller.

E. All blocking must be concrete.

F. All void packing on the first floor level walls must be concrete.

G. All earth rammed tire work must follow articles 1 through 4 of this code.

11. LENGTH OF WALLS
A. In that rammed earth tire walls are not made of a rigid material that is sensitive to expansion and contraction cracks, there is no limit on the length of a earth rammed tire wall.

12. HEIGHT OF WALLS
A. The maximum height for a straight earth rammed tire wall which is an integral part of a structure with a roof or floor load is 10 feet. At this point a wood or concrete bond beam must be installed as per article 8 of this code.

B. The maximum height for a circular earth rammed tire wall which is an integral part of a structure with a roof or floor load is 12 feet. At this point a wood or concrete bond beam must be installed as per article 8 of this code.

C. The maximum height for a free standing earth rammed tire wall that is not a curved or a battered retaining wall or otherwise structurally integrated into a building is 6 feet.

D. There is no maximum height for a battered retaining wall constructed from earth rammed tires. All battered retaining walls must be engineered by a licensed architect or engineer.

13. LOADING OF WALLS

A. Loading on earth rammed tire walls must be **distributed loading** only from joists, beams or rafters setting on a continuous wood or concrete bond beam as per article 8 of this code.

B. **No point or collected loading** is possible on earth rammed tire walls unless special engineering is provided by a licensed engineer or architect.

C. The limits of the **evenly distributed** load an earth rammed tire wall can accept are determined by the bearing capacity of the soil that the earth rammed tire wall is setting on. In cases where an earth rammed tire wall is setting on rock or a concrete foundation which is wider than the tire wall itself and more than typical roof or second story loading is desired, the bearing capacity of the tire wall will be determined by a licensed architect or engineer.

14. FILL OF WALLS

A. Earth rammed tires walls can be filled or rammed with any type of earth, clay, sand or rock fill.

B. All tire casings must be packed tight to 90% compaction with a 6# to 9# sledge hammer. Soft spongy tire packing is not acceptable.

15. VOID FILLING

A. All voids between tires in earth rammed tire walls must be packed solid with mud in a four coat procedure described in Earthship Volume I pages 174-175 unless specific conditions require this packing to be done with concrete as per article 10 of this code.

16. EARTH CLIFFS

A. All Earth cliffs shall be 12" minimum from an earth rammed tire wall.

B. All earth cliffs shall be approved as a result of site and soil inspection by a licensed architect or engineer.

C. Earth cliffs can only occur under non bearing earth rammed tire walls or walls only loaded from one side such as east or west end walls.

17. JOINTS

A. All joints and connections in earth rammed tire walls must must be designed and assembled in such a way so that no voids occur within the earth rammed tire wall. These voids must be filled with concrete or 90% compacted earth contained in a double layer of metal lath or a rubber tire casing.

B. All joints and connections in earth rammed tire walls must employ over lapped tires and joining methods so as not to result in stacked joints occuring over each other.

The regulations for earth rammed tire construction put forth in this code are a guideline relating to structure only and are subject to evolution, refinement, and addendum.

11. THE SURVIVAL POD

THE EARTHSHIP CONCEPT HAS TAKEN SOME FAIRLY RADICAL IDEAS AND EVOLVED THEM INTO A FORM THAT IS PALATABLE TO THE MAJORITY OF THE POPULATION, CONSIDERING THE GRIP OF EXISTING CODES, REGULATIONS, TRADITIONS AND DOGMA. WE THEREFORE STILL USE SOME CONVENTIONAL TECHNIQUES AND MATERIALS LIKE WOOD TRUSSES, FIBERGLASS INSULATION, MODIFIED BITUMEN ROOFING, ETC. AS WE HAVE VENTURED AROUND THE WORLD WITH THE EARTHSHIP CONCEPT WE HAVE OBSERVED THAT IN MANY COUNTRIES WOOD IS SOMETIMES SCARCE AND IS GETTING EXPENSIVE FOR ALL OF US. CONVENTIONAL INSULATION AND ROOFING MATERIALS ARE ALSO HARD TO FIND. **ALUMINUM CANS**, **AUTOMOBILE TIRES** AND **CONCRETE** HOWEVER, SEEM TO BE *EVERYWHERE*. WE DECIDED TO RESPOND TO THIS OBSERVATION WITH A *MORE RADICAL FORM OF THE EARTHSHIP CONCEPT* THAT USES LESS WOOD, NO CONVENTIONAL INSULATION, AND NO MANUFACTURED ROOFING MATERIALS. THESE MATERIALS ARE REPLACED WITH YET MORE RECYCLED BY-PRODUCTS OF THE 21ST CENTURY AND CONCRETE. THIS MORE RADICAL EARTHSHIP WOULD BE, IN TERMS OF INITIAL MATERIALS, CHEAPER THAN THE ORIGINAL EARTHSHIP BUT LESS ACCEPTABLE TO CODES AND REGULATIONS. THERE ARE PLACES (3RD WORLD COUNTRIES) AND SITUATIONS (PEOPLE WITH A LOT OF TIME AND NO MONEY) WHERE THIS APPROACH WOULD HAVE SOME MERIT. WE PRESENT THE SURVIVAL POD, AN ALMOST TOTALLY RECYCLED BUILDING.

Graphics by Claire Blanchard

We were asked specifically in Europe and Bolivia to try to extend the recycling thinking of the basic Earthship a little farther into its *rather conventional roof structures*. The survival pod eliminates the wood beams and/or trusses for roof structure. We have been working with aluminum can/cement domes for many years (see Earthship Volume II, Chapter 11). These domes did not, however, lend themselves to the "U" shaped roofing needs nor the catch water needs. Insulation for these domes has also been an expensive spray-on high-tech problem in the past. We sometimes used double domes with insulation in the middle of the two domes but this was also expensive in that we had to build two domes just to achieve insulation (see Earthship Volume II, p. 213).

In an effort to address these issues, we took the tire "U" and molded it into more of a circle so it would receive a dome.

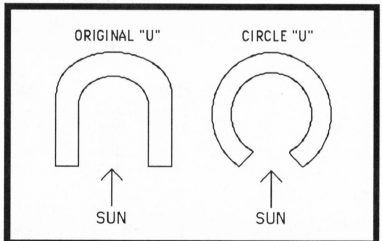

We find this to be satisfactory as the more narrow south opening of the circle could be closed off with glass doors to shut the space off from heat loss through the greenhouse at night. This compensated for the somewhat lower amount of heat gain during the day.

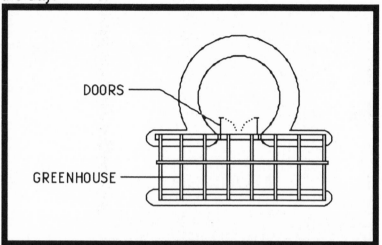

Now with the circular shape we could apply a dome made of aluminum cans and cement (see Earthship Volume II, p. 213). These domes are primarily *perforated cement* domes *formed* with cans. They take more time to build than wood structures but only one skill, minimal tools, and one purchased material - cement. *Concrete domes can be very dangerous if not executed properly.* Consult Earthship Volume II chapter 11 and SSA or an engineer before you proceed. The dome closes with a skylight "turtleneck" at the top and sits on a continuous can/concrete bond beam (see Earthship Volume II, pp. 220-221 and page 165 this Chapter).

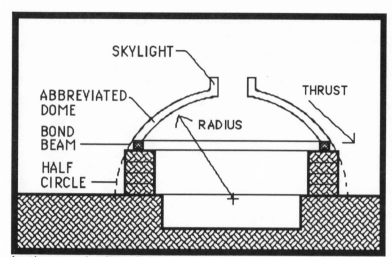

SKYLIGHT

ABBREVIATED DOME

THRUST

BOND BEAM

RADIUS

HALF CIRCLE

In the survival pod we use an abbreviated dome - not a full half circle. This creates more thrust at the point where it joins the tire circle, hence the structural concrete bond beam. We have a slight slope on this bond beam to receive this thrust.

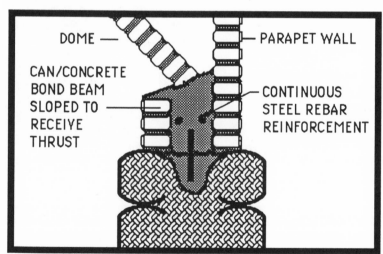

DOME

PARAPET WALL

CAN/CONCRETE BOND BEAM SLOPED TO RECEIVE THRUST

CONTINUOUS STEEL REBAR REINFORCEMENT

Now we have a room enclosed using no wood.

How do we insulate this room in a low tech way with recycled materials and few skills? We take another aluminum can parapet wall up off the bond beam around the edge of the dome.

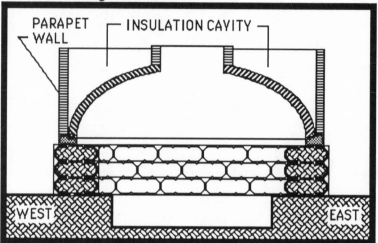

PARAPET WALL

INSULATION CAVITY

WEST   EAST

This creates a cavity for insulation. Many different recycled insulations can be used. If you're in a city, use shredded paper. If you're in the country, use straw. Do not use hay as it may spontaneously combust. If you're near a saw mill use *dry* saw dust. Keep all recycled and organic materials dry or they will compost and become a fire hazard. Other possibilities are scrap stryrofoam, pumice, cloth, etc. This cavity must be lined, before filling, with 6 mil plastic for a typical vapor barrier and after filling, another layer of plastic is advised.

Notice that the can wall forming the cavity is shorter on the south side. This is so the eventual roof covering the cavity can slope to the south for catch water purposes.

208

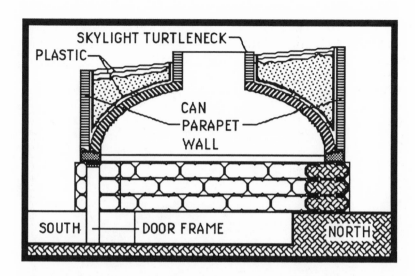

The roof can be made by stretching regular steel rebar from the "turtle neck" of the skylight opening to the can parapet wall around the dome.

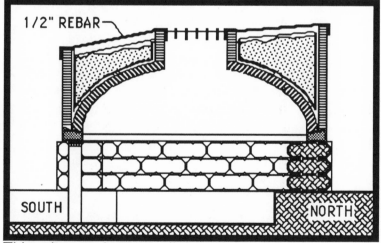

This rebar spokes out all the way around the dome.

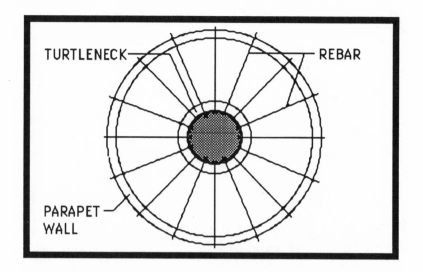

This is then covered with metal lath or a double layer of chicken wire and plastered with 4 coats of regular cement plaster with engineering fibers, scratched after each coat. The final smooth (troweled) coat of plaster can be painted with what ever is available. We use regular latex or an acrylic base paint (see appendix this chapter) to catch clear water.

You now have a **survival pod** using nothing but concrete and recycled free materials. A typical Earthship greenhouse structure can be leaned up against this unit with systems integrated accordingly.

FORMING THE INSULATION CAVITY OF THE CAN DOME

210

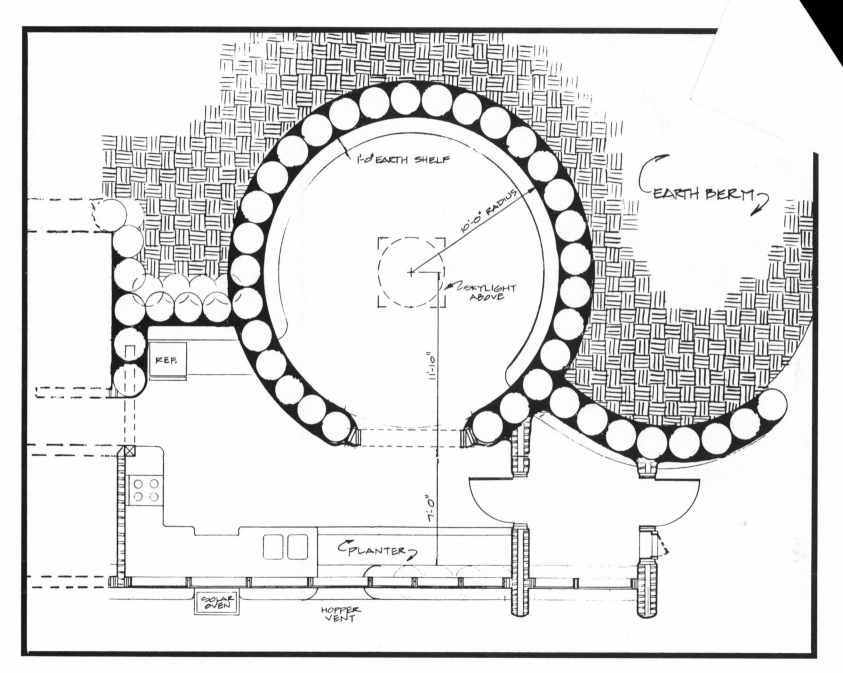

1'-0" EARTH SHELF

EARTH BERM

10'-0" RADIUS

SKYLIGHT ABOVE

11'-10"

7'-0"

REF.

PLANTER

SOLAR OVEN

HOPPER VENT

211

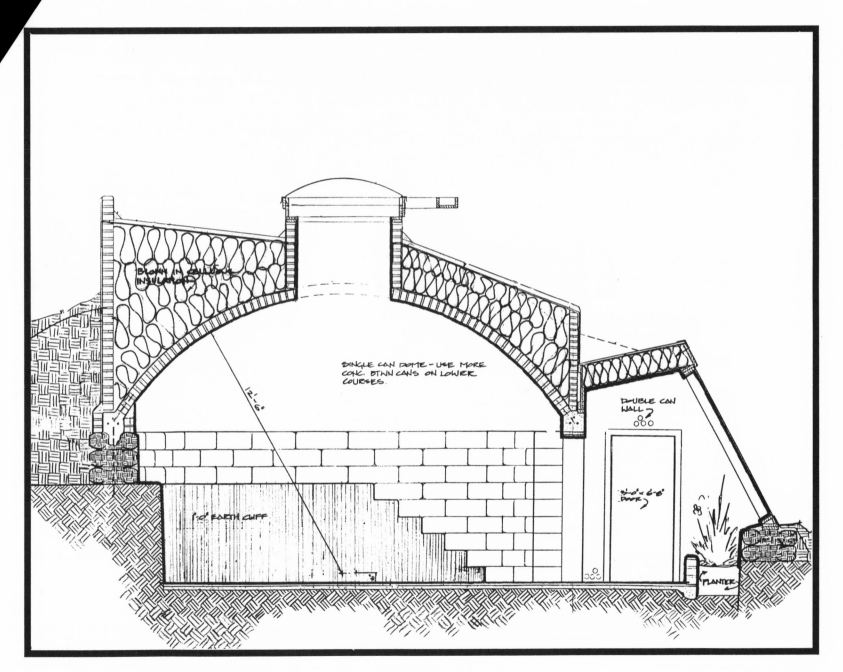

BLOWN IN CELLULOSE INSULATION

SINGLE CAN DOME - USE MORE CONC. BTWN CANS ON LOWER COURSES.

12'-6"

DOUBLE CAN WALL

3'-0" x 6'-8" DOOR

1'-0" EARTH CLIFF

PLANTER

212

This unit can be built almost anywhere on the globe with "local" materials and local unskilled labor. It can certainly be owner built and moved into before (or without) the greenhouse. Many pods of varying diameters can be linked together with a typical Earthship greenhouse.

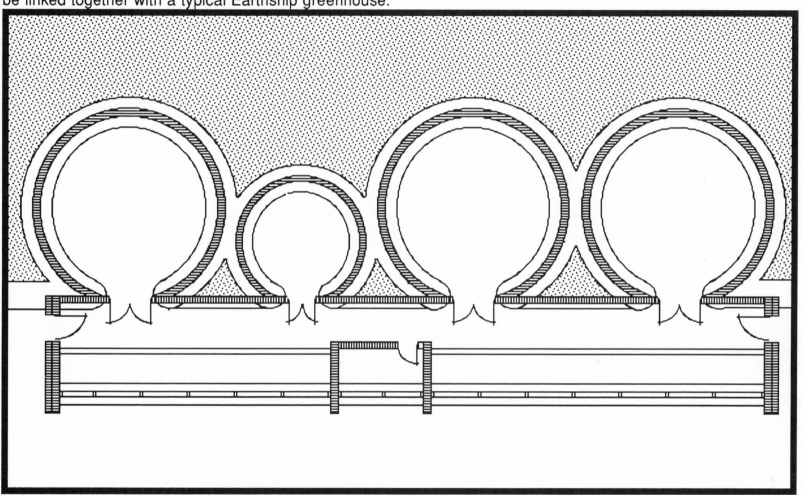

It is truly a cellular "natural" home with by-products that we humans discard from our daily lives.

EARTHSHIP IN JAPAN SHOWING KNITTED IN CONCRETE POST AND BEAM FOR EARTHQUAKE DESIGN

214

12. CLIMATIC ADAPTATIONS

A FOUR WHEEL DRIVE TRUCK DESIGNED FOR STEEP MOUNTAIN ROADS IS AN AUTOMOBILE POWERED BY A GASOLINE ENGINE. A PORSCHE DESIGNED TO GO 200 MPH IS ALSO AN AUTOMOBILE POWERED BY A GASOLINE ENGINE. THESE ARE BOTH TWO DIFFERENT ADAPTATIONS OF THE SAME CONCEPT - *THE AUTOMOBILE*. THE EARTHSHIP CONCEPT - AN INDEPENDENT DWELLING VESSEL CONSTRUCTED FROM TIRES RAMMED WITH EARTH - DESIGNED TO MAINTAIN TEMPERATURE AND HARVEST ENERGY AND WATER FROM ITS IMMEDIATE ENVIRONMENT - IS ALSO CAPABLE OF MANY DIFFERENT ADAPTATIONS. THESE ADAPTATIONS WILL GEAR THE PERFORMANCE OF THE VESSEL TO THE DEMANDS OF ITS LOCAL CLIMATE. IN SOME CLIMATES THE TEMPERATURE CONTAINED BY THE MASSIVE WALLS WILL BE WARMER THAN THE OUTSIDE AND SOLAR ENERGY WILL BE ADMITTED AND STORED. IN OTHER SITUATIONS THE TEMPERATURE OF THE MASSIVE WALLS WILL BE COOLER THAN OUTSIDE AS THEY ABSORB TEMPERATURES FROM THE COOL EVENING AIR AND THE EARTH ITSELF. THE SOLAR ENERGY IN THIS CASE IS BLOCKED WHILE BREEZES AND UNDER GROUND TEMPERATURES ARE ADMITTED. THIS CHAPTER WILL EXPLORE THE VARIOUS WAYS THE EARTHSHIP AND ALL THE SURROUNDING EARTHSHIP HARDWARE IS APPLIED TO RADICALLY DIFFERENT CLIMATES AND SITUATIONS.

Graphics by Claire Blanchard

The principals of an Earthship "U" module are explained in concept in Earthship Volume I. How and why it works and how it evolved are presented there. The evolution of that "U" is presented in this Volume. We have now the high performance generic "U" module.

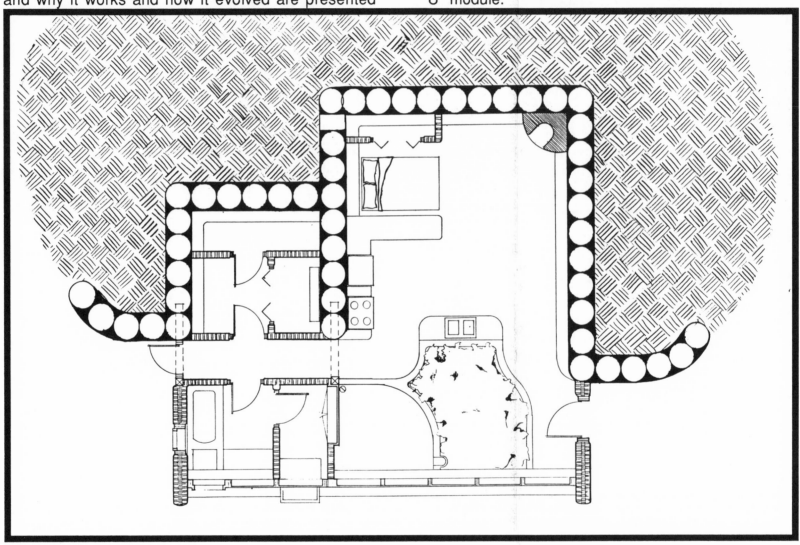

216

If you take a Porsche up into the mountains on a rutted steep muddy road you will be in trouble. This is not the fault of the Porsche. It is the fault of the foolish, ignorant, ill-informed driver who drove it up there. The misuse of an Earthship is just as easy and (to those of us who deal with them everyday) seems just as foolish. The important issue here is that the owner/builders must be aware that **the use of the Earthship concept does require some tailoring to site and climatic specifics.**

While we can provide generic drawings for the modules, we must advise that owner/builders solicit the guidance and counsel of Solar Survival Architecture relative to what modifications are necessary for a specific site or climate. A Porsche is a dream car but it can be a very disappointing experience if you purchased it thinking you could drive it on logging roads in the mountains. You must get the right vehicle for the road you intend to travel on. Likewise, get the right Earthship for the land you intend to build on.

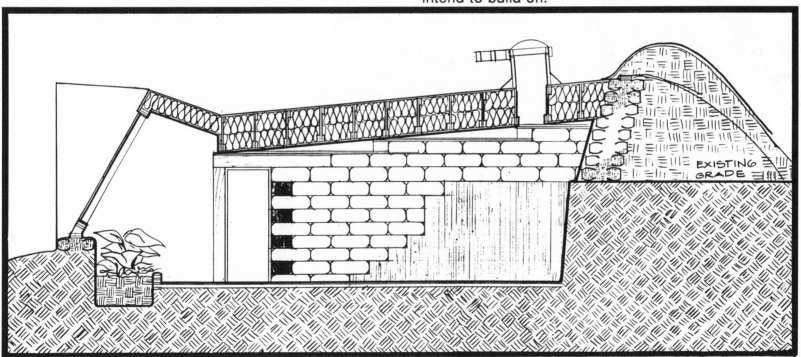

This high performance generic "U" module is designed for 100 degree summers and below zero winters in a generally arid climate (10" total precipitation per year) with reasonably stable soil. Lets take this typical "U" module through several site and climate variations and watch how it adapts. Because of the modular approach - once you understand how to build and/or adapt a single "U" - you can build and adapt the whole home.

UNSTABLE SOIL

All site and climatic conditions are the same as discussed on the previous page for a basic generic "U" except *the soil is unstable*. The solution is simple. Do not use earth cliffs. Excavate down as low as you want but take the tires to the <u>bottom</u> of this excavation, i.e. all the way down to floor level.

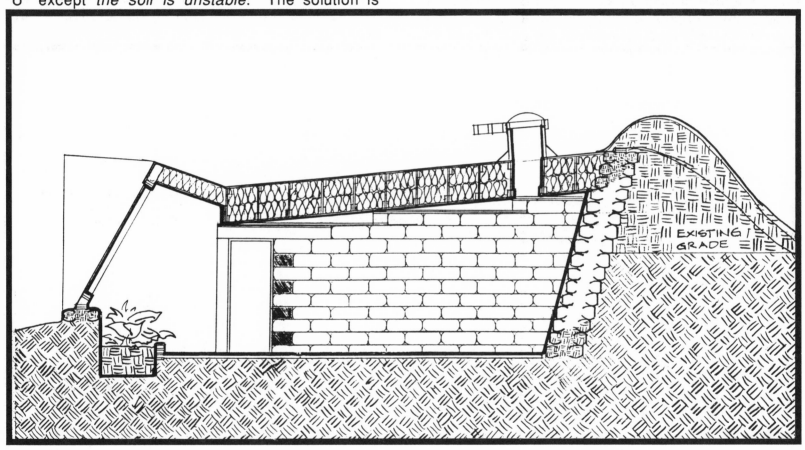

EXISTING GRADE

218

MOIST SOIL - WET CLIMATE - MARSHY LAND

This situation requires that the Earthship be built entirely above ground on a built up base. This base should be machine compacted to 95%. In this situation there is no displaced soil for a complete burial so soil may have to be brought from another location. Then berm against the building as high as you can and insulate and plaster the rest. The rigid insulation goes down below the burial level 2 to 4 feet depending on the depth of the frost line in your area.

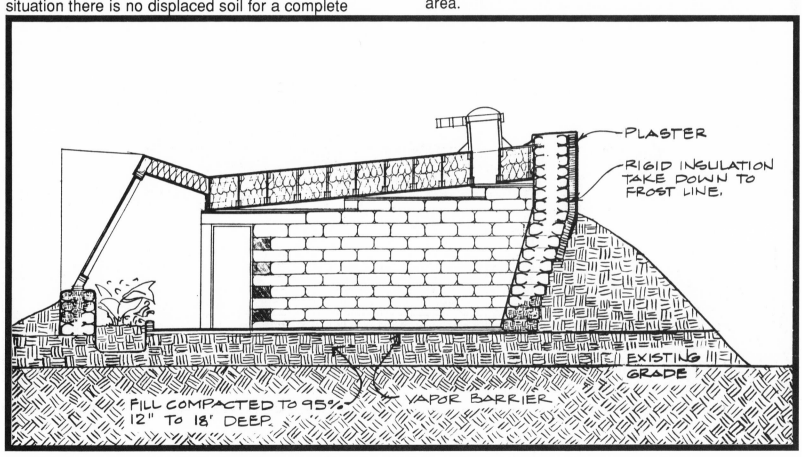

PLASTER

RIGID INSULATION TAKE DOWN TO FROST LINE.

EXISTING GRADE

VAPOR BARRIER

FILL COMPACTED TO 95%. 12" TO 18' DEEP.

EARTHQUAKE ZONES
In areas of the globe that require a structure that will withstand earthquakes the knitted in concrete columns that occur on the ends and corners of the tire walls meet this need. These concrete columns, shown in the above diagram and photograph on the following page, are reinforced with rebar and connect to a concrete bond beam.

EARTHSHIP IN JAPAN UNDER CONSTRUCTION SHOWING KNITTED IN CONCRETE COLUMNS

EXTREMELY COLD - NOT MUCH SUMMER

When there is no real summer and the frost line is more than 4'0" deep, <u>insulate your mass away from the earth</u> as the earth is not warm enough to help maintain the required comfort zone temperatures. In this situation there is no real advantage to going into the earth as it is not going to embrace you with warmth. It is best to build the vessel *on* the earth and completely insulate your mass away from the cold earth. Again as on page 213 there will not be any displaced earth for complete burial so insulation and plaster are required above the burial. This is more expensive than the generic totally buried approach but not as expensive as conventional techniques adapted to the same conditions would be. In this situation it would also be advisable to insulate your mass away from the colder earth.

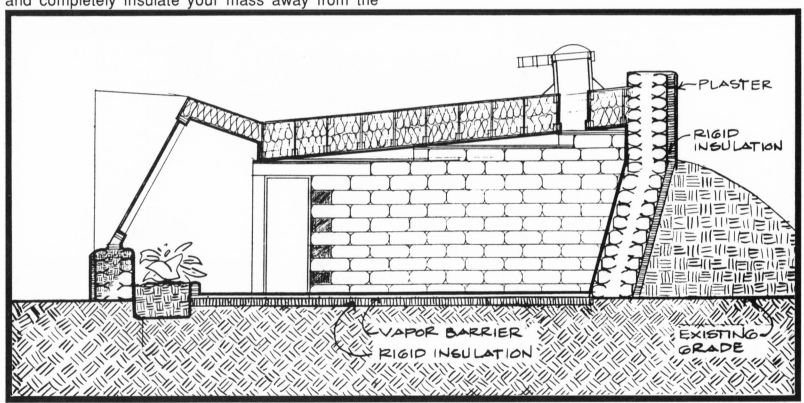

222

ANOTHER EXTREMELY WET OPTION

Some situations such as a sandy beach or a site near a stream that could swell would require a concrete foundation to elevate the structure above ground like any other building. In this situation you may not bury at all so a vertical rear wall can be used with rigid insulation and plaster. An arc is necessary in the rear wall if it is not buried.

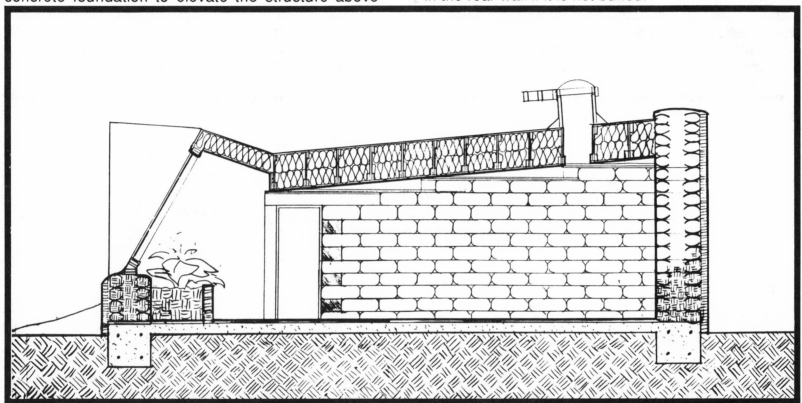

Tire walls are simply big round thermal mass bricks. They can be laid on concrete foundations like any other brick. 90% of the Earthship applications don't require this but it is an option. It is important to note - an Earthship can be built very similar to any other bearing wall building system.

However, no other system has the thermal mass capabilities of the Earthship and the Earthship has many options that conventional methods do not. The generic super economical application of the Earthship may not always be the best for certain situations. Having the need for concrete foundations does not mean you can't have an Earthship.

223

EXTREME WARM AND MOIST - HUMID

Warm, moist, humid climates do not require solar gain. They do not require sloped glass. Dampness could require a concrete foundation as on the previous page, or building on compacted fill as on page 213. Insulating away from the outside heat is necessary. Obviously you wouldn't sink the Earthship in the moist ground. You would enhance the ventilation (see Earthships Volume I, p. 45 and II pp. 146-147 for humidity control). The mass of the tire walls will still help maintain a cooler temperature and there is no easier, more durable thermal mass bearing wall than earth rammed tires. Higher ceilings are also best in this situation.

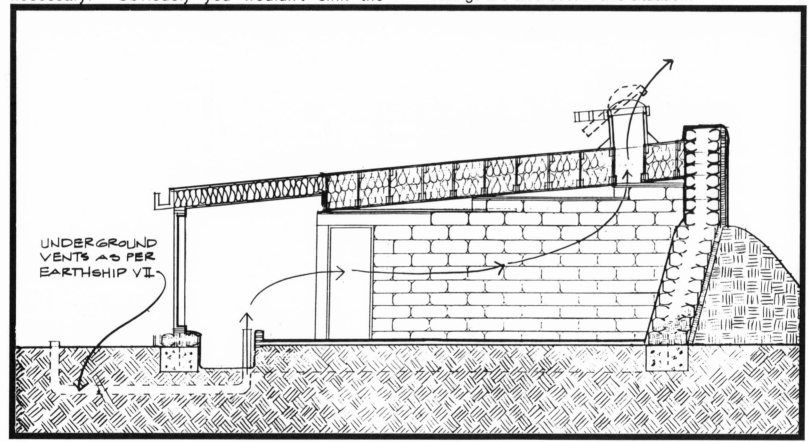

UNDERGROUND
VENTS AS PER
EARTHSHIP VII

Following is a floor plan for an Earthship in Hawaii using some of the above principles.

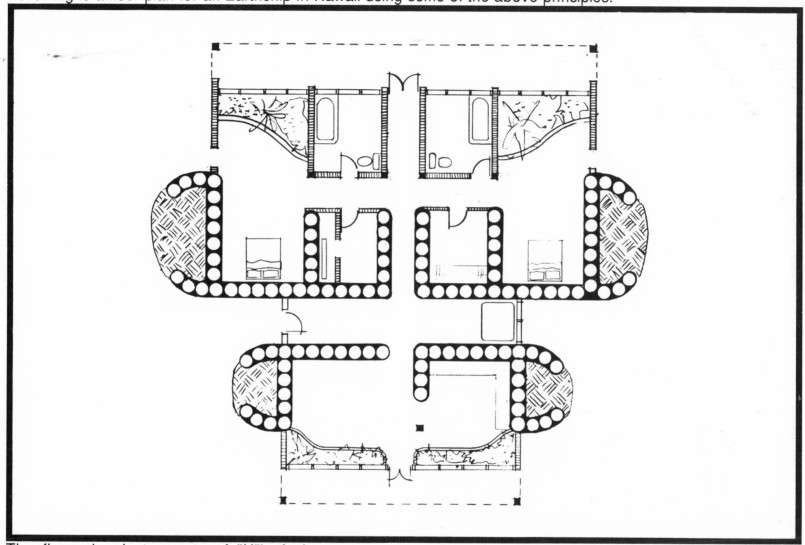

The floor plan is two sets of "U"'s facing out as glazing need not face any specific direction. The building is not buried in the earth due to the damp climate.

It may have concrete foundations under the tire walls. This would be determined by site inspection. The structural concept is still thermal mass "U"'s. Many generic details would apply.

225

HOT / DRY
In this situation going into the earth as far as possible would be advised to reach for the cool earth temperatures. Soil conditions would have to be checked for use of earthcliffs.

Insulation between the mass and the earth would not be necessary. Glazing could be vertical and the building would want to face north. Ventilation would be enhanced. (see Vol. I & II). Now lets introduce a new factor to the Earthship adaptations - wind. Many conventional homes have been blown away by hurricanes and tornados. In these areas, if your home was not blown away, you still could not use it because after these holocausts, gas and power are usually down and water and sewage lines are often damaged. The Earthship can address all these issues. We present THE HURRICANE HOME.

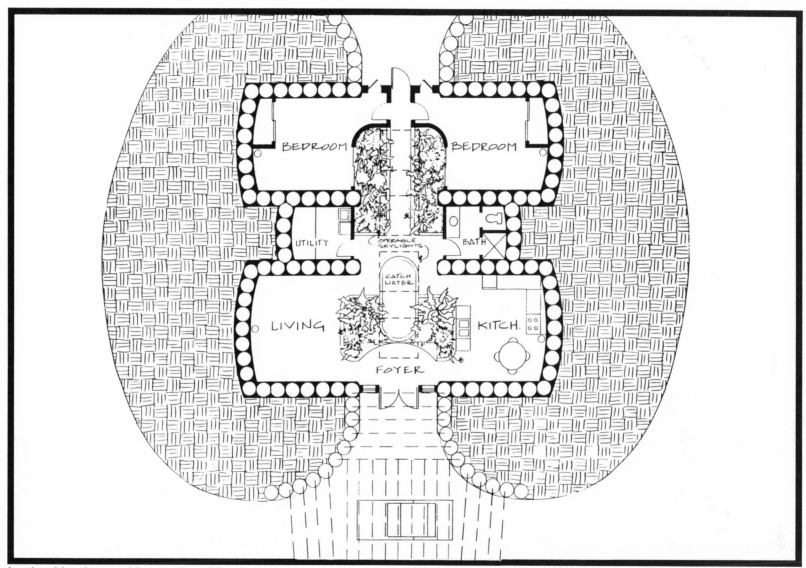

In the Hurricane Home the "U"s face in toward each other so the buried back walls face out to the wind. Large skylights accommodate the central greenhouse area.

Usually hurricanes occur in hot damp climates where solar gain is not required. It is more important to cool the structure than to heat it.

227

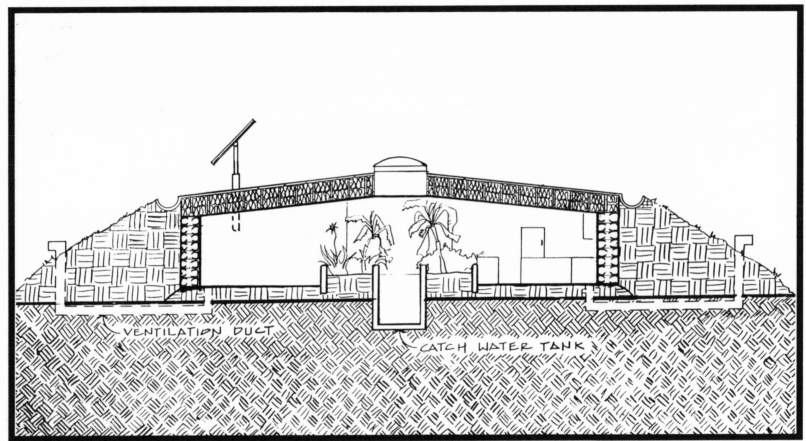

VENTILATION DUCT

CATCH WATER TANK

The "U"'s face inward so no glazing is vulnerable to wind. The building would most often be placed <u>on</u> the ground as most areas hit with hurricanes are wet. The burial would simply take the wind over the building. Completely protected against wind damage, solar panels for power are in a telescopic pipe to be lowered flat on the roof during high winds.

Catch water, solar power, grey water absorption and composting toilets would facilitate total operation of the home when all other homes, dependent on public utilities, would be useless. Gates could protect entrance ways from high winds. The building is elevated so high water would run out.

228

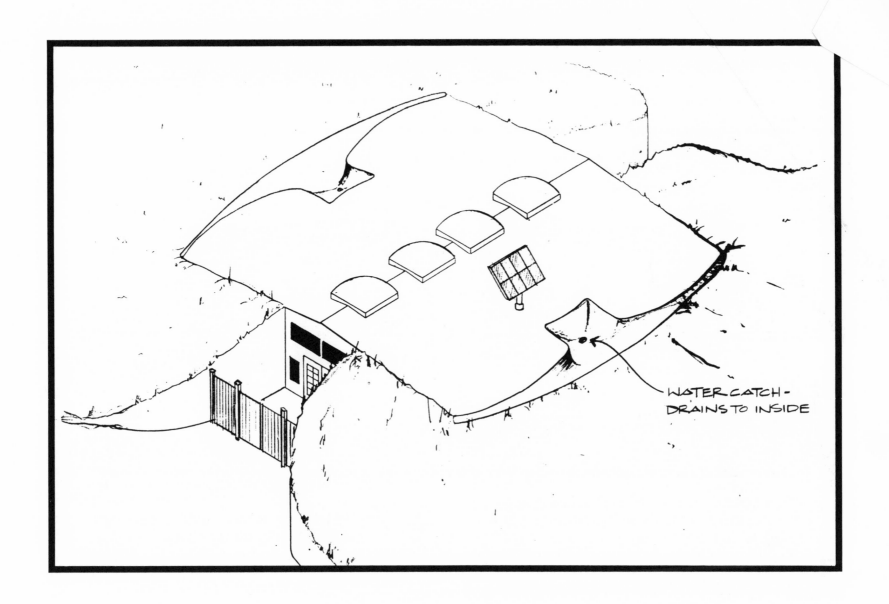

WATER CATCH -
DRAINS TO INSIDE

229

STEPPED APPLICATIONS
Sloped sites facing the sun are obviously the best for Earthships where solar gain is necessary. These sites introduced the option of stepping up the slope as presented in Volume I.

The most economical approach to this is to maintain the generic section and just repeat it in one of two ways. The easiest way is to place the upper level greenhouse wall over the lower level north wall.

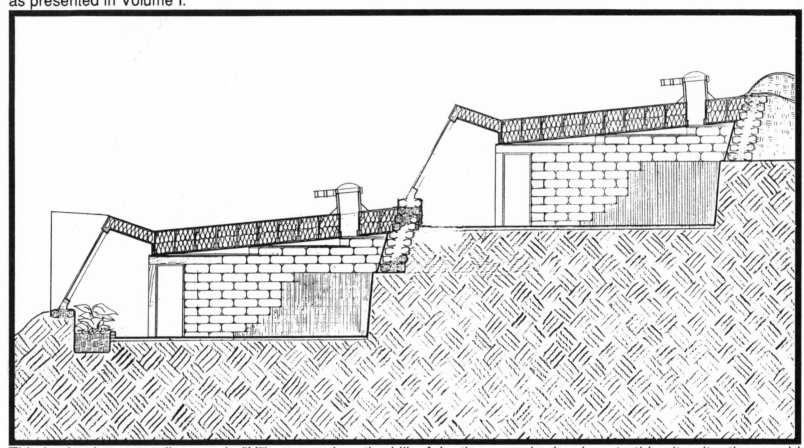

This is simply two totally generic "U"'s stepped up the hill. Adapting generic drawings to this site situation would be fairly easy. Stairs between levels can be carved up into the upper "U" as desired.

The other way is to overlap the "U"'s but try and maintain the generic slope.

This requires a major beam to carry the upper solar face and consequently some columns and footings. There are many other variations but the overlapped approach can get very customized, very quickly.

In any application of the Earthship concept where cost is a factor, the generic configuration must be maintained. Then just apply the various climatic adaptations. Don't try to drive in snow with highway tires.

GENERIC EARTHSHIP AT S.T.A.R. UNDER CONSTRUCTION

232

13. THE NEW GENERICS

THE EARTHSHIP CONCEPT AS PRESENTED IN EARTHSHIP VOLUME I (IN 1990) HAS PROVED TO BE A VIABLE WAY FOR PEOPLE TO BUILD THEIR OWN HOMES. MANY OF THE DETAILS AND METHODS HAVE EVOLVED AS PRESENTED IN PREVIOUS CHAPTERS OF THIS BOOK. HOWEVER THE BASIC "U" SHAPE (OPEN TO THE SUN FOR SOLAR GAIN) CONSTRUCTED OF AUTOMOBILE TIRES RAMMED WITH EARTH FOR THERMAL MASS HAS PREVAILED. THE EVOLUTIONS HAVE SIMPLY MADE IT EASIER AND CHEAPER TO CONSTRUCT, PERFORM EVEN BETTER AND MORE VERSATILE TO VARIOUS CLIMATES. MUCH OF OUR WORK IN THE PAST FEW YEARS HAS BEEN EVOLVING THE *SYSTEMS* THAT MAKE THE STRUCTURE INDEPENDENT. EARTHSHIP VOLUME II (1991) PRESENTED OUR EARLY EFFORTS AND CONCEPTS REGARDING THESE SYSTEMS. AS THESE SYSTEMS CONTINUED TO EVOLVE WE FOUND THAT (LIKE THE "U" MODULE CONCEPT ITSELF) THEY BEGAN TO DICTATE CERTAIN FACETS OF THE BUILDING RELATIVE TO THEIR MAXIMUM PERFORMANCE. WE FOUND OURSELVES TRYING TO *FORCE* THESE SYSTEMS DETAILS AND DEMANDS INTO THE VARIOUS FLOOR PLAN LAYOUTS OF THE GENERIC "U" MODULES. AS THE SYSTEMS CONTINUED TO EVOLVE AND BEGAN TO WORK BETTER AND BETTER, THEIR DEMANDS ON THE FLOOR PLAN LAYOUTS BEGAN TO GAIN MORE AND MORE RESPECT. FINALLY, WE SIMPLY ALLOWED THEM TO DICTATE TO US WHAT THEY REQUIRED FOR ULTIMATE PERFORMANCE MUCH THE SAME WAY WE ALLOWED THE "U" MODULE AND THE TIRE TO DICTATE TO US THE ORIGINAL DESIGN. THIS HAS RESULTED IN WHAT WE CALL THE "NEW GENERICS". THE HIGHEST PERFORMANCE, LOWEST COST, EARTHSHIPS AVAILABLE TO HUMANKIND AT THIS TIME.

Graphics by   Claire Blanchard
Photographs by   Pam Freund

We, as humans needing shelter on Earth in the 21st century, must forget the concept of "house". Unless you are rich or very skilled, the concept of "custom home" or being able to build your own home must also be let go.

The automobile is too evolved to allow each of us to design our own. Designing your own automobile is conceivable but highly impractical and vastly expensive, i.e. virtually not possible. We must choose from what the various automobile companies have provided from their research and development of the many aspects of automobile performance and design. The dwelling vessels for planet Earth in the 21st century <u>must perform</u> and they must be more available to all without selling our souls and destroying our planet. These "Earthships" (like the automobile) are the result of much research and development relative to structure, performance and cost. In automobile selection, there are not many choices other than style, color, degree of luxury and performance. The same is true for the really appropriate and secure living vessel for future dwellers on Earth. *This concept is one of our major discoveries*.

Our experiences over the last twenty years have shown us that the acceptance of this concept by humans would allow us to step back into stride with the rhythms of the universe. We could then participate in our own evolution rather than <u>preventing it,</u> which is currently the case. The bottom line is - we must *change in our minds* before we can change our course. We must do this soon as our current course is leading to extinction of human life. Various animals and plants are illustrating this fact as they simply disappear. Surely we can see that as more and more animals and plants become extinct - humans will eventually follow. Don't we realize that we are in the same river that has carried many creatures before us over the falls of destruction? We are just far enough upstream to go ashore and find a new course, carve a new river, evoke a new concept of living that will carry us (evolve us) gently to the sea of life everlasting instead of the edge of extinction.

The new generic Earthships are a new course, a new concept of living. We recommend them over any custom Earthship design at any price. They are both the most economical and highest performance vessel we can provide at the present time. *Any variation from the dictated design of the new generics will simply cost more and perform less.* We will obviously help anyone in any way we can toward any application of the Earthship concepts, however, those who will get the best performance at the lowest price will be those who can drop the concept of custom home and accept the dictated design of the new generics. From what I have seen through many years of being an architect, my seminars and working with hundreds of people; this is the single most difficult and obvious barrier between people and their homes - **the ability to step out of the dead concept of *house* and into an evolving concept of *living*.** They can choose a crackerbox in Levittown or a Chevy off the lot but want to design their own passive solar, self sufficient Earthship. The new generics can sail us into the future if we can simply get on the boat.

Just as an automobile has a space for an engine and a space for people, an Earthship has a space for support systems and a place for people. Just as this automobile engine is a predesigned functional unit in itself so are the independent mechanical support systems of an Earthship.

The new generics involve two basic structural modules. The already presented "**U**" living module and the new "mechanical" module, an "**mU**". This mechanical module is a synthesized physical and structural arrangement of predesigned mechanical systems and components that support the living modules. It is far more economical to predesign the arrangement of these systems (in their own structural module) relative to their optimum performance than it is to custom arrange and install them in each and every Earthship. Some of the considerations toward this design are as follows:

1. Bathroom must be on front face for warmth without blocking solar gain to the "U" living modules.
2. Solar toilet must be in the front face to function.
3. Pump and filter system (WOM) must be near reservoir and waterfall to accommodate pump limitations and reduce plumbing costs.
4. Power organizer (POM) and battery box must be together under P.V. panels and centrally located to the living spaces.
5. Hot water heater must be near water center (WOM).
6. Power organizer (POM) must be near water organizer (WOM) to accommodate power to pumps with minimum copper wire runs.
7. Refrigerator must be near power organizer (POM) to facilitate minimal gauge copper wire runs.

8. Bathroom and washing machine must be near reservoir to minimize plumbing.
9. Each "U" living module must have adequate ventilation and egress with a minimum amount of detailing and noise from mechanical systems.
10. Sufficient planter space must be allowed to accommodate the wetlands grey water treatment tank.

THE "U" MODULE

There are many types of "**U**" modules. They are basically *spaces* that can be used as kitchen/living/ dining, bedroom, study or any arrangement of the above, i.e. a "**U**" module is a room module typically larger than single rooms in frame houses. As per Chapter 2, the "Jungle" can be placed in any or all of these "**U**"s.

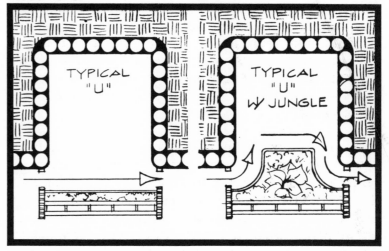

The floor of the jungle area of a "**U**" is dug out and lined for a continuous wetlands grey water treatment tank with plants above (see Chapter 2). This is in effect

235

your "septic tank" room. Originally we planned to close these jungle rooms off from the rest of the Earthship but they have proved to be such delightful spaces that we have started integrating the jungle into typical "U"s. Thus the jungles are part of a room space as well as a grey water treatment facility and a garden for food and flowers. We have grown bananas, grapes, all vegetables, herbs, etc. in these jungle rooms (see Chapter 2). "U" modules, therefore accommodate typical living spaces with or without a jungle.

THE "mU" MODULE

Bathrooms must be on the front face for warmth without back up heat. This results in a space behind the bathroom that receives no solar gain. This space is a logical location for predesigned mechanical and utility components (and storage) both because of its lack of solar gain and its proximity to the bathroom. The "mU"s therefore evolved to accommodate this situation. Since the solar toilet design (see Chapter 4) requires vertical glass, the basic "mU"s are a narrow mechanical "U" with a vertical front face.

In that there are several different applications of the "mU", we have tried to take advantage of this vertical front face (as often as possible) for ventilation and egress windows and doors. This reduces interruptions in the sloped front face fixed glass (see overview page 235) in front of the typical "U" modules. We are, therefore, reducing the detailing and making the generic Earthship more simple and economical.

"mU"1 is the full bath on the front face and utility/power/hot water/food storage in the rear.

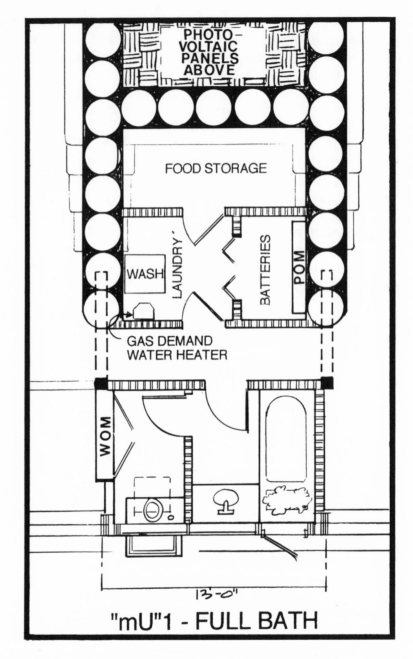

"mU"1 - FULL BATH

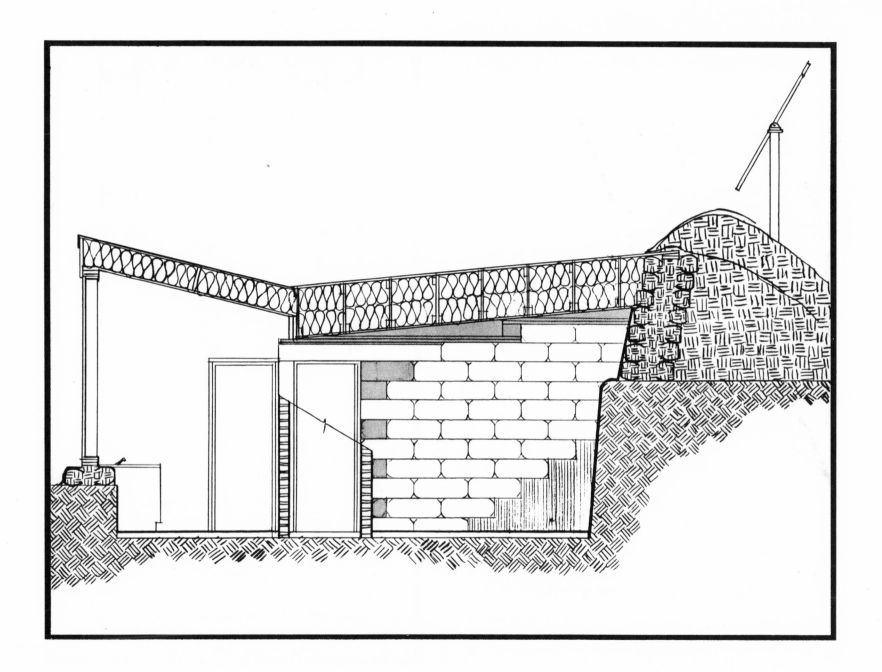

237

"mU"2 is the 1/2 bath on the front face and laundry/storage/power in the rear. "mU"2 accommodates an operable window in the vertical face for ventilation and egress for an adjoining "U" module. Note that both "mU"1 and "mU"2 are designed to accommodate a water organizing module for an adjoining catch water cistern. **It is important to note that like regular "U"s, all "mU"s are structurally identical in section and plan**.

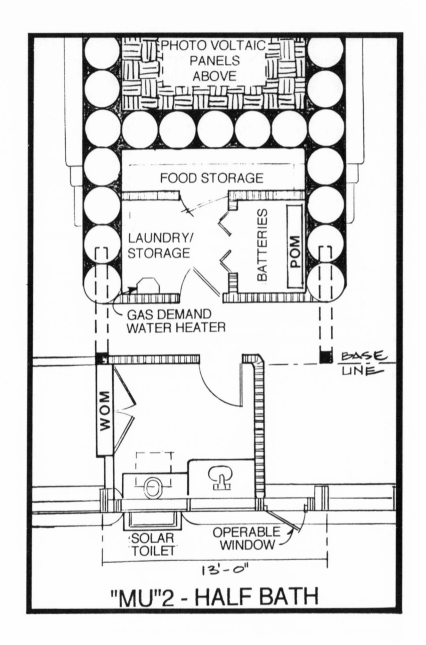

"MU"2 - HALF BATH

238

"**mU**"3 provides egress and ventilation on the front face with storage in the rear. This module is used for egress when bedrooms are desired in the middle of the layout.

Obviously if there is more than one "**mU**" the rear shaded space would not always be needed for mechanical. In the case of more than one "**mU**", the mechanical can be split up with electrical in the rear of one "**mU**" and water/utility in the rear of another. There is never enough storage in any home so the rear of certain "**mU**"s can be used totally for storage.

Any combination of the front and rear uses of these example "**mU**"s can be applied. Remember that the structure of every "**mU**" is the same. The depth can vary ("**U**"s can be deeper or shallower) but the width is better left as designed due to the detailing required for stock sizes of fixed and operable front face windows. If a larger bathroom is desired (a wider "**mU**") the sizes of the front face windows would have to be changed and this would probably result in a custom piece of thermal glass as compared to the stock sized thermal glass shown. The result would simply be a little more architectural and construction expense.

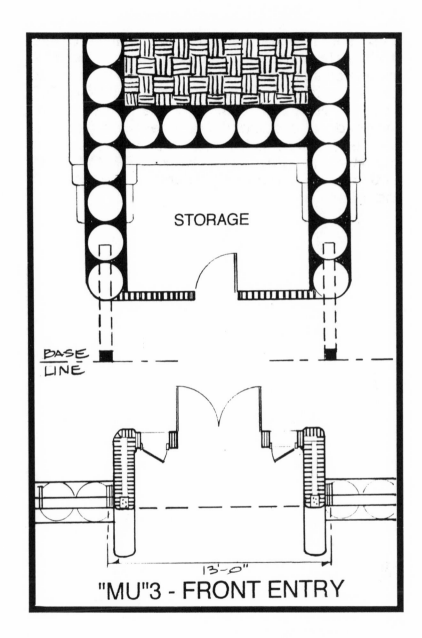

STORAGE

BASE LINE

13'-0"

"MU"3 - FRONT ENTRY

239

There are obviously many combinations of "U"s and "mU"s. Below is a one bedroom generic floor plan using two "U"s and one "mU".

Egress and ventilation are achieved on the ends of the building so we have no interruptions in the fixed glass in front of the typical "U"s

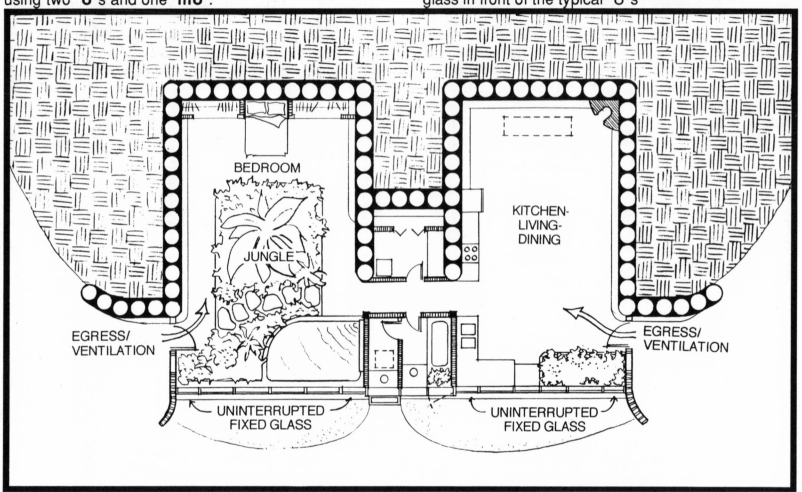

BEDROOM

JUNGLE

KITCHEN-LIVING-DINING

EGRESS/VENTILATION

EGRESS/VENTILATION

UNINTERRUPTED FIXED GLASS

UNINTERRUPTED FIXED GLASS

Another important consideration in arranging the modules is that the only way two regular "**U**" modules can be placed next to each other is when they are both being used for kitchen, living, dining, or study. Two bedroom "**U**" modules cannot be placed together in the middle of the plan as egress and ventilation cannot be adequately accommodated. Both are required by code. Thus, when arranging living modules, an "**mU**" must occur every one or two "**U**"s. The types of "**U**"'s and "**mU**"s are the variables.

In the arrangement below, the front face does not need to be interrupted with various operable window types for ventilation and egress as both are achieved in the "**mU**" or on the ends. This keeps the front face detailing to a minimum which keeps costs down. Operable windows most economically occur on the east and west or in "mU" modules with vertical front faces.

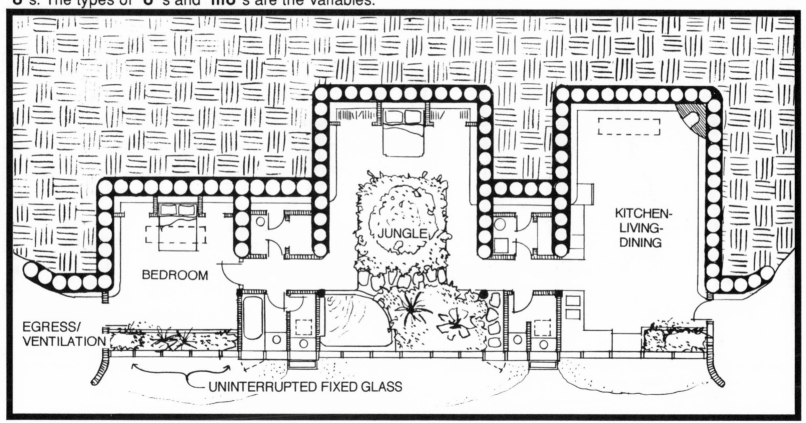

JUNGLE

KITCHEN-
LIVING-
DINING

BEDROOM

EGRESS/
VENTILATION

UNINTERRUPTED FIXED GLASS

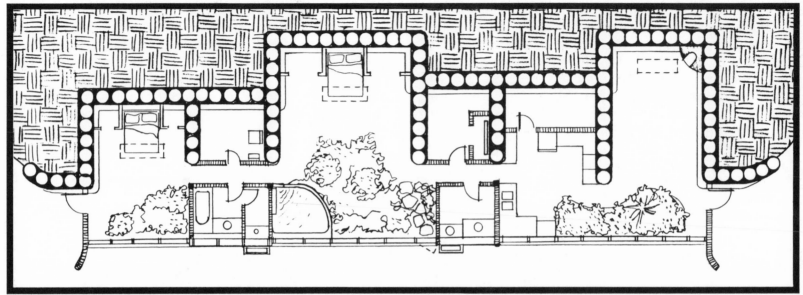

These typical generic plans are basic examples of how a variety of requirements are met in a generic format.

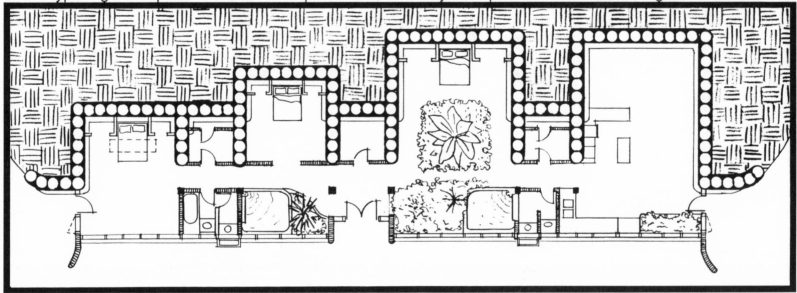

242

A TYPICAL GENERIC OVERVIEW. NOTICE THE VERTICAL GLASS AREA DEPICTING THE "mU"

Now we have uninterrupted fixed glass front face detailing (see overview previous page) with two basic structural modules both of which are very simple to build. This leaves the owners with the task of arranging various different types of "mU" and "U" modules to tailor the concept to their needs. This is the most economical and highest performing application of the Earthship concept to date. Of course there can be custom applications but the architectural and construction costs (and degree of difficulty) go up and performance usually goes down. *This new generic method is the way to be successful in building your own home out of pocket.* As soon as you drift from this method, costs go up. Solar Survival Architecture has provided a new generics information package in an effort to enlighten prospective clients on the most economical way to proceed with getting an Earthship. *We have seen too often that an owner's desire for customization is what makes their projects grow in cost and diminish in performance.*

A basic construction sequence of a typical new generic "U" is on the following four pages. We recommend sinking them into the ground as much as 6'-0" where soils will allow to use more natural earth cliffs and less tire work. This obviously reduces costs. However, when soil stability does not allow this, the entire "U" (or building) can be built on the surface of the ground and earth can be bermed up around it. Tire work can also be taken down to the bottom of the excavation to avoid earth cliffs when instability of soil demands this. Both of the above situations will require slight architectural modifications to the generic drawings. Solar Survival Architecture should be consulted in both the

above instances. See Chapter 13, Climatic Adaptations.

The analogy of the automobile has served us well here, to illustrate the importance of using predesigned systems and modules to keep cost down and performance up. There is, however, a very important difference between Earthships and automobiles that needs to be emphasized. While the new generic Earthships offer the high performance and low cost of a mass produced automobile, the Earthship makes its own "fuel", catches its own water, puts out no air or noise pollution and can go anywhere.

MATERIAL AVAILABLE

New Generic package $5.00
     This package explains how to apply the generic approach and develop or choose your own tailored floor plan.

New Generic Construction Drawings $1,500.00
(with video and books)
     These are architect stamped detailed drawings (26 pages) including all mechanical for a generic Earthship based on your tailored generic floor plan.

All prices subject to change after the printing of this book.

244

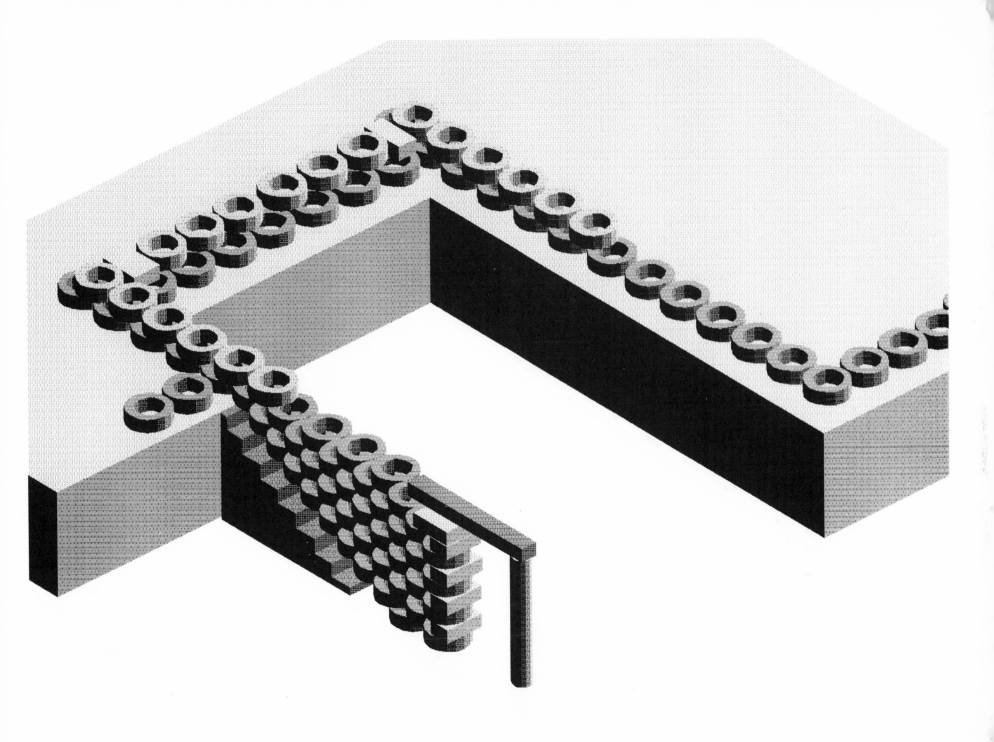

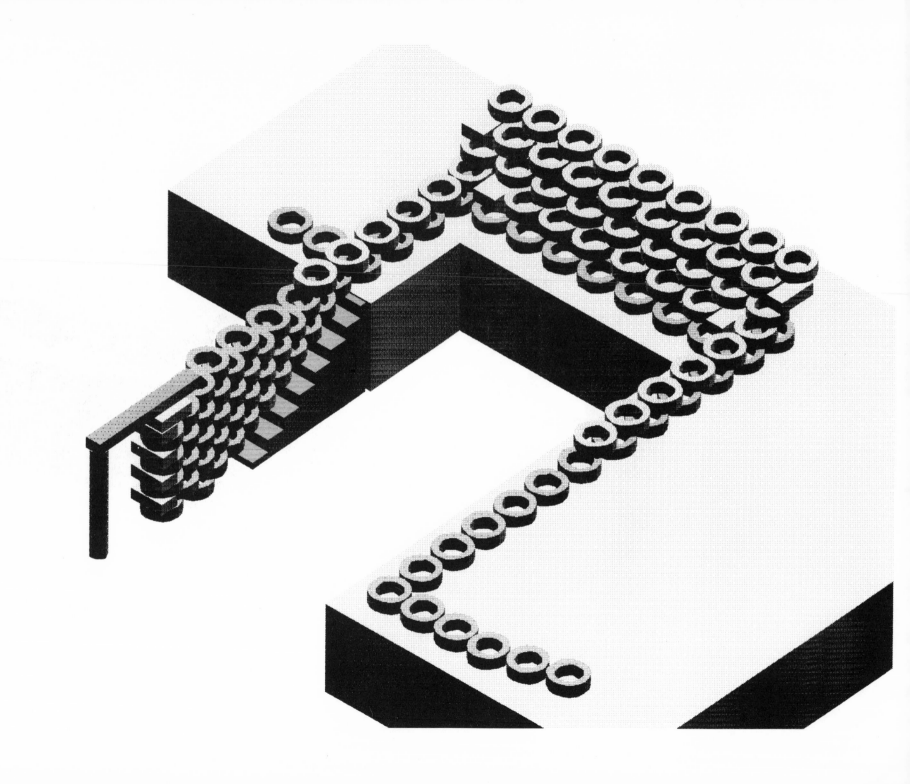

I WAS RUNNING ON A MOUNTAIN TRAIL ABOUT 3 MILES FROM CIVILIZATION. I WAS HEADING UP TO THE CREST OF ONE OF MANY LITTLE PEAKS ALONG THE TRAIL. AS I NEARED THE PEAK I HEARD WHAT SOUNDED LIKE WIND BLOWING THROUGH THE TREES. THE SOUND GOT LOUDER AS I REACHED THE PEAK. THE OXYGEN "INTOXICATION" WHILE RUNNING ON HIGH ALTITUDE UP AND DOWN HILLS TENDS TO REMOVE ONE FROM THE CLARITY OF THE "REALITY" AT HAND. I DID NOTICE, HOWEVER, THAT THERE WERE NO TREES MOVING IN THIS "WIND". IT GOT VERY LOUD AT THE PEAK LIKE IT WAS RIGHT IN MY EARS. THEN AS I PASSED THE PEAK IT BEGAN TO DIMINISH. THIS ALL HAPPENED IN A FEW SECONDS. I STOPPED TO FIGURE OUT WHAT WAS GOING ON. I LOOKED BACK AND THERE RIGHT BY THE TRAIL WAS A LARGE GREEN RATTLESNAKE ALL COILED UP AND RATTLING. IT WAS RIGHT BY THE TRAIL. I HAD RUN PAST WITHIN 3 FEET OF IT. THE LOUD NOISE OF THE RATTLE VIBRATION IS WHAT SOUNDED LIKE THE WIND. I SHUDDERED TO THINK HOW CLOSE I HAD COME TO IT. WITH THE THOUGHT OF WHAT COULD HAVE HAPPENED TO ME (SNAKE BITE THREE MILES OUT ON FOOT) I PICKED UP A ROCK AND THREW IT AT THE SNAKE. I MISSED. AFTER MISSING WITH A COUPLE MORE ROCKS I FINALLY PICKED UP A FAIRLY LARGE ROCK AND HIT IT IN THE HEAD. THE SNAKE WAS HURT - IT BEGAN STRIKING ITS OWN TAIL AND FLOPPING AROUND. I HAVE KILLED AND EATEN RATTLE SNAKES BEFORE AND THIS THOUGHT WAS IN MY MIND. HOWEVER, I DIDN'T WANT TO CARRY IT HOME THIS TIME SO I LEFT IT THERE STRIKING AT IT'S TAIL. ON THE WAY HOME I BEGAN THINKING WHY I REALLY KILLED IT. IT WASN'T REALLY FOR FOOD OR THE SKIN. I KILLED IT FROM THE FEAR OF WHAT IT COULD HAVE DONE. THE FACT IS *IT WARNED ME ONLY*. IT COULD HAVE STRUCK AS I WENT BY BUT IT DIDN'T. I REACTED TO ITS WARNING NOT ITS ATTACK. IT ACTUALLY HAD EVERY RIGHT TO WARN ME. I HEARD ITS WARNING FROM MANY YARDS AWAY. TOO OFTEN FEAR OF WHAT COULD HAPPEN CAUSES THE SAME REACTION AS IF IT ACTUALLY DID HAPPEN. A WARNING IS DIFFERENT FROM AN ATTACK. I KILLED THE SNAKE BECAUSE OF WHAT IT COULD HAVE DONE - NOT BECAUSE OF WHAT IT DID - IT DID NOTHING.

FEAR REACHES BEYOND CONSCIOUSNESS AND STRIKES FASTER THAN LOGIC.

WE MUST HAVE A LIFE WHERE THERE IS NO FEAR.

DOME OF THE DEGAN AND SIEGAL EARTHSHIP, SANTA FE NEW MEXICO

EPILOGUE

Most of us are aware of the fact that insurance companies dictate what procedures doctors can perform and when they can perform them. Likewise mortgage companies dictate what kind of housing can be built and when it can be built. Insurance companies also have a hand in this. Power brokers dictate what kind of decisions congressmen and women make and when they make them. We can and do point the finger at these corporate/political "villains", but do we realize that many of us work for them or otherwise depend upon and support them?

This situation is very much like a cancer infested human body. The cancer (the villain) is actually a <u>part</u> of the body and the body is part of the cancer. We are <u>part</u> of the villain that controls us. *We are the problem*. Nothing will evolve in a different direction as long as we support the villains by allowing them to support us. *We and the villains are co-dependant.*

How futile it appears when any political leader presents a plan of attack on how to make this co-dependency work. If you were on a sinking ship would you want to be dependent on a predominantly white male life boat full of leaks with no gas, no oars and seven people fighting over which way to go, or would you want to be independent and have your own life jacket?

I once heard a cancer patient say "I'm dying, don't waste my time". We are all dying, why waste time? Lets grab a life jacket and all help each other. The **Earthship** and its related concepts **is** a **life jacket**. *It won't let you sink*. You still have to kick and swim and position yourself in movement toward the shore, <u>but it won't let you sink</u>.

The concept for a cancer starts with a single mutant cell that is "born" within the existing activities of the body. Whether the cell multiplies into a tumor or a rampant "family" running through the body it still lives *within the existing activities of the body*. The body feeds the cancer as it feeds itself. The original cancer cell found a way to survive and multiply from the <u>processes already taking place in the body</u>. This sounds a lot like insurance companies, mortgage companies and politics. They have become malignant tumors inhibiting our "body processes".

The *concept* of cancer can be applied to cancer itself in an effort to <u>eliminate cancer</u>. Imagine planting a cell within a cancerous tumor that functions in relation to the tumor exactly like the cancerous tumor itself relates to the human body. The "anti-cancer" cell is planted in the tumor and lives from the *existing activities of the tumor*. It grows and becomes an "anti-tumor" within the tumor. This is an Aikido approach to cancer and to life on Earth in the later part of the twentieth century.

A major part of the concept of the Earthship is that it can be owner built without a mortgage payment. Now, without a mortgage payment no one can tell you what the building must look or function like to assure resale. This means <u>one person</u> is not being manipulated by and dependant on the mortgage and insurance companies. This is little more than a "cell" in the whole cancerous scheme of things in the "civilized" world. Now, this Earthship needs no centralized electric power, water or sewage support so it further becomes an "anti-cell" with respect to other "tumors" in our society such as power companies, water controllers, and politically "stained" sewage systems. This Earthship is a little cell of life that was born out of the system but is not a functioning part of the system - much like a cancer cell. Now, this Earthship multiplies much like a cancer cell. It worked so well for its owner that others wanted one and lo, we see many Earthships multiplying into an "anti-tumor" within the system - *a community*. This community grows within the system and begins to displace and render useless certain aspects of the system. The system becomes weaker and the concepts of the community become stronger. **Human interest and support will simply gravitate to that which takes care of it best**. No amount of political promises and television ads or even dogmatic legal threats can compete with the snowballing effect of ***people choosing life over waning survival***. In this analogy, all malignant aspects of our civilization will simply starve. They will not have to be cut out, fought, disguised, or otherwise reckoned with. They will simply starve. We are feeding them. All we have to do is stop feeding them and feed ourselves.

The cancer analogy is not new. A photo of a group of cancer cells has been blown up while an aerial photo of Los Angeles was reduced and both looked the same. The cancer concept is alive and well on the planet earth both within the human body and without. What **is** new is the "cancer within a cancer" concept. This is new as a way of dealing with cancer within the human body and a way of dealing with "cancers" on the planet earth.

Many seemingly valid new inventions, cures for diseases, and social reforms are scrapped because of lack of funds and support. I submit that they are not valid if they need continuous, conscious support and/or funds from the very malignancy they are fighting. The "land build" concept (which is fueled from by products and redirected existing forces in our society) is a "cancer within a cancer" application and so is the Earthship itself.

The new concepts for the future must come from an "immaculate conception" and must thrive on conceptual and physical by-products of the beast.

Cancer does not need the conscious mental and physical support of the human body. That is why it is so feared. Likewise, our solutions and reactions to the various forms of the cancer that we are facing (both within the human body and around the earth) must not need the support of the very "tumors" they are trying to replace. Our new ages will be like the phoenix rising from the ashes of the dying ages. This is a fact of physics and metaphysics. The only question is *will the human being be able to pass through the vortex of the death of the old and the birth of the new?* This is our choice - **to participate in our own evolution** or to perish as the universe continues to evolve in spite of us.

Much attention is being given toward trying to create employment for humans on earth so that they may keep up with the ever growing cost of living. Although many seem to think they understand why the cost of living (i.e. the cost of survival) continues to swell, no one can control it. It continues to grow year after year. Our lenders' and politicians' approach to this problem is a "catch up football" approach. Keep creating jobs so people can keep paying for the ever increasing cost of living. A tremendous amount of money has to be injected into the economy to finance the creation of these often meaningless jobs. This gives people a chance (if they can handle a little stress) of staying in the race to keep up with inflation.

All my life I have seen inflation somehow racing across the sky with employment and income of the masses feebly trying to just stay in the race but usually losing ground. Hence, *the rat race*.

This is what I have grown to see as "life" on this planet. I am not playing this game anymore. Let me ask some questions. Why is the focus of attention always on jobs and employment? Why isn't anyone able to slow up or stop inflation so that jobs and employment can coast a while?

What is inflation? Inflation is essentially the rising cost of living. This is shelter, food and energy. Shelter is the single largest investment that the average human ever spends. An effect on the "price" of shelter would therefore be an effect on inflation. An effect on shelter, energy and food would result in a significant effect on inflation. The graphic result would be as follows.

We are always trying to speed up employment and income. Why not put that energy towards slowing up or even stopping inflation? This should not be attempted with numbers, banks, interest rates, charts, politicians' promises or economists. This should be done by us, *the people*. We are not dependent on ghost economics and figurehead politicians for our way of life. We do not have to ask their permission to change our focus. We simply have to look at and observe the phenomena and simple logic will show us that rather than trying to stress our "rat wagon" to keep up with the cost of living,

let's attack the cost of living.

The Earthship concept does this. We can literally slash the power of inflation. Imagine (as we have said before) no mortgage payment, no rent, no utility bill and living in a situation where you can grow much of your own food year round.

Suppose you are trying to dislodge a rock and you have been pushing in one direction with all your might for quite some time but to no avail. Often you simply try pushing in another direction and sometimes you get results. Why have all of our approaches toward trying to fight the world of economics been with economic weapons? Economic survival is nothing more than a ruthless game and we do not have to play it. Money has become the sea of life and everyone needs a boat. The sea keeps getting rougher and the boats keep getting more elaborate, but never elaborate enough for a comfortable ride. We do not have to stay here. There is land out there where you don't need a financial boat, you just need an Earthship.

The real dream application of the Earthship concept is for people to buy memberships in land users associations for relatively small amounts of money. They build their own independent, food producing, homes for a fraction of the cost of having a conventional home built and end up with little or no mortgage payment and no utility bills. The result of this is a serious reduction in power of the "inflation" wagon.

Now, without major portions of revenue going to shelter and nothing going to utilities and less going to food, *we have a LIFE not just a grueling race.* This whole process creates jobs relative to the building of Earthships and their various components as well as some management and office work relative to the land users association and various businesses. The result of this is that employment and income can catch up to inflation (cost of living.)

When we stop trying to catch up, the race becomes just a ride. Of course if the government got behind this kind of program it could help, although I wonder if they could keep from bureaucracizing it to a standstill. The opportunity, however, is there without any kind of help. One grain of sand at a time can eventually tip the scales.

One Earthship at a time can change the world. The land users associations both rural and urban (see Chapter 8) set the stage for Earthship development. They are the "soil" from which Earthship communities can grow.

The trick here is the individual approach. These concepts can and have stopped inflation (the race) for people *on an individual basis*. When many people have been affected individually you have a *movement.* Our world - our reality - our problems are too big for thin blanket approaches such as mass creation of jobs and massive welfare programs that actually fuel the fires of inflation. We need a program that allows each individual to stop inflation for themselves. This will take the burden off of the already over-burdened government. The governments greatest burden is itself. How can it take care of us? ***We must not only help ourselves - we must eventually help our government. When the masses are all quietly and peacefully sailing through life in Earthships maybe we can throw a life preserver to the bureaucrats.***

Imagine you are riding on a school bus down a highway. The road slowly gets worse and worse and eventually the pavement runs out and you are on a dirt road. This road deteriorates more and gets very treacherous for the big bus. Then the bus gets a flat tire but still tries to keep going - thumping along up the bumpy hills and around the sharp curves going slower than you could walk. If the road kept deteriorating to nothing more than a trail, at some point you would eventually make the decision to *get out of the school bus and walk.* Now is the time. The school bus is on a *one* dimensional journey. There are, however, many dimensions into which we can journey. The Earthship is a good vessel for that journey. It can cross the seas between us and freedom.

In *one* dimensional thinking there is *one* response to a situation.

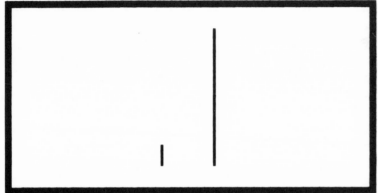

You are the short line in the above diagram. Your object is to conform. You have one choice - grow.

In a *two* dimensional world there are *two* responses to a situation.

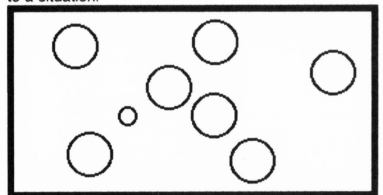

You are the little circle in the above diagram. Your objective is to conform. You have *two* choices -grow or shrink the others. The point is there are *two* choices.

Three dimensional thought gives you *three* choices, grow, shrink the others, or join the others.

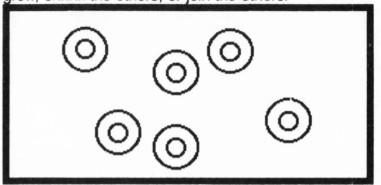

In *four* dimensional thought you have *four* choices - grow, shrink the others, join the others, or have the others join you.

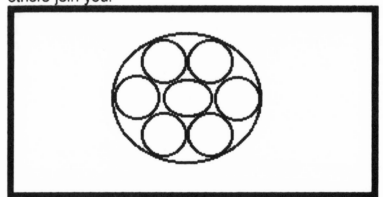

Five dimensions - grow, shrink the others, join the others, have the others join you, change the rules.

And so on.

Power is a matter of how many choices you have. How do you get these choices? You create/invent them. Everything is a choice. Only one choice is right for any given situation. The more choices, the more of a bank of responses to any one situation. This "bank" is a method of maneuverability through the physical world. It is at our disposal. We may use it to direct our evolution.

On behalf of the entire Solar Survival staff

Thank You

Michael Reynolds